Flex Appeal

Flex Appeal

A Vegetarian Cookbook
for Families

with
Meat-Eaters

PAT CROCKER *and* NETTIE CRONISH

whitecap

EDITOR: Elizabeth McLean
DESIGNER: Diane Robertson
COVER DESIGNER: Andrew Bagatella
FOOD PHOTOGRAPHER: Pat Crocker
PROOFREADER: Joan Templeton

Printed in Canada

Library and Archives Canada Cataloguing in Publication

Crocker, Pat, author

Flex appeal : a vegetarian cookbook for families with meat-eaters

/ Pat Crocker and Nettie Cronish.

Includes index.

ISBN 978-1-77050-188-1 (pbk.)

1. Vegetarian cooking. 2. Cooking (Meat). 3. Cookbooks.

I. Cronish, Nettie, 1954-, author II. Title.

TX837.C748 2014   641.5'636
C2013-908277-8

The publisher acknowledges the financial support of the Government of Canada through the Canada Book Fund (CBF) and the Province of British Columbia through the Book Publishing Tax Credit.

14 15 16 17 18 5 4 3 2 1

 This book was printed on chlorine-free paper and made with 10% post-consumer waste.

To busy people

who want to eat

and be healthy

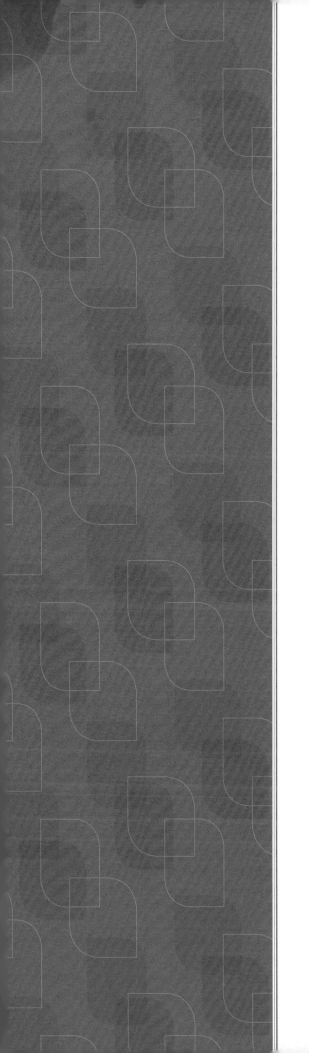

Contents

Introduction

We are constantly striving to think beyond "meat and potatoes with a salad thrown in for good luck." We have struggled with the constraints of our own concepts of healthy food, family preferences and the pressure of dwindling time and energy at the end of the workday. And we are both fiercely devoted to eating mindfully, which for us means not only being aware of the way we taste and ingest food but also being aware of the journey that food took to get to our tables.

The aim of this book is to give you strategies for cooking and eating in the ways that you already know are the healthiest—using high-quality plant-based ingredients, less meat and fewer dairy products.

Almost all of the recipes in this book can be prepared in under an hour and the ingredients are easily found, sometimes in the freezer and even, sometimes, in a package, jar or can. They have been family- and friend-tested and we know that they have a broad appeal while being easy on the cook. "Honest and healthy" and "pure and simple"—these were the principles we followed while we created what we think are exceptional, delicious, flexible dishes.

MEET THE AUTHORS!

The Enlightened Vegetarian: Nettie

At the age of 17, I became an evangelical vegetarian. Blame it on Paul McCartney. At any family or social event, I would spell out in detail all the terrific reasons for going vegetarian. My idealism knew no bounds. The world would be a better, greener place with fewer factory farms, I would say. Changing your culinary focus from meat to veg only required a change in your attitude, I believed. What I neglected to take into account was just how convenient meat is to eat. Changing your culinary focus requires well-written recipes, an equipped kitchen and the time to shop and cook.

Forty years ago, it was a very isolating experience to be veg. The counterculture image prevented any scientific data from being acknowledged. Today, due to mounting scientific evidence that higher-fat and meat-based diets are factors in heart disease and strokes, people are occasionally eating vegetarian meals. But many people have no interest in giving up meat, dairy, eggs and poultry. Vegetarian and vegan diets are too difficult, for lots of reasons, for many people to follow. Nowadays I would simply encourage people to follow an omnivorous diet that is moderate, ethical, respectful and delicious. Your eating style is a mindset.

My family has chosen not to be vegetarian. As my three children became teenagers, they became very curious about all kinds of food. It was time for them to make their own culinary decisions without my disapproval. We all needed to find a level of tolerance, whether we were cooking at home or dining out. It has not been easy but we maintained our ability to communicate and the respect we share is mutual.

In this book, we demonstrate any one recipe two ways. By utilizing the same basic recipe, we can share a meal and not feel bullied about choices. At the same time, we can control the amount of sugar, salt and quality of fat we use in our cooking. Our book will allow you to prepare recipes with lots of choice in a minimum of time. Drop the labels. Life is too short. Long live beans and grains.

The Enlightened Meat-Eater: Pat

Less is more; humane and fair are essential—these are the new standards of the enlightened meat-eater. But is the reality of health and compassion consistent with actual practice? According to a report by the United Nations Food and Agriculture Organisation and reported by *The Economist*, Americans, Australians, Canadians, Israelis, New Zealanders, Spaniards and people from the Bahamas and Luxembourg consumed on average between 216 and 300 pounds (98.1 and 136.5 kilograms) of meat per person in 2007.[1]

For human and environmental health, the international Slow Food organization recommends in its booklet "Too Much at Steak" that we eat under 100 grams or about 3½ ounces of meat per day—roughly the weight of an unpeeled Clementine orange. According to Canada's 2011 Food Guide, the recommended daily serving of fish, meat or poultry for teenagers and adults can be up to 7½ ounces (212 grams) for males and 5 ounces (142 grams) for females, although it recommends eating meat alternatives, such as beans, tofu and nuts, often. The United States Department of Agriculture recommends that a healthy daily diet should include 5½ to 6 ounces (156 to 170 grams) from the meat/beans group (including meat, fish, poultry, eggs, nuts, seeds, beans and peas).

So are we actually eating between 3½ and 7½ ounces of meat in one day?

In 2007, Americans ate 276.5 pounds (125.4 kilograms) of meat per person, which amounts to about 12 ounces (340 grams) per person every day. Any way you compare the numbers, that's far more meat than is considered either healthy or environmentally sustainable.

As meat-eaters, we do have a long way to go towards mindful eating, but many are seeing the light, and I believe that in the years since those figures were published in *The Economist* in 2007, people living in industrialized nations have begun to follow a new dietary path. In fact, according to Statistics Canada, by 2009 Canadians consumed about

1 Revised table published May 2, 2012. Viewed at www.scribd .com/doc/91840616/Meat-Consumption-Per-Person.

Meet Nettie

What do you call yourself?

I call myself a Natural Foods Chef/ Vegetarian Ambassador. Introducing new ingredients and easy-to-prepare recipes inspires people.

Favourite ingredients?

Avocados. They are a fruit but we use them as a vegetable. Never refrigerate! Serve on toast with sprinkles of sea salt. I adore blood oranges, beets, vanilla beans and watermelon.

Favourite meal?

Linguini with Leeks, Olive Oil and Garlic (page 89) served with arugula and grape tomatoes.

Comfort food?

Coconut milk–infused basmati rice with ripe mango slices

Necessary extravagance?

Bamboo cutting boards

Always in the refrigerator/ pantry?

Frozen wild blueberries and organic cashew nut butter

Culinary inspiration?

Findhorn Organic Farm, Scotland

Favourite restaurant?

Ursa, in downtown Toronto, because of the excellent quality of the ingredients and the use of dehydration and sprouting on their menu.

Signature dish?

Split Pea and Cashew Loaf (page 163) served with Thai Slaw (page 147) and Tomato Avocado Crostini (page 25). Nice texture contrasts with a lot of CRUNCH.

NETTIE CRONISH is a natural foods chef, culinary instructor and cookbook author. Her three vegetarian cookbooks, *Nettie's Vegetarian Kitchen*, *New Vegetarian Basics* and *The Complete Idiot's Guide to Being Vegetarian in Canada*, are cornerstones of the Canadian vegetarian scene.

Nettie is the chair of the Women's Culinary Network and a board member at Fairtrade Canada.

Meet Pat

What do you call yourself?

I actually coined the term Culinary Herbalist to describe what I do because, while I'm not a medical herbalist, I do specialize in cooking with herbs.

Favourite ingredients?

Rosemary is my favourite herb for specific dishes, but garlic and thyme are my go-to, everyday herbs. Other fave ingredients: Chinese "forbidden" black rice, roasted red peppers, maple syrup, smoked salt and pepper

Favourite meal?

Lamb tagine cooked with Moroccan Spice Blend, roasted vegetables and Chinese black rice.

Comfort food?

Scalloped potatoes, macaroni & cheese

Necessary extravagance?

18/10 grade (high-quality, food-grade) stainless steel tools

Always in the refrigerator/pantry?

My own Ras el Hanout spice blend (a version of Garam Masala, page 179)

Culinary inspiration?

The Herbfarm, Seattle, Washington

Favourite restaurant?

Blue Hill at Stone Barnes, Tarrytown, in New York. The farm, the century barns, the sustainable food and the organic gardens combine to make it work.

Signature dish?

I visited the spice market in Istanbul and wrote a tagine cookbook, and I love cooking with my own spice blends. When I'm home cooking for my family, I use the tagine two or three times a week. Moroccan Vermicelli with Lentils is a fast, easy and delicious one-pot food and my homemade Moroccan spice blends lend an authentic taste. (For the dish, see page 102. For the spice blend, see page 181.)

Home economist (BAA, Ryerson University), food writer and photographer, Pat is passionate about health, herbs and food. Her books have won international awards (Best in the World for *The Juicing Bible*) and she was awarded the Gertrude B. Foster Award for Excellence in Herbal Literature by the Herb Society of America. She develops recipes using the produce from her local Community Supported Agriculture program, Green Being Farm, and her herb garden.

81 pounds (36.8 kilograms) of red meat and poultry per person, or about 3½ ounces (100 grams) daily. More and more people are choosing less meat, meatless days and vegetarian alternatives often enough to make a difference in their lives and the health of the planet.

Another innovation catching on in North America is Community Supported Agriculture (CSA), which involves a direct connection between farmers and their local communities, as consumers invest in the farm's success and receive healthy local food in return. CSA allows farmers and communities to share in the risk and the bounty of small, organic farms. Supporting local, organic foods is a mindful act, because it reinforces our commitment to sustainable food.

Mindful Eating: The Flex Approach

There are lots of great reasons to eat less meat and there are so many good resources outlining environmental issues (including water, land, plant, animal and insect well-being), human health, animal dignity and the economic rights of farmers. (See the Resources section on page 207 for a short list.)

Industrialized factory farming is based on speed, quantity and profit. When we eat cheap, poor-quality meat, we feed into a system that caters to thoughtless consumption, which leads to the continuation of poor meat production. Providing cheap meat in huge quantities means using inhumane practices of shortening animals' life cycles, growing chemical-dependent, soil-depleting crops to feed animals, caging animals and using drugs as prevention against diseases that are often caused by those same production methods.

There are alternatives to supporting such an unhealthy and unsustainable approach to food. Some people choose a strict vegan or vegetarian diet. Others decide to eat fewer animal products, choosing quality over quantity. When we seek out organic, free-range and drug-free meat and dairy products from animals that have been humanely raised on small, mixed-crop farms, the quality of both the food and the environment is maintained. For this, we agree to pay farmers fairly for their efforts.

In addition to concerns about food animal production, it's also important to consider how vegetable and fruit products are produced and marketed. When buying foods that are produced or grown outside Canada and the US, such as chocolate, coffee, sugar, vanilla, bananas and coconut oil, the Fair Trade mark ensures that the quality of the food is excellent and that producers have been treated fairly.

Consumers who are well-informed have the ability to challenge the way much of their food is grown, produced and sold.

If you want to continue to eat meat but also to contribute to sustainable agriculture and improve your diet, we encourage you to focus on two things: making wise meat purchases and creating strategies for eating less meat. This is what we mean by the term "mindful eating." Below are some of the flexible meat techniques we use.

Nettie's Favourite Tools

KitchenAid stand mixer: Versatile and durable, stand mixers free up your hands. They whip faster, beat longer and knead evenly compared to hand mixers. KitchenAid is the most durable, lasts a lifetime anad has lots of attachments. See image **1**.

Food Scale: Electronic scales are compact, accurate and storable. A scale accurately weighs such foods as butter, nuts, chocolate and flour, and many recipes are based on weight measurements, not volume. There's always empty space in a measuring spoon or cup. Your scale should have metric measurements. See image **2**.

Salad Spinner: Use the bowl and ventilated basket to store washed salad greens in the refrigerator. It keeps greens fresh. Salad spinners are available in a variety of sizes. See image **3**.

Vegetable Steamer: Available in different shapes and sizes, steamers fit into small pots and saucepans. The colour and texture of steamed vegetables are always better than boiled. See image **4**.

Citrus Reamer: A reamer allows juice to be extracted completely from fruit with just a few turns of the wrist, resulting in more juice with less effort. See image **5**.

Pat's Favourite Tools

Global knives: I test-drove them in the store to feel their heft and shape in my hand. I like knives with a metal handle because of the risk of bacteria hovering in and under a wooden handle. I keep them sharp. See image **6**.

Cast Iron Pans: For beautiful, even heat, season skillets and bakeware and learn to use them properly. You will pass them on to your heirs. See image **7**.

Bamix: After 30 years of grinding spices for my spice blends, I can say that this is the perfect tool for the job. The size and shape of both the bowl and the knife enable you to grind spices to the desired texture. See image **8**.

Emile Henri Bakeware: This glazed ceramic bakeware and cookware is beautiful. Some is flame-proof, so it can sit on a gas or electric stovetop. See image **9**.

Mortar and Pestle: I like cast iron mortars to grind spices because of their resistance to hard seeds and bark, but prefer porcelain for pesto, salsa verde and other green sauces because there is more of a macerating effect. See image **10**.

Strategies for Eating Less Meat

- Use meat and dairy products as a condiment. Thinking of meat and dairy as one small addition to a dish or a meal helps you to reduce the amount used. Artisanal cheese, shaved or slivered chicken or beef, pulled pork, bacon, chopped ham, pancetta and nitrite-free sausage all add big flavour in small amounts to the main event: vegetable-based dishes.

- Have breakfast for dinner. We've included a whole chapter on Breakfast Dinners that take advantage of the great source of protein from eggs. Try our Basque Eggs or Sweet Potato Hash and Halloumi. They're satisfying, quick and easy to prepare at the end of a workday.

- Try the vegetarian version of any recipe in this book first. Of course you can add small amounts of meat to most of the recipes, but we think the vegetarian versions are delicious and satisfying enough to please most meat-eaters.

- Turn salad into supper. Our hearty warm and cold salads are satisfying enough to make a meal. That's because we use substantial winter and root vegetables, nuts and nut butters, seeds, legumes (like lentils and black beans), cheese, miso and tofu for their tasty protein.

- Go with the grain. Hearty grains like quinoa and amaranth, spelt, barley and rice add dimension to vegetarian fare. All of the grains we use are good sources of protein, are easy to cook and can be cooked and frozen for quick access later.

- Try tofu or tempeh, you just might like it. Choose organic, extra-firm tofu (because of its meaty texture) and marinate it in your favourite sauce before adding to kebabs for the grill or crumbling over roasted vegetables.

- Create leftovers on the weekends. If you have committed meat-eaters to satisfy, indulge in one weekend meal of beef, pork, lamb, chicken or fish, but keep portions to healthy amounts and whisk leftovers into the refrigerator before diners can reach for seconds. It's easy to chop and measure 1- or 2-cup (250 or 500 mL) amounts to freeze for use another day. Weekends are also a great time to make tomato sauce or cook dried beans in order to save time on weeknights.

- Use every bit of the organic meat you buy. Freeze meat bones along with vegetable trimmings and make soup stock when you have enough.

the new organic farmer

Meet Tarrah Young. She holds a degree in environmental biology from the University of Guelph in Ontario and runs Green Being Farm (see Resources on page 207) with her husband Nathan Carey in south-western Ontario. Tarrah chose to study organic agriculture because of her deep concern for the environment. She looks at organic farming as a positive and tangible way to be an environmental activist.

Green Being Farm is a small, mixed farm specializing in pastured animals and vegetables. It is devoted to embodying organic and humane principles while remaining economically viable. The cattle and sheep on Green Being Farm help to keep it fertile, and because they are dispersed over the land, grazing instead of being fed soy and corn with antibiotics, they are efficient converters of the farm's resources. The chickens and pigs, while still being able to range free, are fed a balanced diet of wheat, oats, peas and

buckwheat along with some corn and soy. All of their animals make their marginal land productive and sustainable.

Tarrah and Nathan (and a crop of other young farmers like them) care about the land, the plants and their animals. They are using the Community Supported Agriculture (CSA) system as a method of distributing their high-quality food to the local community in return for the promise of a decent return for their efforts. If you come to dinner at Pat's house anytime from November through February, you will taste first-hand the exceptional vegetables that Tarrah provides to her CSA members.

Tarrah's mix of rare-breed hens, Berkshire pigs, Red Poll cows and Katahdin sheep have free access to green forage. No preventive medicines, hormones, additives or genetically modified plant foods are given to her animals.

Make Wise Meat Purchases

- Go small or buy from the source. Most meat sold in supermarkets and large grocery chains is from large industrial farms. If you live in the city, finding farmers' markets, small, private butchers and other outlets that only sell local meat from ethical, humane farmers may be a challenge, but more such retail outlets are opening as more people seek them out. We list some organizations that can help in the Resources section on page 207.

- Be content to pay more. If the meat is cheap, its quality is poor and its production exploits the land, the animal and you. By eating less, you should be able to afford to pay fair prices for high-quality meat.

- Buy small amounts (unless you are planning for leftovers) that can be used within a few days. Having less fresh meat on hand helps you to be creative in using less and going meat-free more often.

- Look for and be flexible about the amount of fat in meat because, along with tremendous flavour, fat can be a sign of well-being in animals.

- Go for the giblets. You can save money by learning how to cook less popular cuts of meat such as organ meats and tougher cuts such as shoulder and blade. Using all parts of the animal, not just the most popular cuts, means that you are part of the mindful act of making use of the whole animal.

- Be flexible and mix it up. If you or your dinner guests are huge beef (or chicken or pork) eaters, make a point of trying different breeds, cuts and types of meat, including game and fish.

- Buy local heritage breeds. Many organic farmers are raising native and heritage breeds. By seeking them out, you are supporting a healthy local economy as well as genetic diversity. For the most part, heritage and native breeds are raised by ethical methods without industrial farming practices, so that preventive drugs aren't necessary.

about cooking oils

In our recipes, we recommend cooking with olive oil only at low to medium temperatures, and with coconut or avocado oil at higher temperatures. Olive oil breaks down into damaging components under high cooking temperatures, so coconut and avocado oil are safer choices.

High-quality oils such as avocado oil are more expensive but are well worth the price. When you shop for oils, watch for sales and buy the best quality you can afford. Canola oil can be used as a cooking oil, but if you do use it, look for organic brands. We recommend this because organic canola oil is made from non-genetically modified rapeseed and is not over-refined. Mass-produced, cheaper oils are made from genetically modified, chemically sprayed crops and are over-refined to extend their shelf life. (See the Glossary on page 203 for more information on individual oils.)

Because we have been thinking about you during the creating, testing and development of all aspects of this book, we would love it if you want to contact us. How did we do? Do you have comments or suggestions? Do you have a favourite recipe set? And if you've changed it, how did you make it your own? If you love Nettie's Zucchini Mushroom Moussaka, tell her! If you secretly sneak Pat's Salted Dulce de Leche Tarts with Chocolate Ganache to work, share that with her!

You can contact Pat at pcrocker@riversongherbals.com and Nettie at nettiecronish@rogers.com.

Basque Eggs

☐ FLEX APPEAL HAM OR BACON

This recipe has become one of my favourite breakfast dinners and it's different each time I make it, depending on who is home and what I have in the refrigerator or pantry. It's so easy that, after you make it once, you will be able to whip it up anywhere, anytime, without even glancing at the recipe. Adding a good local cheese, or trying whatever frozen greens you have on hand (and for the meat-eaters whatever cooked meat or seafood you have on hand) keeps it interesting. —Pat

FLEX APPEAL

MAKES 2 SERVINGS

½ cup (125 mL) chopped cooked ham or bacon

After step 2, sprinkle the ham over half of the vegetables in the pan before continuing with step 3.

MAKES 4 SERVINGS

2 Tbsp (30 mL) olive or avocado oil

1 onion, chopped

8 oz (250 g) mushrooms, sliced

1 Tbsp (15 mL) butter or olive oil

1 potato

2 cups (500 mL) chopped fresh, or thawed and drained, frozen spinach

4 large eggs

1 tsp (5 mL) paprika

1. In a cast iron or heavy-bottomed skillet, heat the oil over medium heat. Add the onion and sauté for 5 minutes or until soft and translucent. Add the mushrooms and cook, stirring occasionally, for 3 to 5 minutes or until the mushrooms are soft and have released their juices.

2. Add the butter, reduce the heat to low and grate or thinly slice the potato into the mixture. Stir well, cover the pan and cook, stirring occasionally, for 8 to 10 minutes or until the potato is tender-crisp. Stir in the spinach, cover and cook for 2 to 3 minutes or until wilted.

3. Make 4 little hollows in the vegetable mixture and break an egg into each. Cover the pan and cook for 5 to 8 minutes or until the whites are firm and opaque and the yolks are still runny. If you prefer firm yolks, break the eggs and cook for 1 or 2 minutes more, or until hard.

4. Garnish the eggs with the paprika. Use a spatula to lift the eggs and vegetables onto 4 warmed serving plates.

42   Flex Appeal

How to Use Our Flex Recipes

As far as we know, our "flexitarian" books are the only cookbooks that provide directions to weave meat portions into strictly vegetarian recipes while keeping the two options separate, so that you can satisfy both vegetarians and non-vegetarians with one recipe.

The vegetarian recipe is listed front and centre on the page. If you want to make only the vegetarian dish, simply follow the main recipe. If you want to include non-vegetarian portions, the flex instructions tell you how to prepare and include the meat or fish.

Most of the recipes serve 4 to 6 vegetarians, with the number of vegetarian servings listed in the main recipe. Most of the flex options allow for 2 meat portions (the number of meat servings is listed in the flex option). Should you wish to feed 4 meat-eaters, simply double the ingredients in the flex option. You **do not** need to double any of the ingredients in the main recipe unless you plan to serve double the number of vegetarian portions or to allow for leftover servings.

appetizers and snacks

Olive, Walnut and Mushroom Pâté

RECIPE NOTE

If you buy sliced green olives, it will save the tedious job of slicing them, but be sure to drain them well. If you are using pitted whole olives, you only need to halve them.

MAKE-AHEAD STRATEGY

Make this pâté up to 3 days in advance. Cover tightly and refrigerate until ready to serve.

The consistency, and to some degree the flavour, of this spreadable mixture is similar to a chicken liver pâté. Of course, it is vegetarian and if olive oil were used in place of the butter, it would be vegan, but check out "What makes it work?" before replacing the butter. Use as a cocktail spread for crackers or crostini or with sliced cucumbers. It also makes a great spread for a sandwich or wrap, or toss ½ cup (125 mL) of the spread with 2 cups (500 mL) cooked rice for a delicious pilaf. —Pat

MAKES 2¼ CUPS (560 mL)

2 Tbsp (30 mL) olive or avocado oil	1 cup (250 mL) walnut halves or pieces
1 onion, chopped	½ cup (125 mL) sliced or halved green olives (see Recipe Note)
3 cloves garlic	½ cup (125 mL) chopped fresh parsley
1 lb (500 g) button or cremini mushrooms	½ tsp (2 mL) coarse salt or to taste
3 Tbsp (45 mL) butter	

1. Preheat the oven to 400°F (200°C).

2. In a skillet, heat the oil over medium heat. Sauté the onion for 5 minutes or until soft.

3. Meanwhile, using a food processor, chop the garlic. Add half of the mushrooms to the bowl and pulse until coarsely chopped.

4. Add the butter to the onions in the skillet and let melt. Stir in the chopped mushrooms and garlic. Quarter the remaining mushrooms and add to the skillet. Reduce the heat and cook, stirring often, for 15 minutes or until the mushrooms are soft and have released their juices.

5. Meanwhile, spread the walnut pieces over a rimmed baking sheet in one layer. Toast for 3 to 5 minutes or until lightly browned. Let cool.

6. When the mushrooms have released their juices, increase the heat to medium and boil for 3 to 5 minutes or until the juices have evaporated (the mixture should not be extremely dry). Let cool.

7. In a food processor, finely chop the toasted walnuts. Add the cooled mushroom mixture and olives and process until smooth. Add the parsley and pulse to combine. Taste and add salt as desired. Scrape into a bowl, cover tightly and refrigerate until ready to serve.

Olive, Walnut
and Mushroom
Pâté

Mediterranean Eggplant Spread and Grilled Pita

I like to use the deep purple–skinned eggplant variety that is available in most supermarkets. Their silky texture and ability to absorb flavour make them an essential ingredient in Middle Eastern, Indian and Mediterranean cuisines. Broiling the eggplant will blister the skin and allow you to scoop out the pulp within 20 minutes. You can use any type of nut butter in place of the tahini if you like. Look in your cupboards or refrigerator and use almond, cashew, peanut or hazelnut butter, whatever you have on hand. I once combined several leftover nut butters and dubbed it "mystery nut butter," and it has been a family favourite ever since. This spread has a caviar-like consistency and is terrific with celery, toast or pitas. —Nettie

MAKES 4 SERVINGS

2 medium purple eggplants

1 cup (250 mL) plain or Greek yogurt

3 cloves garlic, finely chopped

⅓ cup (80 mL) freshly squeezed lemon juice

¼ cup (60 mL) tahini (see About Tahini, page 17)

⅛ tsp (0.5 mL) black pepper

¼ tsp (1 mL) sea salt

⅓ cup (80 mL) chopped fresh Italian parsley

½ cup (125 mL) diced tomatoes, fresh or canned

3 Tbsp (45 mL) olive or avocado oil

Grilled Pita (recipe follows)

1. Preheat the oven to broil (500°F/260°C). Move the oven rack to top position.

2. Pierce the eggplants several times all over with a fork and place on a parchment paper–lined, rimmed baking sheet. Broil, turning occasionally, for 20 minutes or until the skins are browned and the centres soft. Skin will char and blister and the flesh will collapse.

3. Transfer the eggplants to a cutting board. Let cool. Slice the eggplants in half lengthwise and scrape out the pulp.

4. In a food processor or blender, purée the eggplant pulp until smooth. Add the yogurt, garlic, lemon juice, tahini, pepper and salt and process for 1 minute or until puréed.

5. Transfer the mixture to a serving platter or bowl. Sprinkle with the parsley and tomato. Drizzle with the olive oil and serve with the Grilled Pita.

Grilled Pita

MAKES 32 TRIANGLES

4 pita breads	½ tsp (2 mL) ground cumin
3 Tbsp (45 mL) avocado oil	

1. Brush the pita breads with oil and sprinkle with the cumin. Grill over a medium flame for 1 minute or until browned. (If using an oven, preheat the oven to broil (500°F/260°C) and move the oven rack to the top position. Arrange the pitas in 1 layer on a parchment paper–lined baking sheet and broil for 1 minute.)

2. Cut each pita into eighths.

Spicy Sweet Potato Dip

This is a perfect fall recipe. Served with long slices of celery and cucumber, this dip will be scooped up by children and adults alike. I often serve it in half a scooped-out purple cabbage with a garnish of green herbs. —Nettie

MAKES 4 CUPS (1 L)

1 Tbsp (15 mL) caraway seeds	2 cloves garlic, finely chopped
6 cups (1.5 L) sweet potato cubes (1-inch/2.5 cm cubes)	¼ cup (60 mL) chopped fresh mint
1 tsp (5 mL) finely chopped ginger	1 Tbsp (15 mL) finely chopped fresh red chili pepper
¼ cup (60 mL) freshly squeezed lime juice	¼ tsp (1 mL) sea salt
¼ cup (60 mL) olive or avocado oil	⅛ tsp (0.5 mL) pepper

1. Heat a small, heavy-bottomed skillet or sauté pan over medium heat. Add the caraway seeds, stirring constantly to prevent burning, and toast for 1 minute.

2. Add enough water to reach the bottom of a collapsible steamer set in a saucepan and bring to a boil on high heat. Place the sweet potato cubes in a steamer basket, cover and steam for 10 minutes on medium-high.

3. Remove from the steamer and cool in a large bowl for 5 minutes. Transfer to a food processor and purée.

4. Add the toasted caraway seeds, ginger, lime juice, oil, garlic, mint, chili pepper, salt and pepper to the food processor. Blend for 3 minutes or until smooth, scraping down the sides occasionally.

MAKE-AHEAD STRATEGY

This dip freezes really well and can be kept in the freezer for up to 3 months. Thaw in the refrigerator overnight or on the counter for 2 hours.

Tahini, Miso and Herb Pâté

Pâtés are luxurious. This vegetarian version will melt in your mouth. Serve with your favourite baguette or use as a filling for celery or mini pitas. —Nettie

MAKES ½ CUP (125 mL)

½ cup (125 mL) tahini (see About Tahini)

1 clove garlic, finely chopped

½ tsp (2 mL) dried oregano

1 Tbsp (15 mL) finely chopped fresh basil

1 Tbsp (15 mL) rice miso

1 Tbsp (15 mL) sweet white miso

1 Tbsp (15 mL) finely chopped green onions

½ cup (125 mL) water

1. In a small, heavy-bottomed skillet, roast the tahini over medium heat, stirring constantly, for 3 to 5 minutes. The tahini will turn light brown and stick to the pan. Transfer to a small bowl and cool for 10 minutes.

2. In a food processor, combine the cooled tahini, garlic, oregano, basil, miso and green onions. Process for about 1 minute or until puréed. With the motor running, add the water in small amounts until the mixture is smooth and creamy.

about tahini

Tahini is simply ground sesame seeds, although it varies in oil content. Generally used in small amounts, tahini thickens and adds a nutty flavour to hummus, baba ghanoush and halva. When you buy tahini in a can or jar, it will have a layer of oil on top of a thick paste. It is important to stir the oil back into the paste so it is distributed evenly. If the tahini you have is thick and dry, add more water as needed.

about miso

Miso is made from soybeans that are soaked, steamed and inoculated with a bacterial culture. Cooked grains (rice, barley, buckwheat) are added to the fermentation process along with salt. Miso is cultured between 3 months and 3 years. Each type has its own distinct flavour, colour and aroma. Sweet miso is yellow or white, low in salt and ferments in 2 to 8 weeks. Miso with a higher salt content is darker in colour, fermented longer (up to 3 years) and is marketed as rice, barley or brown rice miso. I think it looks like chopped liver, vegan style.

Miso is a living food, full of enzymes and active cultures that are beneficial to your health. Organic, traditionally made Japanese miso is the best kind to buy. It is sold in plastic tubs in the refrigerated section of most supermarkets as well as health food stores and will keep for 6 months, refrigerated. It is a terrific ingredient to have in your kitchen, especially when replacing salt.

Feta-Stuffed Figs
◻ FLEX APPEAL PROSCIUTTO

This recipe is super easy and superb, but relies on plump, fresh figs. The soft, almost over-ripe, squishy texture of fresh figs makes them precious when they are at their best. Sun-loving figs are grown in warm places around the world and must be carefully packed so that they do not split and spoil before (or just after) you get them. If you live in British Columbia, California or the southern US, local figs are available in early summer and again in late summer or early fall. If fresh figs are not available, you can substitute fresh dates. —Pat

FLEX APPEAL

MAKES 6 SERVINGS

6 slices prosciutto or thinly sliced cooked ham

After step 2, wrap a slice of prosciutto or ham around the outside of 6 of the feta-stuffed figs. Secure with a toothpick.

MAKES 12 STUFFED FIGS

12 ripe fresh figs (see Recipe Note)

4 oz (125 g) feta cheese, drained and cut into twelve ½-inch (1 cm) cubes

1. Slice the figs from the top almost to the base. Turn and slice at a 90° angle almost to the base.

2. Press 1 feta cube into the centre of each fig.

RECIPE NOTE

You can use Adriatic, Black Mission, Calimyrna, Kadota or Brown Turkey figs (in photo) for this recipe. Some, such as Black Mission, are much sweeter than others, so experiment with as many varieties as you can find.

MAKE-AHEAD STRATEGY

Stuff and, if desired, wrap figs with prosciutto up to 24 hours in advance. Store in an airtight container in the refrigerator. Bring to room temperature before serving.

FLEX APPEAL Prosciutto

Date and Fig Tapenade with Mixed Greens

In this recipe, you can also use all figs or all dates. I love to combine them, especially after they have been grilled. This recipe is a reflection of Mediterranean cuisine. —Nettie

MAKES 4 SERVINGS

4 fresh or dried Medjool dates, pitted and halved

4 ripe fresh figs, halved

4 plum tomatoes, halved

⅓ cup (80 mL) olive oil

1 clove garlic, finely chopped

2 Tbsp (30 mL) finely chopped fresh basil

sea salt and black pepper

3 cups (750 mL) mixed salad greens

3 Tbsp (45 mL) olive or avocado oil

2 Tbsp (30 mL) freshly squeezed lemon juice

¼ lb (125 g) pitted black olives, quartered

¼ lb (125 g) feta cheese, crumbled

¼ cup (60 mL) fresh chopped parsley

1. Preheat the grill to medium heat.

2. Combine the dates, figs and tomatoes in a medium bowl.

3. In a separate bowl, whisk together the ⅓ cup (80 mL) oil, and the garlic, basil, salt and pepper to combine. Pour over the date mixture and toss to coat.

4. Grill the coated dates, figs and tomatoes over the preheated grill for 3 minutes on each side, turning once, or until lightly browned. Let cool, then thinly slice.

5. Place the salad greens in large bowl. Mix the 3 Tbsp (45 mL) oil and the lemon juice together. Pour over the greens and toss using tongs to evenly coat. Divide the salad greens into 4 bowls.

6. Mix the grilled dates, figs and tomatoes with the olives and feta cheese in a medium bowl. Divide the tapenade evenly among the 4 salad bowls. Sprinkle with parsley.

USING A STOVETOP GRILL

Use a cast iron or heavy grilling pan to grill fruits and vegetables. Heat the grilling pan over medium-high heat. Once the pan is hot, reduce the heat to medium-low. Slicing food into uniformly sized pieces allows them to cook evenly and they are less likely to burn or fall apart.

about dates and figs

Dates and figs can be bought fresh or dried and are stored differently. Fresh dates are stored in a plastic bag in the refrigerator and dried dates are stored in an airtight container at room temperature. Fresh figs should be refrigerated in a perforated plastic bag if not eaten within 36 hours.

TIME-SAVING STRATEGY

Wash your leafy greens ahead of time and keep them crisp in the refrigerator.

MAKE-AHEAD STRATEGY

Delicious hot or cold, the tapenade mixture can be grilled ahead of time, stored in a covered container in the refrigerator and brought to room temperature when ready to use.

Caramelized Onion and Pear Tart
☐ FLEX APPEAL BACON

I like the versatility of the filling for this tart. Without the pastry, you can use the caramelized onion-pear mixture as a spread for crackers or raw vegetable rounds. It serves as a condiment for grilled vegetables or meat dishes. You can use it in place of mayonnaise in sandwiches, and it's fantastic teamed with sharp cheddar cheese in a grilled sandwich. —Pat

FLEX APPEAL

MAKES 4 TO 6 SERVINGS

4 strips side bacon, chopped

In a skillet over medium-high heat, cook the chopped bacon, stirring frequently, for 4 minutes or until browned and crisp. Using a slotted spoon or lifter, transfer the bacon bits to a paper-lined plate and let drain.

Sprinkle evenly over one half of the baked tart in step 7.

MAKES 8 TO 12 SERVINGS

1 egg, room temperature

1 Tbsp (15 mL) milk

½ pkg (17.3 oz/490 g) frozen puff pastry sheets (see Recipe Note), thawed

3 Tbsp (45 mL) olive oil

3 large sweet onions, thinly sliced

2 Bartlett pears, cored and thinly sliced

2 Tbsp (30 mL) maple syrup or honey

1 Tbsp (15 mL) balsamic vinegar

20 pitted black olives, halved

1. Preheat the oven to 375°F (190°C).

2. In a bowl, whisk together the egg and milk to make an egg wash.

3. Spread the puff pastry on a pizza stone or a parchment paper–lined, rimmed baking sheet. Turn up the edges and pinch the corners to form a ½-inch (1 cm) lip all around.

4. Lightly brush the edges of the pastry with the egg wash.

5. Prick the centre of the pastry sheet with a fork. Chill in the refrigerator for 30 minutes.

6. Meanwhile, in a skillet or Dutch oven, heat the oil over medium heat. Add the onions and sauté for 5 minutes. Add the pears and cook, stirring frequently, for 5 minutes. Drizzle the maple syrup and vinegar overtop, reduce the heat to low and cook, stirring frequently, for 15 minutes or until the onion and pear are soft and the mixture has turned a dark caramel colour.

7. Spread the onion mixture over the chilled pastry and top evenly with the olives. Bake for 30 minutes or until the pastry edges are golden brown and the bottom is firm. Let cool to room temperature before serving.

FLEX
APPEAL
Bacon

Caramelized
Onion and
Pear Tart

RECIPE NOTE

Most frozen puff pastry packages contain
2 unrolled squares or 2 pre-rolled sheets.
For this recipe, use either 1 pre-rolled sheet
or 1 unrolled square (you can roll it out
to a rectangle). Thaw the pastry in the
refrigerator.

PLAN-AHEAD STRATEGY

Make double the vegetarian recipe. Cool one
tart and freeze for a future meal.

MAKE-AHEAD STRATEGIES

· You can't roll out the pastry until you are ready to make the tart, but you
can prepare the onion mixture in step 6 up to 2 days in advance. Store the
cooled mixture in a covered container in the refrigerator and bring to room
temperature before spreading over the pastry.

· The tart may be baked, cooled and frozen in a zip-top freezer bag for up to
2 months. To reheat, remove from the freezer bag, place on a parchment
paper–lined baking sheet or preheated pizza stone and warm in a 350°F
(180°C) oven for 15 to 20 minutes or until heated through.

continued on next page ›

❯ *Caramelized Onion and Pear Tart continued*

about this recipe

What makes it great?

The tart-sweet flavours of the caramelized onions, honey and balsamic vinegar in the filling are the perfect blend to produce a complex and satisfying taste and silky soft texture.

How do the onions caramelize?

The first thing to know is that one of the essential techniques for this recipe is to slice the onions very thin. You can't really do this by hand, so use either a hand-operated mandoline (as shown in image ❶) or the slicing disc of a food processor. Choose the thinnest size of blade available. For this recipe, I used a portable mandoline because it's quick, but the slicing disc of a stand mixer or food processor works just as well.

Secondly, you need to cook the onions in a heavy-bottomed skillet or Dutch oven so that you can turn down the heat and let the onions "sweat" to bring out the natural sugars in them. The final product should look like image ❷.

Why brush the pastry with an egg wash?

The "wash" of egg and milk makes the surface of the pastry brown and shiny while it is baking (see image ❸).

Why prick the pastry?

The holes allow the pastry to cook flat. By punching tiny holes in the pastry using a fork (see image ❹), you are creating vent holes so that as the pastry cooks and steam builds, it can escape without causing the pastry to bulge out. You usually prick pastry that will be used as a tart or pie base. You don't always need to prick puff pastry, especially when you want a puffy hors d'oeuvre or pie topping.

How is the bacon added?

This is one of the easiest ways to provide a meat-flex element to a dish. The bacon is chopped and cooked over medium-high heat for about 5 minutes or until it is crisp (see image ❺).

Once there are no visible signs of fat on the bacon bits, lift out the crispy bacon using a slotted lifter or spoon and let drain on absorbent towels or paper (see image ❻). You can set aside the bacon until the last minute before it is sprinkled over one half of the tart.

Cheddar and Salsa Tortillas
☐ FLEX APPEAL TUNA

This is a favourite after-game snack for my son, 14-year-old Emery, who plays Select hockey for the Forest Hill Falcons. It's quick and easy to prepare. You can use mild, medium or hot salsa depending on your taste. —Nettie

MAKES 8 SERVINGS

eight 6-inch (15 cm) whole-wheat flour or gluten-free tortillas

1 cup (250 mL) grated cheddar cheese

2 cups (500 mL) tomato salsa

⅓ cup (80 mL) chopped red onion

⅓ cup (80 mL) chopped fresh basil

¼ tsp (1 mL) ground cumin

2 cups (500 mL) shredded iceberg lettuce

3 tomatoes, diced

1 cup (250 mL) Greek yogurt or sour cream

1. Preheat the oven to 400°F (200°C).

2. Arrange the tortillas in one layer, flat on a parchment paper–lined, rimmed baking sheet. Sprinkle the cheese evenly overtop. Bake for 4 to 6 minutes or until golden brown. Remove from the oven but leave on the baking sheet. ←

3. In a medium bowl, toss together the salsa, onion, basil and cumin. Spoon the salsa mixture over the tortillas.

4. Return to the oven and bake until heated through, about 5 minutes. Top each tortilla with some lettuce, tomato and yogurt.

FLEX APPEAL

MAKES 2 SERVINGS

1 can (6 oz/175 g) flaked tuna

Drain the tuna and break it up with a fork. In step 2, spoon tuna over 2 of the tortillas before sprinkling with cheese.

RECIPE NOTES

· To locate a good-quality canned tuna, do some research. Your local health food store is a good resource (see also "Mindful Eating" in the Introduction). Many cans have a toxic coating called bisphenol A. If you can, buy canned goods that do not use this coating.

· Tuna packed in olive oil is gaining in popularity because people enjoy the flavour, but if you are calorie counting, tuna packed in water is less caloric. One 6 oz (175 g) water-packed can of tuna will weigh ¼ lb (125 g) when drained.

PLAN-AHEAD STRATEGY

It is hard to cook for a crowd. Everyone has her or his favourite level of heat. Some want mild; others crave extra spicy. A simple way to present options is to coordinate the type of tortilla (gluten-free, spinach-flavoured) with the level of heat. A colour-coded chart will tell people which tortillas are gluten-free, mild or spicy.

Crispy Nori and Walnut Snack

This flavourful Japanese-inspired recipe is very easy to prepare. Nori is a sea vegetable that has been dried and pressed into sheets. It is most commonly used to wrap rice or as the exterior of sushi rolls. —Nettie

MAKES 4 CUPS (1 L)

½ cup (125 mL) walnuts

3 cups (750 mL) crispy brown rice cereal

5 sheets nori, sliced into small, thin slivers (see Recipe Note)

2 Tbsp (30 mL) white miso

1 tsp (5 mL) toasted sesame oil

1 Tbsp (15 mL) agave nectar

2 tsp (10 mL) wasabi powder

½ tsp (2 mL) sea salt

¼ cup (60 mL) olive oil

1. Preheat the oven to 350°F (180°C).

2. Arrange the walnuts in one layer on a parchment paper–lined, rimmed baking sheet. Toast in the oven for 5 minutes.

3. Transfer to a large bowl and cool for a few minutes. Add the cereal and nori. Toss well.

4. In a mini food processor or blender, combine the miso, sesame oil, agave nectar, wasabi powder and salt. Add the oil and process until smooth.

5. Pour overtop the walnut-cereal-nori mixture. Toss to coat evenly.

6. Arrange the mixture in one layer on the baking sheet. Bake for 15 minutes, stirring 3 times, until browned.

7. Transfer to a bowl and serve.

RECIPE NOTE

Available in packages of 10 or 50, nori will last a long time in its protective wrap, especially if you keep it dry. Store in an airtight package or container.

Tomato Avocado Crostini

This spread can easily be made into two separate spreads: instead of mixing the tomatoes or avocados together with the other ingredients, keep them separate and make a tomato spread and an avocado spread. (But I prefer the combined version!) The tomato-avocado mixture also makes a delicious addition to salads and pita pockets. During winter, I have used half a 14 oz (398 mL) can of organic diced tomatoes in place of fresh tomatoes. It all depends on what you have available. —Nettie

MAKES 4 SERVINGS

3 Tbsp (45 mL) coconut or avocado oil, divided

1 garlic clove, minced

2 Tbsp (30 mL) chopped fresh basil

1 Tbsp (15 mL) freshly squeezed lime juice

¼ tsp (1 mL) sea salt

2 tomatoes, diced

1 small ripe avocado, mashed

8 slices (1 inch/2.5 cm) whole wheat baguette bread or bread of your choice

1. Preheat the grill to medium-high or use a grill pan on the stove over medium heat.

2. In a bowl, mix 2 Tbsp (30 mL) of the oil, and the garlic, basil, lime juice, salt, tomatoes and avocado.

3. Grill the bread over a preheated grill for 2 minutes each side. Lightly brush with the remaining 1 Tbsp (15 mL) oil. Spread an equal amount of the tomato-avocado mixture on each slice of grilled bread.

MAKE-AHEAD STRATEGY

Prepare the tomato-avocado mixture up to 2 days ahead and store in an airtight container in the refrigerator.

about avocados

Do you consider an avocado to be a fruit or a vegetable? They are a fruit and are in season during spring and summer. The Haas variety from California and the Fuerte from Florida are the most popular and available to buy. I recommend buying underripe avocados at least 3 days before you need them. Leave them at room temperature and always cut them in half lengthwise.

Cheddar
Mushroom
Caps with
Asparagus and
Balsamic Glaze

about mushrooms

The most common edible mushrooms are *Agaricus bisporus*, which were the first mushrooms to be cultivated for the French king, Louis XIV. *Agaricus* boasts several species and varieties, including the common white button mushroom.

When the brown or cremini strain of the common domesticated *Agaricus bisporus* mushroom is allowed to grow to full maturity, the large, flat, open-capped adult form is called portobello.

CLEANING: There is always a lot of discussion about whether to wash mushrooms. If you like, you can quickly rinse the mushrooms in a colander, tossing with your clean fingers, draining and drying immediately with a dish towel or paper towel. Or if the mushrooms look fairly clean, you can just use a dry or slightly damp paper towel (or a soft bristle brush), to wipe or brush the cap. Trim the ends of the stalks after cleaning.

STORING: Keep in a paper bag or wrap in paper towels and store in the produce drawer of the refrigerator.

Cheddar Mushroom Caps with Asparagus and Balsamic Glaze

These cheesy tidbits are a delicious, fast and easy appetizer when served simply over a bed of spring greens. Alternatively, cut them in half, spear them with a toothpick and pass them on a plate. For a luncheon main dish, serve them over rice or with flatbread. —Pat

MAKES 4 SERVINGS

4 large portobello mushrooms

16 asparagus spears

2 to 3 Tbsp (30 to 45 mL) olive or avocado oil

½ cup (125 mL) grated sharp cheddar cheese

1 cup (250 mL) fresh spring greens

¼ cup (60 mL) Balsamic Glaze (recipe follows)

1. Preheat the oven to 375°F (190°C).

2. Clean the mushroom caps and trim the stems. Place gill-side down on a parchment paper–lined, rimmed baking sheet. Arrange the asparagus spears in one layer around the mushrooms on baking sheet. Drizzle the oil over the vegetables. Bake for 15 minutes or until the mushrooms are tender when the point of a knife is inserted into the flesh. Test the asparagus and remove to a plate if tender or turn and leave on the baking sheet.

3. Using tongs, turn the mushrooms so that the gill side is up. Spoon 2 Tbsp (30 mL) of cheese into each mushroom. Bake for 4 to 5 minutes or until the cheese melts.

4. Arrange 4 asparagus spears over each mushroom and serve overtop the spring greens.

5. Drizzle with the Balsamic Glaze or pass the glaze separately.

continued on next page ›

> *Cheddar Mushroom Caps with Asparagus and Balsamic Glaze continued*

Balsamic Glaze

MAKES ¾ CUP (150 mL)

1 cup (250 mL) balsamic vinegar	2 tsp (10 mL) tamari or soy sauce
3 Tbsp (45 mL) liquid honey	

1. In a saucepan, combine the vinegar, honey and tamari. Bring to a boil over high heat. Reduce the heat to low and simmer for about 20 minutes or until thick and syrupy. Let cool.

MAKE-AHEAD STRATEGIES

- You can cook the asparagus and mushrooms as directed in step 2 up to 4 hours in advance, and refrigerate on the baking sheet. Bring to room temperature before continuing with steps 3 to 5.

- Make the Balsamic Glaze up to 2 weeks in advance. Store in a jar or other tightly covered container in the refrigerator. Bring to room temperature before using.

about balsamic vinegar

Distinctly Italian, oak-aged balsamic vinegar is rich, dark and complex in flavour (ranging from tart to sweet). Genuine balsamic vinegar is only made in Modena, Italy, and its history dates back to the Middle Ages. The Maison Orphée brand is a product of Italy, certified organic and aged in oak barrels for 3 years. See image ❶.

Exceptional balsamic vinegar is highly prized—this bottle sells for €150 in Milan. Our advice is to spend as much as your budget will allow on top-quality, genuine balsamic vinegar and use it sparingly. See image ❷.

Cornmeal-Coated Cheesy Mushroom Balls

I love to combine fresh and dried mushrooms for complex flavours. Button mushrooms are delicious. The secret is to cook them long enough to evaporate their water content and concentrate on added flavour. Look for mushrooms that are almost perfectly white with tightly closed caps. Dried mushrooms can be very expensive. Porcini mushrooms (also known as cèpes), are prized for their meaty texture and taste. Soak dried mushrooms until they are plump and softened. —Nettie

MAKES 9 TO 12 SERVINGS

Cream Cheese Filling

½ cup (125 mL) dried mushrooms (porcini, morels, shiitake)

1 cup (250 mL) cream cheese

3 Tbsp (45 mL) chives or green onions, thinly sliced

1 Tbsp (15 mL) chopped fresh basil

½ tsp (2 mL) salt

⅛ tsp (0.5 mL) pepper

Mushroom Balls

36 button mushrooms, 1 to 2 inches (2.5 to 5 cm) in diameter (see Recipe Note)

¾ cup (185 mL) cornmeal

¼ cup (60 mL) tan and black sesame seeds

1 tsp (5 mL) salt

3 large eggs

½ cup (125 mL) coconut or avocado oil, divided

1. To make the filling, in a bowl, cover the dried mushrooms with 2 cups (500 mL) boiling water and soak for 15 minutes. Strain the reconstituted mushrooms over a bowl, pressing out all the soaking liquid. Set the soaking liquid aside for another use. Remove the stems and chop the mushrooms.

2. In a bowl, combine the chopped mushrooms, cream cheese, chives, basil, salt and pepper. Mix well and set aside.

3. To make the mushroom balls, remove the stems from the button mushrooms. Slice ¼ inch (6 mm) off the flat side of each cap. Press 1½ tsp (7.5 mL) of the cream cheese filling into each mushroom cap.

4. In a bowl, mix the cornmeal, sesame seeds and salt together.

5. In another small bowl, break the eggs one at a time and beat.

6. Dip 1 stuffed mushroom ball into the beaten eggs, coat well and then roll in the cornmeal mixture, pressing the mixture onto any uncovered areas. Repeat until all mushroom balls have been coated. Chill for 15 minutes in the refrigerator.

7. In a large skillet, heat ¼ cup (60 mL) of the oil over medium-high heat. Add half the mushroom balls and fry for 8 minutes or until lightly golden all over. Remove with a slotted spoon and drain. Repeat with the remaining oil and mushroom balls.

Dilled Chèvre Pops

◻ FLEX APPEAL SHRIMP

These pops are easy to make and easy to eat while still being sociable at a cocktail party. For the vegetarian pops, try rolling the cheese balls in chopped nuts instead of the panko crumbs. For the seafood option, try cooked crab or lobster instead of shrimp, or roll the pops in crispy bacon bits. You can use almost any green herb (or spice) here. —Pat

FLEX APPEAL

MAKES 8 POPS

½ cup (125 mL) chopped cooked shrimp

ground paprika

2 additional breadsticks

After step 2, remove half of the cheese mixture to a separate bowl and stir in the shrimp. Continue with step 3. Sprinkle the shrimp balls with paprika before placing them on the serving platter.

MAKES 12 POPS

¼ cup (60 mL) panko crumbs or finely chopped nuts

2 Tbsp (30 mL) finely grated Parmesan cheese

4 oz (125 g) chèvre at room temperature

4 oz (125 g) cream cheese at room temperature

2 sprigs fresh dill, finely chopped, plus extra for garnish

12 breadsticks

1. In a bowl, combine the panko and Parmesan. Spread evenly over a rimmed baking sheet.

2. In the same bowl, combine the chèvre and cream cheese with chopped dill.

3. Using a 1 oz (30 g) scoop, form into balls and place on the panko-Parmesan mixture on the baking sheet. Roll the cheese balls to coat with the mixture.

4. Arrange the balls on a serving platter and spear each with a breadstick. Garnish with fresh dill if desired.

MAKE-AHEAD STRATEGY

Form the pops up to 24 hours in advance. Store in an airtight container in the refrigerator. Bring to room temperature before serving.

Dilled
Chevre
Pops

Spiced Bean Cakes and Lime Cream
☐ FLEX APPEAL CRAB

I like that these cakes are baked instead of fried because this technique uses less oil. You can make these cakes tamer or hotter by adding less or more jalapeños. The Lime Cream is an optional accompaniment; for a change, top the cakes with fruit or vegetable preserves, chili sauce or salsa instead. These cakes also make a sturdy base for poached eggs or for nut spreads or cheese for an easy, portable lunch. For bite-sized hors d'oeuvres, make the cakes smaller in size and double the yield. —Pat

FLEX APPEAL

MAKES 6 CAKES

1 can (6 oz/175 g) lump crabmeat, rinsed and drained

After step 3, remove half of the bean mixture to a separate bowl and stir in the crabmeat. Divide the crab mixture into 6 equal portions and the vegetarian mixture into 4 equal portions and continue with step 5.

MAKES 8 CAKES

3 Tbsp (45 mL) olive or avocado oil

1 onion, chopped

4 green onions, sliced

4 cloves garlic, finely chopped

1 jalapeño, finely chopped

1 Tbsp (15 mL) Moroccan Spice Blend (page 181)

1 can (19 oz/540 mL) black-eyed peas, drained and rinsed (see Recipe Note)

1 large sweet potato, peeled and coarsely grated

1 large egg, lightly beaten

½ tsp (2 mL) coarse salt

½ cup (125 mL) Lime Cream (recipe follows)

1. Preheat the oven to 375°F (190°C).

2. In a skillet, heat the oil over medium heat. Sauté the onion for 5 minutes or until soft. Stir in the green onions, garlic, jalapeño and spice blend. Cook, stirring frequently, for 3 to 5 minutes or until the vegetables are soft and fragrant. Let cool slightly.

3. Meanwhile, in a bowl, using a fork or potato masher, mash the black-eyed peas, leaving about one-quarter of them whole. Stir in the sweet potato, egg and salt, and mix well. Stir in the onion mixture.

4. Divide into 8 portions of equal size.

5. Arrange the portions about 1 inch (2.5 cm) apart on 2 rimmed baking sheets. Using a fork, pat into compact, round shapes and flatten to about ½ inch (1 cm) thick. Bake in 350°F (180°C) oven for 15 minutes, turn over and bake for 8 minutes more.

6. Serve with the Lime Cream alongside.

Lime Cream

MAKES ½ CUP (125 mL)

½ cup (125 mL) reduced fat sour cream

½ lime, juiced

---

1. In a bowl, combine the sour cream and lime juice.

MAKE-AHEAD STRATEGY

This recipe is easily doubled to make extra for freezing. Bake and cool completely, then stack with parchment paper between the cakes and pack in sealable freezer bags or airtight containers. Freeze for up to 2 months. Thaw in the refrigerator and reheat on a baking sheet in a 350°F (220°C) oven for 10 minutes or until heated through.

RECIPE NOTE

I like black-eyed peas in this recipe because of their soft and creamy texture, but Nettie tells me that a good organic canned brand can be hard to find. You can always use black beans, kidney beans, lima beans or even chickpeas in this recipe.

Spicy Lentil Pinwheels

Spicy Lentil Pinwheels
☐ FLEX APPEAL CHICKEN

These spicy, samosa-style rolls of tender lentils are great for a grab-and-go lunch, easy to make and baked, not fried. If you have cooked potatoes or other vegetables on hand, you can chop them and add up to 1 cup (250 mL) to the filling. Turkey works just as well as chicken here. —Pat

MAKES 18 PINWHEELS

4 tsp (20 mL) coconut or avocado oil

½ onion, chopped

1 clove garlic, finely chopped

1 tsp (5 mL) curry powder or garam masala

1 cup (250 mL) cooked lentils (see Recipe Note)

½ cup (125 mL) fresh or frozen peas

2 Tbsp (30 mL) coarsely chopped walnuts

1 Tbsp (15 mL) freshly squeezed lemon juice

½ pkg (17.3 oz/490 g) frozen puff pastry sheets, thawed

¼ cup (60 mL) melted butter

1. Preheat the oven to 425°F (220°C).

2. To make the filling, heat the oil in a skillet over medium-high heat. Sauté the onion for 5 minutes or until soft. Add garlic and curry powder and cook, stirring frequently, for 2 minutes. Remove from the heat and add the lentils, peas, walnuts and lemon juice. Set aside.

3. To assemble the pinwheels, pat the pastry into a rectangle on a lightly floured work surface. Cut the pastry in half crosswise. Pile the filling along the long sides of each pastry half. ←

4. Roll up each pastry half and place seam-side down on a pizza stone or parchment paper–lined baking sheet. Chill in the freezer for about 20 minutes.

5. Cut the pastry rolls into ¾-inch (2 cm) slices and place in one layer on the pizza stone or parchment paper–lined baking sheet. Brush with melted butter and bake for 10 to 12 minutes or until the pastry is golden.

continued on next page >

FLEX APPEAL

MAKES 9 PINWHEELS

3 oz (90 g) shaved chicken or turkey

In step 3, after placing the lentil filling, top one of the pastry halves with the shaved chicken before rolling the pastry.

> Spicy Lentil Pinwheels continued

RECIPE NOTE

Dried lentils are easy to cook because they do not require soaking. Use green, black, brown, yellow or red lentils and rinse well before cooking. To make 1 cup (250 mL) cooked lentils, measure 2 cups (500 mL) water and bring to a boil. Add ½ cup (125 mL) lentils, stir and simmer for 15 to 20 minutes or until tender. Drain and rinse. Note: Adding salt to the cooking water retards the cooking of dried lentils, peas and beans and they will not become tender. Always add salt after cooking lentils.

TIME-SAVING STRATEGY

Use frozen or canned cooked lentils and use any leftover amount in other recipes.

MAKE-AHEAD STRATEGIES

- Prepare filling up to 2 days ahead, wrap tightly and refrigerate until ready to make pinwheels. Bring to room temperature before baking.
- Pinwheels may be baked, cooled, wrapped and frozen for up to 3 months. To reheat, remove from wrappings, place on a cookie sheet or preheated pizza stone and warm in a 350°F (180°C) oven for 15 to 20 minutes or until heated through. Pinwheels that have been frozen and reheated are softer than those baked fresh.

PLAN-AHEAD STRATEGY

Make twice the amount of filling, mix half with tomato sauce and use as a topping for pasta or rice. The filling can also be frozen for up to 3 months and added to soups or stews.

breakfast dinners

Classic Mushroom Omelette *38*
FLEX APPEAL Ham, Sausage, Bacon, Turkey
or Seafood

Apple Cinnamon French Toast *40*

Mediterranean Frittata *41*
FLEX APPEAL Chorizo

Basque Eggs *42*
FLEX APPEAL Ham or Bacon

Huevos Rancheros *46*

Red Potato, Mushroom and
Red Pepper Hash *47*

Tempeh Scramble *48*
FLEX APPEAL Italian Sausage

Timely Tacos *51*

Mango, Cherry and Cottage Cheese
Burritos *53*
FLEX APPEAL Turkey

Sweet Potato, Halloumi and
Avocado Hash *54*
FLEX APPEAL Ham

Classic Mushroom Omelette

☐ FLEX APPEAL HAM, SAUSAGE, BACON, TURKEY OR SEAFOOD

Omelettes are so versatile. You can whip one up with almost any vegetable or pantry staple. I love the combination of mushrooms, onions, celery and herbs served with homemade chili sauce (as shown), but cooked fresh (or canned) asparagus with fontina cheese or leeks and fresh thyme are other tasty combinations. For a Mediterranean flavour, try roasted red peppers, spinach, tomatoes and feta cheese. —Pat

FLEX APPEAL

MAKES 1 SERVING

2 Tbsp (30 mL) cooked, shredded or finely diced ham, sausage, bacon, turkey or seafood

In step 5, top one half of the cooked vegetables with your choice of meat before folding the omelette.

about this recipe

What makes it work?

Cooking the onions and mushrooms in butter makes them taste divine. If you prefer, you can substitute olive or avocado oil for the butter.

Using the right utensils and paying attention to cooking temperature will ensure a perfect omelette every time.

MAKES 2 SERVINGS

2 Tbsp (30 mL) butter

1 onion, chopped

1 celery stalk, chopped

¼ lb (125 g) cremini mushrooms, sliced

2 tsp (10 mL) fresh thyme leaves

sea salt and pepper

4 large eggs, at room temperature

2 Tbsp (30 mL) water

¼ cup (60 mL) shredded cheddar cheese, plus 2 Tbsp (30 mL) for garnish

½ cup (125 mL) Sweet Thai Chili Sauce (page 184) (optional)

1. Warm 2 plates in a 200°F (95°C) oven.

2. In a skillet, melt 1 Tbsp (15 mL) of the butter over medium heat. Add the onion and sauté for 3 minutes. Add the celery and mushrooms and cook, stirring occasionally, for 5 minutes or until the onions are soft and the mushrooms are brown and their juices have evaporated. Stir in the thyme and season with salt and pepper. Using a slotted spoon, transfer the vegetables to a bowl and keep warm.

3. In a bowl, whisk together the eggs, water and a few more grinds of salt and pepper. Add the remaining 1 Tbsp (15 mL) butter to the skillet and melt over medium heat. Tilt the pan to cover the bottom evenly with butter.

4. Add the egg mixture to the pan and cook just until the eggs have begun to set around the outside edges, about 30 seconds. Using a spatula, lift the cooked eggs at the far side of the pan and gently push them toward the centre, tilting the pan to allow the uncooked liquid egg on top to flow underneath. Cook for 30 seconds or until the egg liquid has set around the outside edges. Repeat the process of lifting the cooked eggs, pushing them to the centre and letting the uncooked egg on top flow underneath to be cooked.

Classic Mushroom Omelette

5. When there is no more liquid egg mixture on top and the eggs are almost completely set but still slightly moist on top, sprinkle the cooked vegetables over one half of the omelette in the pan. Sprinkle ¼ cup (60 mL) of the cheese over the vegetables.

6. Using the spatula, fold the untopped half of the omelette over the filled half to create a half-moon shape. Cover and cook for 30 seconds. Cut in half and slide onto heated plates. Garnish each half omelette with 1 Tbsp (30 mL) shredded cheese and half of the chili sauce, if desired.

RECIPE NOTES

- Well-seasoned cast iron or heavy-bottomed stainless steel pans are best for cooking omelettes. Some recipes call for a non-stick pan, but using only medium to medium-low heat and coating a pan with butter will prevent sticking. An 8-inch (20 cm) pan with curved sides is ideal for a 4-egg, 2-serving omelette.

- If you wish to serve 4 people, double the recipe, cook half to make one 2-person omelette and repeat for the second omelette. Keep the first omelette warm in the oven.

Apple Cinnamon French Toast

You know that expression "one bad apple can spoil the whole bunch"? Well, it's true. I always separate any bruised or less than 100% specimens. I keep apples in the refrigerator in a plastic bag with a few strategically placed holes. We don't want the apples to shrivel and we want to prevent excessive moisture build-up. Sturdier, late season apples retain their shape when cooked. Empire, Gala, Pippin and Ida Red are good choices for the apple cinnamon sauce recipe (maple syrup, move over). Returning from a trip, I often have this dish for dinner because it's easy to prepare and digest. —Nettie

MAKES 6 SERVINGS

2 cups (500 mL) vanilla almond, soy or regular milk	¼ tsp (1 mL) sea salt
½ cup (125 mL) Apple Butter (page 181)	2 Tbsp (30 mL) salted butter, divided
1 tsp (5 mL) pure vanilla extract	12 slices (½ inch/1 cm thick) challah (egg bread) or soft crusty French bread
½ tsp (2 mL) ground cinnamon	Apple Cinnamon Sauce (recipe follows)

1. Combine the milk, apple butter, vanilla, cinnamon and salt in a blender or food processor. Blend for 30 seconds or until smooth. Pour into a bowl.

2. Heat 1 Tbsp (15 mL) of the butter in a large skillet over medium heat. Dip the bread slices into the milk batter, coating evenly. Cook for 3 to 5 minutes on each side, or until lightly browned. Add the remaining 1 Tbsp (15 mL) butter to the skillet as needed.

3. Serve the Apple Cinnamon Sauce over the cooked toast or pass separately.

Apple Cinnamon Sauce

RECIPE NOTE

You can use pears combined with apples for the sauce. Over-ripe and slightly bruised fruit (with bruised spots removed) are terrific ingredients that pack a lot of flavour if not beauty.

MAKES 2 CUPS (500 mL)

1 Tbsp (15 mL) salted butter or coconut oil	3 Tbsp (45 mL) sugar
4 large apples, peeled, cored and thinly sliced (see Recipe Note)	½ tsp (2 mL) ground cinnamon
	1 Tbsp (15 mL) freshly squeezed lemon juice

1. Heat the butter in a skillet over medium-high heat. Add the apples and cook for 5 minutes or until softened. Reduce the heat to medium and add the sugar and cinnamon. Stir and cook for 5 minutes. Add the lemon juice, stir, remove from the heat and set aside.

Mediterranean Frittata

☐ FLEX APPEAL CHORIZO

A frittata has similar ingredients to those of a classic omelette but is filled with more ingredients and is cooked in the oven, which makes it a perfect brunch or dinner dish. In this Mediterranean-flavoured recipe, olive oil replaces butter. When meat is added to frittata, the popular choice is chorizo: a fresh or cured pork sausage seasoned with dried smoked paprika that originated in Spain. You can use breakfast or sweet Italian sausage if you prefer them to chorizo. —Pat

MAKES 4 SERVINGS

2 Tbsp (30 mL) olive or avocado oil

1 onion, chopped

1 Tbsp (15 mL) finely chopped fresh oregano (see Recipe Note)

¼ cup (60 mL) chopped roasted red pepper or cooked artichokes (see Time-Saving Strategy)

8 large eggs

¾ cup (185 mL) milk

sea salt and pepper

¼ cup (60 mL) crumbled fresh goat cheese

1. Preheat the oven to 400°F (200°C).

2. In a skillet, heat the oil over medium heat. Add the onion and sauté for 5 minutes or until soft and transparent. Remove from the heat and stir in the oregano and red pepper. Toss to mix well.

3. Lightly oil a 10- × 15-inch (25 × 39 cm) baking dish and spread the vegetable mixture evenly over the bottom.

4. In a bowl, combine the eggs, milk and a few grinds of salt and pepper. Whisk until well blended.

5. Pour the egg mixture over the vegetables in the baking dish. Sprinkle the goat cheese evenly over all. Bake for 25 to 30 minutes or until puffed and golden.

RECIPE NOTE

If you don't have fresh oregano, use other fresh green herbs, such as thyme, sage or rosemary. You can use just one or a combination of herbs in this recipe.

FLEX APPEAL

MAKES 2 SERVINGS

4 oz (125 g) fresh chorizo or sausage (see Time-Saving Strategy)

Before starting the recipe, cook the fresh chorizo. Remove the meat from the casing and in a skillet, heat 1 Tbsp (15 mL) olive or avocado oil. Add the chorizo and cook, stirring frequently, for 7 to 10 minutes, breaking up the meat with the back of a wooden spoon. When cooked through, the meat shows no signs of pink. Set aside.

In step 5, sprinkle the cooked chorizo over half of the frittata before adding the goat cheese.

TIME-SAVING STRATEGIES

- You can save time by using canned artichokes and roasted red peppers (drain well before adding to the pan).

- You can save time by using ½ cup (125 mL) diced fermented, cured or smoked chorizo, which does not need to be cooked ahead of time, instead of fresh chorizo.

Basque Eggs

FLEX APPEAL HAM OR BACON

This recipe has become one of my favourite breakfast dinners and it's different each time I make it, depending on who is home and what I have in the refrigerator or pantry. It's so easy that, after you make it once, you will be able to whip it up anywhere, anytime, without even glancing at the recipe. Adding a good local cheese, or trying whatever frozen greens you have on hand (and for the meat-eaters whatever cooked meat or seafood you have on hand) keeps it interesting. —Pat

FLEX APPEAL

MAKES 2 SERVINGS

½ cup (125 mL) chopped cooked ham or bacon

After step 2, sprinkle the ham over half of the vegetables in the pan before continuing with step 3.

MAKES 4 SERVINGS

2 Tbsp (30 mL) olive or avocado oil

1 onion, chopped

8 oz (250 g) mushrooms, sliced

1 Tbsp (15 mL) butter or olive oil

1 potato

2 cups (500 mL) chopped fresh, or thawed and drained, frozen spinach

4 large eggs

1 tsp (5 mL) paprika

1. In a cast iron or heavy-bottomed skillet, heat the oil over medium heat. Add the onion and sauté for 5 minutes or until soft and translucent. Add the mushrooms and cook, stirring occasionally, for 3 to 5 minutes or until the mushrooms are soft and have released their juices.

2. Add the butter, reduce the heat to low and grate or thinly slice the potato into the mixture. Stir well, cover the pan and cook, stirring occasionally, for 8 to 10 minutes or until the potato is tender-crisp. Stir in the spinach, cover and cook for 2 to 3 minutes or until wilted.

3. Make 4 little hollows in the vegetable mixture and break an egg into each. Cover the pan and cook for 5 to 8 minutes or until the whites are firm and opaque and the yolks are still runny. If you prefer firm yolks, break the eggs and cook for 1 or 2 minutes more, or until hard.

4. Garnish the eggs with the paprika. Use a spatula to lift the eggs and vegetables onto 4 warmed serving plates.

Basque
Eggs

RECIPE NOTES

For variety, you can:

· Omit the mushrooms and add half a green
  or red bell pepper, chopped, with the onion
  in step 1.

· Add grated carrot, turnip or parsnip with
  the potato in step 2.

· Add 2 finely chopped garlic cloves with the
  potatoes in step 2.

· Omit the mushrooms and add 2 quartered
  tomatoes with the spinach or in place of the
  spinach in step 2.

· Add 2 Tbsp (30 mL) chopped fresh basil or
  1 Tbsp (15 mL) fresh thyme leaves with the
  spinach in step 2.

· Sprinkle ¼ cup (60 mL) grated cheese over
  the vegetables after adding eggs in step 3.

continued on next page ›

about this recipe

What makes it great?

It's easy, it's fast and it's nutritious. And if that isn't enough, you can make it with staple ingredients that you may already have on hand.

What makes it work?

The key to cooking the vegetables fast is to slice or shred them very thin. For this, you can use the slicing or shredding disc of a food processor, but I find it is just as easy to use a hand-held, flat, stainless steel shredder. A small, lightweight mandoline is great for superfine slicing. These tools store easily and are easy to use and clean.

What is essential?

In this recipe, it's the quality of the pan. Good-quality, well-seasoned skillets make stovetop cooking a pleasure. Look for stainless steel pans with a copper core (they're heavy on the bottom) or cast iron, because they conduct heat well and stay hot at very low temperatures. In fact, to keep starchy food such as raw potatoes and protein food such as eggs from sticking, it's important to always use low heat. But if the pan doesn't retain heat well, the food won't cook properly. Once you understand how to season and clean your skillet and use heat to control sticking, you will be happy with the results and your food will be safer in pans that are not coated with plastic or chemicals.

To season cast iron or non-stick stainless steel skillets: Heat the oven to 300°F (150°C) and turn it off. Cover the bottom of the pan with salt and pour cooking oil into the pan until it reaches a depth of 1 inch (2.5 cm). Let stand in the heated oven for 12 hours. On the stovetop over medium-high heat, heat the oil until very hot (but not smoking). Let cool slightly, discard oil and wipe pan thoroughly with paper towels while the pan is still very warm. You can do this once or twice a year as a proactive approach to maintaining the patina on your pan or if it comes in contact with water.

To care for a seasoned skillet: Do not immerse in water or wash the seasoned pan after use. Simply sprinkle salt in the bottom of the warm skillet and wipe clean with paper towels, then wipe using a damp towel.

With cast iron or other heavy-bottomed skillets, you can heat the oil in the pan over medium to medium-high heat and sauté onions and other vegetables over medium or medium-low heat, but always use medium-low for protein or starchy foods. If you do this, the oil will be healthier because it is not overheated and you won't have sticking problems.

Can I use a tagine for this dish?

Yes! A tagine works well for this dish because the steam created by the domed lid cooks the eggs perfectly.

about eggs

What makes them so nutritious?

As a relatively inexpensive food, eggs deliver important nutrients. They contain high-quality protein and a significant amount of absorbable iron, as well as being an important source of choline, a nutrient important for its role in fetal brain development and in memory function. Eggs are one of the few natural food sources of vitamin D.

The antioxidant carotenoid pigments are the phytonutrients that give the yolks their rich yellow colour. These pigments help protect the eye against macular degeneration and they're higher in eggs from free-range hens.

What about their colour?

The colour of the shell—which can be white, brown, green or blue—comes from the pigments that are deposited on the egg as it makes its way through the oviduct. Generally, most hens with white feathers and earlobes (such as the white leghorn) lay white eggs, whereas brown eggs usually come from hens with red feathers and red earlobes (like the barred rock or cuckoo maran). Some breeds with red earlobes (the ameraucana, for example) may lay blue or green eggs.

As for the colour of the yolk, pasture-raised hens that get lots of greens in their diet produce eggs that have a deep orange colour (due to an abundance of the carotenoid pigments mentioned above) and are naturally higher (up to 30% higher) in omega-3 fatty acids.

Why are eggs important in cooking?

· Whole eggs give structure to sauces, baked goods and dishes such as beans or meatloaf because when heated, the proteins form a firm web that holds ingredients together.

· When beaten, whole eggs trap air, which swells when heated and puffs out to leaven cakes, breads and other baked products.

· The whites, yolks or the whole beaten egg helps to brown and glaze pastry and breads when brushed on just before baking.

· Egg yolks bind and thicken sauces such as mayonnaise and hollandaise.

· Egg yolks create a creamy smooth texture in custards, sauces and fillings.

· Egg whites contain no fat and help give extra puff to baked soufflés, angel food cakes and cream puffs.

Huevos Rancheros

A good salsa, either store-bought or homemade, is a great pantry staple. I seem to be always trying new ones, so my cupboard is well stocked most of the time. You can use flour or corn tortillas (as used in traditonal Mexican cooking) as the base, but when I have Indian naan or other good flatbread I use one of them instead. This is an incredibly fast meal; for a heartier dinner, serve the huevos rancheros with cooked whole grains such as wheat berries, brown rice or amaranth. —Pat

MAKES 4 SERVINGS

1½ cups (375 mL) tomato or green salsa	4 large eggs
2 cups (500 mL) refried beans	sea salt and pepper
1 flatbread or naan, or 4 small tortillas	½ cup (125 mL) crumbled feta cheese
3 Tbsp (45 mL) coconut or avocado oil, divided	¼ cup (60 mL) chopped fresh cilantro or flat-leaf parsley

1. Preheat the oven to 200°F (95°C).

2. In a saucepan over low heat, warm the salsa. Keep warm, stirring occasionally.

3. In another saucepan over low heat, warm the refried beans. Keep warm, stirring occasionally.

4. Divide the flatbread into 4 pieces. Place on a parchment paper–lined, rimmed baking sheet and drizzle with 1 Tbsp (15 mL) of the oil. Cover with foil and keep warm in the oven.

5. In a skillet, heat the remaining 2 Tbsp (30 mL) oil over medium-high heat. Crack the eggs into the pan and season with salt and pepper. Cover, reduce the heat to medium-low and cook until the whites are set, about 2 minutes for sunny side up. If desired, carefully flip the eggs and cook for 1 minute or until the yolks are firm.

6. Spread the warm refried beans over flatbread. Place the eggs over the beans, overlapping if necessary. Spoon the warm salsa over the eggs and top with the cheese and cilantro.

Red Potato, Mushroom and Red Pepper Hash

Hash always tastes better when the potatoes have been precooked because all their starch has been released. They are also a perfect thickening agent. Precooking saves time too. Cast iron skillets make the best hash. —Nettie

MAKES 6 SERVINGS

1 lb (500 g) small red potatoes, quartered

3 carrots, cut into ½-inch (1 cm) slices

3 Tbsp (45 mL) coconut or avocado oil

2 Tbsp (30 mL) butter

1 red onion, chopped

1 cup (250 mL) button mushrooms

1 red bell pepper, thinly sliced

1 tsp (5 mL) dried thyme leaves

1 tsp (5 mL) rinsed capers

1 tsp (5 mL) sea salt

¼ tsp (1 mL) black pepper

½ cup (125 mL) crème fraîche or sour cream, for garnish

chopped chives, for garnish

1. Bring a pot of salted water to a boil over high heat. Add the potatoes, cover and reduce the heat to medium-low. Simmer for 5 minutes. Add the carrots and cook for 10 minutes or until the vegetables are tender when pierced with the tip of a knife. Drain and set aside.

2. Heat the oil and butter in a skillet over medium-high heat. Add the onion and cook for 5 minutes, stirring occasionally. Add the mushrooms, bell pepper, thyme and capers. Cook for 5 minutes or until the vegetables are soft. Add the cooked potatoes and carrots, then the salt and pepper. Mix well.

3. Cook over medium heat, stirring occasionally, for 6 to 8 minutes or until a golden crust forms on the potatoes.

4. Divide among 6 bowls and top with the crème fraîche and chives.

Tempeh Scramble

☐ FLEX APPEAL ITALIAN SAUSAGE

This is a quick, easy-to-prepare breakfast dinner that is very versatile. You can serve this dish with leftover rice or toast, or wrapped in a burrito. I have prepared a variation of this scramble with 8 oz (250 g) crumbled tofu instead of tempeh and ½ tsp (2 mL) of turmeric (to give the tofu the same colour as eggs) and it was sensational. —Nettie

FLEX APPEAL

MAKES 2 SERVINGS

> 1 Tbsp (15 mL) olive or avocado oil
>
> 6 oz (175 g) hot or sweet Italian sausage, cut into ½-inch (1 cm) pieces

In step 2, while the vegetables are cooking, heat the oil in a skillet over medium heat. Add the sausage pieces and cook, stirring occasionally, for about 6 to 8 minutes or until the pieces are browned and cooked through.

In step 3, before adding the tempeh, remove 1 cup (250 mL) of the vegetable mixture and set aside. When the sausage is cooked, add the reserved vegetable mixture to the sausage in the skillet and heat through.

In step 4, divide the tempeh scramble among 4 bowls instead of 6. Divide the sausage scramble between 2 bowls. Garnish with the pumpkin seeds.

MAKES 6 SERVINGS

> ¼ cup (60 mL) plus 2 Tbsp (30 mL) coconut or avocado oil, divided
>
> 8 oz (250 g) package frozen tempeh, thawed and crumbled (see About Tempeh)
>
> 1 cup (250 mL) chopped red onion
>
> 3 cloves garlic, minced
>
> ½ cup (125 mL) grated carrot
>
> 1 cup (250 mL) thinly sliced red bell peppers
>
> 2 cups (500 mL) Swiss chard or spinach, thinly sliced
>
> 1 Tbsp (15 mL) freshly squeezed lemon juice
>
> 1 fresh green chili, finely chopped
>
> ½ tsp (2 mL) ground cumin
>
> 1 Tbsp (15 mL) chopped fresh basil
>
> 1 tsp (5 mL) sea salt
>
> ½ cup (125 mL) toasted pumpkin seeds (see Recipe Note)

1. In a wok or skillet, heat ¼ cup (60 mL) of the oil over medium-high heat. Add the tempeh and cook, stirring frequently, for 8 to 10 minutes or until reddish brown. Transfer to a lint-free cloth or paper towel using a slotted spoon. Wipe the wok clean of any residual bits.

2. Add the remaining 2 Tbsp (30 mL) oil to the wok over medium heat. Add the onion and sauté for 5 minutes or until soft. Add the garlic and cook, stirring constantly, for 1 minute. Stir in the carrot, peppers, chard, lemon juice, chili, cumin, basil and salt. Cook, stirring often, for 5 minutes.

3. Add the cooked tempeh to the wok. Cook, stirring constantly, for 2 to 4 minutes or until the tempeh is heated through.

4. Divide the tempeh scramble among 6 bowls and garnish with the pumpkin seeds.

about tempeh

A high-protein soy food, tempeh is made by inoculating crushed cooked soybeans with the bacteria *Rhizopus oligosporus,* then incubating them at a high temperature. The fermentation process enhances the flavour and breaks down the soybeans' complex proteins, fats and carbohydrates to make them easily digestable.

Tempeh is sold fresh and frozen, and will keep in the freezer for up to 6 months. It will thaw overnight in the refrigerator or within 3 hours unrefrigerated. Fresh tempeh has a shorter expiry period than frozen, so always check the expiry date. One problem I have encountered with fresh tempeh is its inability to absorb a marinade due to its high water content.

I prefer Noble Bean tempeh made in Perth, Ontario. It has a firm, chewy texture and is drier than most tempeh sold fresh.

RECIPE NOTE

Heat a medium-sized, heavy-bottomed skillet over medium-high heat. Add pumpkin seeds and dry-roast, stirring constantly with a wooden spoon, for 3 to 5 minutes or until lightly browned. Transfer to a small bowl.

Timely
Tacos

1

2

Timely Tacos

Kids and adults love these nutritious all-in-one packets. Don't like tomatoes? Easy, just sub-stitute diced avocado or artichoke or frozen peas. No-go for the black beans? No sweat, just scoop canned baked beans right out of the can. Feta or soft goat cheese in the refrigerator but no cheddar? No problem. In fact, you can take away and add ingredients to your heart's content and the eggs will bring them all together. —Pat

MAKES 8 TACOS

2 Tbsp (30 mL) olive or avocado oil, divided	1 cup (250 mL) cooked black beans, rinsed and drained
1 onion, chopped	½ cup (125 mL) frozen or canned, drained corn kernels
½ red bell pepper, finely chopped	
6 large eggs	four to six 6-inch (15 cm) soft corn or wheat tortillas or hard, pre-folded tacos (see Recipe Note)
2 Tbsp (30 mL) water	
sea salt and pepper	½ cup (125 mL) grated cheddar cheese
1 cup (250 mL) mini tomatoes (cherry or grape), quartered	1 cup (250 mL) tomato salsa (optional)

1. Preheat the oven to 350°F (180°C).

2. In a skillet, heat 1 Tbsp (15 mL) of the oil over medium-high heat. Reduce the heat to medium-low and cook the onion, stirring frequently, for 5 minutes or until soft and translucent. Add the red pepper and cook, stirring frequently, for 3 minutes.

3. Meanwhile, in a bowl, whisk together the eggs and water. Season with salt and pepper.

4. Add the remaining 1 Tbsp (15 mL) oil to the skillet and heat on medium-high. Reduce the heat to medium-low, pour the egg mixture into the skillet and cook, stirring and scraping up the cooked eggs from the bottom of the skillet for 3 minutes or until eggs are firm but still moist.

5. Turn the heat off and add the tomatoes, beans and corn to the eggs and stir until heated through.

6. Using a ⅓ cup (80 mL) measure, spread warm filling from the skillet onto one half of a soft tortilla (or scoop into a hard, pre-folded taco). Sprinkle 1 Tbsp (15 mL) cheese overtop. Fold soft tortillas in half and place on a parchment paper–lined, rimmed baking sheet (or stand hard tacos upright on the baking sheet).

7. Warm in the oven for 1 to 2 minutes or until the cheese is melted. Serve with salsa, if desired.

continued on next page >

RECIPE NOTES

- Tortillas may be made from corn or wheat and they may be either soft or crisp. You can use either soft corn or wheat tortillas or hard, pre-folded tacos in this recipe. See image ❶.

- The key to great scrambled eggs is to use low heat and remove the pan from the heat when the eggs are set but still moist. In this recipe, the cooked eggs are mixed with other ingredients, stuffed or wrapped and warmed in the oven, so you don't want them dry from the start. Be careful toward the end of the cooking stage in step 4 and remove the pan from the heat while the eggs are still moist on top, as you can see in the photograph. See image ❷.

> Timely Tacos continued

about mini tomatoes

This recipe calls for mini tomatoes; a cherry variety is called Golden Honey Bunch.

You can also use grape tomatoes.

The difference between the two types is in their shape: cherry tomatoes are round and grape tomatoes are oval or teardrop in shape. Most varieties of mini tomatoes are sweet and there are several varieties that you can easily grow in containers or purchase from a market garden.

Storing Mini Tomatoes: Rinse under warm running water and pat dry. Tomatoes are best (and will keep up to 10 days) if stored at cool (45 to 60°F/7 to 15°C) room temperatures. If you don't have a cool storage space, keep tomatoes in the refrigerator. They will keep there for up to 5 days.

Serving Mini Tomatoes: If eating tomatoes raw, always serve at room temperature for best flavour.

Mango, Cherry and Cottage Cheese Burritos
☐ FLEX APPEAL TURKEY

Beans and dried fruit are excellent burrito fillings. Add pressed or regular cottage cheese and you have a creamy, sweet mixture that tastes great any time of the day. Use canned small red beans, black beans or pinto beans, or mix any leftover cooked beans together. These burritos freeze well too. —Nettie

MAKES 6 SERVINGS

½ cup (125 mL) diced dried mango (see Recipe Note)

½ cup (125 mL) dried cherries

¾ cup (185 mL) apple juice

one 1-inch (2.5 cm) cinnamon stick

1 small jalapeño, seeds removed, finely chopped, or ½ tsp (2 mL) chili powder (optional)

1 can (14 oz/398 mL) pinto beans, drained and rinsed

½ tsp (2 mL) sea salt

1½ cups (375 mL) 2% pressed or regular cottage cheese

2 Tbsp (30 mL) chopped fresh parsley

six 10-inch (25 cm) flour or gluten-free tortillas

1. In a saucepan, combine the mango, cherries, apple juice, cinnamon stick and jalapeño, if using. Cook, stirring frequently, over low heat for 5 minutes.

2. Add the beans and bring to a boil over high heat. Reduce the heat and simmer, uncovered, for 5 minutes, stirring often. Discard the cinnamon stick. Add the salt, cottage cheese and parsley.

3. In a large skillet, warm each tortilla over medium heat for 2 minutes, turning once.

4. As each tortilla is warmed, remove from the heat and place ¾ cup (185 mL) of filling down the centre, leaving 1 inch (2.5 cm) uncovered at bottom and top. Fold the bottom and the top over the filling; fold the sides overtop to close. ←

RECIPE NOTE

Organic dried fruit is my favourite snack on a car journey. It takes a long time to soften the piece of dried fruit and the flavour is intense. One time, I went to prepare this recipe and my son Cameron confessed to eating up my dried mango supply. I substituted pineapple, but could have used banana chips as well.

FLEX APPEAL

MAKES 2 SERVINGS

½ cup (125 mL) cooked, skinless, boneless turkey or chicken strips

In step 4, top the filling on 2 of the tortillas with the turkey strips before folding the tortillas.

Sweet Potato, Halloumi and Avocado Hash
▢ FLEX APPEAL HAM

FLEX APPEAL

MAKES 2 SERVINGS

½ lb (250 g) diced cooked ham

After step 5, top 2 of the dishes with ham.

RECIPE NOTE

Most halloumi requires soaking in water to remove excess salt. A brief soak in cool water will reduce the salinity while maintaining the flavour and texture.

about halloumi

Originally a Cypriot specialty that is thousands of years old, halloumi cheese holds its shape when grilled or fried; the surface caramelizes and the interior is soft and smooth, with a subtle salty presence. A delicate shade of ivory, with a slightly porous texture, this cheese can be used in many ways and incorporated into many dishes.

The texture of the halloumi cheese combines so well with the black beans and avocado. This dish is beautiful to look at with its contrasting textures. Try serving the hash in half a pita, in half a cantaloupe or rolled in a wrap. —Nettie

MAKES 6 SERVINGS

2 cups (500 mL) sweet potato, cut into 1-inch (2.5 cm) cubes

4 Tbsp (60 mL) coconut or avocado oil, divided

½ tsp (2 mL) ground cumin

1 jalapeño, finely diced, or ½ tsp (2 mL) chili powder

4 green onions, trimmed and thinly sliced

10 oz (300 g) grape or cherry tomatoes, halved

1 can (19 oz/540 mL) black or red beans, drained and rinsed

2 cups (500 mL) spinach leaves

⅔ lb (350 g) halloumi cheese, grated (see Recipe Note)

1 firm, ripe avocado, coarsely chopped

¼ tsp (1 mL) sea salt

¼ tsp (1 mL) pepper

1. In a saucepan, cover the sweet potatoes with water and cook over medium-high heat for 10 minutes or until tender. Drain and set aside until cool enough to handle.

2. Heat 2 Tbsp (30 mL) of the oil in a large saucepan over medium heat. Add the cumin and cook, stirring for 30 seconds. Add the cooled sweet potatoes and cook, stirring often, for 4 to 5 minutes or until golden. Transfer to a bowl.

3. Wipe the saucepan clean of any residual bits and heat the remaining 2 Tbsp (30 mL) oil over high heat. Add the jalapeño, green onions, tomatoes, beans and spinach. Cook for 4 minutes. Add the grated cheese and cook, stirring frequently, for 5 minutes.

4. Add the sweet potatoes back to the pan and cook for another 2 to 4 minutes or until the potatoes are heated through. Remove the pan from heat and stir in the avocado. Add salt and pepper.

5. Spoon the hash onto 6 serving dishes.

skillet suppers and stir-fry dinners

Corn and
Lentil
Fritters

about chickpea flour

Chickpea flour, also known as besan, channa flour or gram flour, is made by grinding raw chickpeas (also known as garbanzo beans) to a fine powder. It's the perfect flour for making fritters, patties or vegetable cakes because it firms up and holds the vegetables and other ingredients together.

If you can't find chickpea flour at your supermarket, try Indian, Turkish, Spanish or even Italian food specialty stores. You can make your own by processing small amounts of chickpeas (½ cup to 1 cup/125 mL to 250 mL) at a time in a blender or food processor. The fineness of the powder will depend on the quality of the equipment used.

Corn and Lentil Fritters
☐ FLEX APPEAL SHRIMP

These little packages of pure flavour are fabulous! The secret is in the chickpea flour. Top these versatile fritters with yogurt, guacamole, sour cream, salsa, chili sauce, peanut butter or other spreads, pâté, fruit chutney, jam or other preserves. Serve them with Thai Slaw (page 147) or sliced tomatoes and spinach (steamed or raw) drizzled with herbed oil. Use them as the base for poached eggs or for fried egg sandwiches. Make a grilled cheese or panini sandwich with fritters in place of bread slices. These are just a few hints about how to use these fritters, but you will see the potential once you try them. —Pat

MAKES 8 FRITTERS

½ cup (125 mL) chickpea flour (see About Chickpea Flour)	sea salt and cracked black pepper
½ tsp (2 mL) baking powder	1½ cups (375 mL) corn kernels (see Recipe Note)
¼ cup (60 mL) milk	½ cup (125 mL) brown or yellow cooked lentils (see Recipe Note)
1 large egg	2 green onions, chopped
3 to 4 Tbsp (45 to 60 mL) coconut or avocado oil, divided	1 Tbsp (15 mL) chopped fresh sage

1. Preheat the oven to 350°F (180°C).

2. In a bowl, whisk together the flour and baking powder. Whisk in the milk, egg and 1 Tbsp (15 mL) of the oil. Add a few grinds of salt and pepper. Add the corn, lentils, onions and sage. ←

3. In a skillet, heat 1 Tbsp (15 mL) of the oil over medium-high heat. Using a ¼-cup (60 mL) dry measure, scoop the batter into the skillet and flatten slightly. See images ❶ and ❷.

4. Cook in batches, adding oil to the skillet as needed, for 2 to 3 minutes on each side or until golden. Drain on absorbent paper.

5. Transfer to a heatproof platter or baking sheet and keep the fritters warm in the oven while you cook the remaining batter.

continued on next page >

FLEX APPEAL

Any finely chopped, cooked meat will work in these fritters, but shrimp are easy to use if you have them on hand in the freezer. You do not need to thaw the shrimp before using— simply rinse and let sit while you prepare the fritter batter. The shrimp are easier to chop when slightly frozen. See image ❸.

MAKES 5 FRITTERS

- ¼ cup (60 mL) chickpea flour
- ¼ tsp (1 mL) baking powder
- 1 large egg
- 1 Tbsp (15 mL) milk
- 2 to 3 Tbsp (30 to 45 mL) coconut or avocado oil, divided
- 1 cup (250 mL) chopped cooked shrimp (about 14 large)
- 4 small fresh sage leaves and 5 fresh thyme sprigs (optional)

In a bowl, whisk together the flour and baking powder. In a separate bowl, whisk the egg, milk and 1 Tbsp (15 mL) of the oil. Whisk the egg mixture into the flour mixture. Set the batter aside while preparing the corn-lentil mixture in step 2.

After step 2, divide the corn-lentil mixture in half and add the extra batter and the shrimp to one half. Continue with step 3, placing a sage leaf on top of each vegetarian fritter and a thyme sprig on each shrimp fritter to mark them, if desired.

> Corn and Lentil Fritters continued

RECIPE NOTES

- You can use fresh, frozen or canned corn kernels in this recipe. If you use frozen corn, thaw the kernels before adding, and if you use canned corn, drain it well.

- To cook lentils, simmer ¼ cup (60 mL) lentils in ½ cup (125 mL) water for 20 to 30 minutes or until tender. If you use canned lentils, you can use the leftovers in salads, stir-fries and casseroles.

- You can replace the lentils with cooked beans or vegetables, or a combination of vegetables and nuts.

- Add 1 tsp (5 mL) of Tex-Mex or Moroccan Spice Blend (page 181) to jazz up the flavour.

PLAN-AHEAD STRATEGY

Double the recipe and enjoy these for breakfast the next morning. They're great at room temperature or toast them and serve with jam or preserves. They also freeze well in an airtight container for up to 2 weeks.

Falafel with Spiced Tahini Dressing

This makes a terrific appetizer, main course or side dish. I like to serve falafels inside a pita pocket garnished with lettuce and tomatoes, on top of pasta with a tomato sauce, or beside cooked leafy greens and a baked root vegetable. The key to a satisfying vegetarian meal is flavour and texture. —Nettie

MAKES 6 SERVINGS

1 can (14 oz/398 mL) chickpeas, drained and rinsed

⅓ cup (80 mL) chopped red onion

½ cup (125 mL) all-purpose flour, divided

½ tsp (2 mL) sea salt

1 clove garlic, minced

1 tsp (5 mL) ground cumin

¼ tsp (1 mL) ground cayenne pepper

1 tsp (5 mL) baking powder

3 Tbsp (45 mL) chopped fresh basil

¼ cup (60 mL) olive or avocado oil

1¼ cups (310 mL) Spiced Tahini Dressing (recipe follows)

TIME-SAVING STRATEGY

Canned beans are essential for the pantry, especially when lack of time is a factor and everything cannot be prepared from scratch.

1. Combine the chickpeas, onion, 3 Tbsp (45 mL) of the flour, salt, garlic, cumin, cayenne and baking powder in a food processor or blender. Process for 2 minutes or until a coarse purée forms. Add the basil to mixture. Process for 30 seconds to blend.

2. Sprinkle a large plate with the remaining flour. Roll level tablespoons (15 mL) of the chickpea mixture into balls. Roll the balls in flour to coat well.

3. In a skillet, heat the oil over medium heat. Fry the chickpea balls until deep brown, turning once at 3 minutes. Transfer the balls to paper towels or a dish towel to drain. Serve with the tahini dressing.

Spiced Tahini Dressing

MAKES 1¼ CUPS (310 mL)

½ cup (125 mL) tahini (see About Tahini, page 17)

1 Tbsp (15 mL) olive oil

3 Tbsp (45 mL) freshly squeezed lemon juice

1 tsp (5 mL) grated lemon zest

1 clove garlic, finely chopped

½ tsp (2 mL) smoked paprika or paprika

½ tsp (2 mL) ground cumin

½ tsp (2 mL) salt

1 cup (250 mL) vegetable stock or water

MAKE-AHEAD STRATEGY

The Spiced Tahini Dressing can be made in advance and kept in an airtight container in the refrigerator for up to 5 days.

1. In a food processor, process the tahini, oil, lemon juice and zest, garlic, paprika, cumin, salt and stock for 1 minute or until smooth.

Skillet Fava Bean Paella

☐ FLEX APPEAL CHICKEN AND SHRIMP

Traditional, Valencia-style paella is loaded with chicken, seafood, sausage and even fish and is meant to serve a very large family or as a feast. Since paella always contains rice, the dish likely originated in the wet lowlands near Valencia on the Mediterranean coast of Spain where the Moors cultivated rice. The name comes from the large, shallow, cast iron skillet used to prepare the dish. Our lightened, flexible version includes tempeh and fava or lima beans as the vegetarian protein and a slimmed-down quantity of chicken and/or shrimp. You can also add fresh mussels or clams along with shrimp in place of the chicken. —Pat

FLEX APPEAL

MAKES 2 SERVINGS

    2 skinless chicken thighs or legs
    6 fresh or thawed, frozen cooked shrimp

After step 2, transfer 1 cup (250 mL) of the rice mixture into a separate pan. Stir 1 cup (250 mL) of the broth into the original skillet and the remaining 1 cup (250 mL) broth into the second pan. Add the chicken to the second pan.

Bring both pans to a boil, cover, reduce the heat to medium-low and simmer for 40 minutes or until the rice and chicken are cooked. Chicken is cooked when a thermometer inserted into the centre of the flesh reads 165°F (74°C).

Add the shrimp to the cooked chicken-rice mixture and stir until heated through.

MAKES 4 TO 6 SERVINGS

    1 pinch (about 20 strands) saffron (see Buying Saffron)
    2 cups (500 mL) vegetable broth
    2 Tbsp (30 mL) coconut or avocado oil
    1 onion, chopped
    1 leek, white and pale green parts only, sliced

    ½ red bell pepper, chopped
    3 cloves garlic, finely chopped
    ½ cup (125 mL) short brown rice (see Time-Saving Strategy)
    1 cup (250 mL) cooked fresh fava beans or 1 can (10 oz/ 284 mL) lima beans, drained

1. In a bowl, combine the saffron with the broth and set aside.

2. In a large skillet or tagine, heat the oil over medium-high heat. Sauté the onion and leek for 5 minutes. Stir in the red pepper and garlic and cook, stirring frequently, for 3 minutes or until the vegetables are soft and fragrant. Add the rice and cook, stirring frequently, for 1 minute.

3. Stir in the saffron-flavoured broth and bring to a boil. Cover the pan, reduce the heat to medium-low and simmer for 40 minutes or until the rice is cooked.

4. Stir in the beans and heat through.

TIME-SAVING STRATEGY

Using white rice instead of brown will cut the cooking time by 10 or 15 minutes.

about this recipe

What makes it work?

To experience a true Spanish flavour, using saffron (*Crocus sativus*) is essential because there is no other spice or herb that has its unmistakable musky, floral aroma and flavour.

Buying saffron

The threads or filaments, as they are called, are actually the dried stigmas of the flower. It is best to buy them whole because ground saffron is easily adulterated and is often stale. Look for small amounts of the deep red Spanish or Kashmiri saffron filaments and store them in an airtight container out of the light and heat. See image ❶.

A spice seller measures out saffron in the ancient spice market of Istanbul. See image .

Parmesan Quinoa Sliders

This recipe has it all—flavour, texture, fibre and protein—and is quick to prepare. Serve sliders with pasta and tomato sauce, or with hot or cold salads, or add them to wraps and pitas. Float sliders on top of soups (see Beet Soup, page 126) or crumble over stews. You can also use the uncooked mixture as a stuffing for cabbage rolls, bell peppers, mushroom caps and zucchini boats. —Pat

MAKES 16 SLIDERS

3 cups (750 mL) vegetable broth	¼ cup (60 mL) chopped walnuts or almonds
1½ cups (375 mL) tan-coloured quinoa, rinsed (see Recipe Note)	3 cloves garlic, finely chopped
½ cup (125 mL) whole grain breadcrumbs	2 Tbsp (30 mL) ground flaxseed
⅓ cup (80 mL) grated Parmesan or cheddar cheese	1 Tbsp (15 mL) tamari or soy sauce
¼ cup (60 mL) finely chopped green onions or chives	1 tsp (5 mL) apple cider vinegar
	2 large eggs, lightly beaten

1. In a saucepan, bring the broth to a boil. Add quinoa and cook over medium heat, stirring often, for 12 to 15 minutes or until liquid has been absorbed.

2. Meanwhile, in a bowl, combine the breadcrumbs, cheese, onions, walnuts, garlic, flaxseed, tamari and vinegar. Stir in the cooked quinoa and let stand for 10 minutes or until mixture is cool enough to handle. Add eggs and mix well.

3. Lightly oil a cast iron grilling pan. Heat the pan over medium-high heat for 2 or 3 minutes. Using a ¼-cup (60 mL) dry measure or ice cream scoop, scoop out one measure of the mixture and place in the pan. Flatten to about 1-inch (2.5 cm) thick with the back of a wooden spoon. Repeat until the pan is full, without crowding the sliders. Cook for 5 minutes, flip and cook the opposite side for 5 minutes. Repeat with the remaining mixture.

RECIPE NOTE

Use the tan-coloured variety of quinoa because it cooks in 12 to 15 minutes.

MAKE-AHEAD STRATEGY

Sliders may be made ahead, formed, tightly covered and refrigerated for up to 2 days. Bring to room temperature before cooking.

TIME-SAVING STRATEGY

Make double the quantity of these tasty sliders. After cooking, cool and then wrap them individually and freeze for up to 3 months. To reheat: remove from wrappings, place on a baking sheet or preheated pizza stone and warm in a 350°F (180°C) oven for 15 to 20 minutes or until heated through.

about quinoa

What is it?
While used like a grain, quinoa is actually the small seeds of a plant (*Chenopodium quinoa*) native to South America. The Incas considered its power to be almost supernatural and we now know that quinoa is high in protein and entirely gluten-free. See image ❶.

What about the different varieties?
There are over a dozen varieties of quinoa, some grown in North America, and the most popular is the tan-coloured variety. The red (called Red Inca) and black seeds may be slightly higher in proteins and calcium, but they take longer to cook. Look closely at the photographs on this page and you will see several different colours of quinoa seeds, including the tan, black and red seeds that are most widely available. The tan variety takes 12 to 15 minutes to cook, the red takes 18 to 25 minutes and the black can take up to 30 minutes to cook.

Why rinse?
Quinoa resembles millet in size. A bitter, resin-like substance called saponin protects it, which if not rinsed off, gives a bitter taste to the seeds. We recommend rinsing even if the label says "pre-rinsed." See image ❷.

To rinse: Measure quinoa into a fine mesh strainer and hold under cold running water for 3 to 5 minutes or until the bubbles subside. Drain well.

Why toast?
Toasting quinoa brings out the natural nutty flavours of the seeds and helps to keep the grain intact while it is cooking. To save time, we have skipped this step, but you can try it to see if you like the results. See image ❸.

To toast: Rinse and drain the quinoa well. In a large skillet, spread quinoa in one layer. Toast over medium-high heat for 5 to 7 minutes or until seeds begin to pop. Remove before the seeds begin to smoke.

about this recipe

What makes it great?
The high protein and calcium in quinoa makes these sliders exceptional snacks and main dish additions.

How do I make them uniform?
We use an ice cream scoop to form the sliders and gently flatten them with the back of a wooden spoon to about 1 inch (2.5 cm) thick. See images ❹ and ❺.

Can I use an oven?
Yes, but the sliders won't be as crispy on the outside as when they're grilled. To bake: Preheat the oven to 350°F (180°C) and line 2 baking sheets with parchment paper. Scoop out a measure of the mixture as described in step 3 and place on one of the baking sheets. Repeat for the remaining mixture, placing 8 scoops on each baking sheet. Flatten to about 1 inch (2.5 cm) thick with the back of a wooden spoon. Bake for 10 minutes. See image ❻.

Ratatouille and Polenta
☐ FLEX APPEAL GROUND LAMB

We all know that the Mediterranean diet promotes good health. The cuisine's time-honoured, traditional ingredients—olive oil, eggplant, zucchini and tomatoes—reflect the region's vegetable bounty and encourage us to use them in simple, delicious ways. —Nettie

FLEX APPEAL

MAKES 2 SERVINGS

1 Tbsp (15 mL) coconut or avocado oil

6 oz (175 g) ground lamb

In a skillet, heat the oil over medium-high heat. Add the ground lamb, stirring and breaking it up with the back of a wooden spoon. Cook for 5 to 7 minutes, or until browned through and with no trace of pink remaining. Drain off the fat. After step 3, top 2 of the polenta pieces with the lamb and continue with step 4.

RECIPE NOTE

Polenta has been a staple ingredient in Italian cuisine for centuries. The best polenta is made from whole corn kernels that are ground between millstones in order to retain the nutritious germ and flavour. Look for stone-ground, whole-grain, ready-to-heat polenta.

Polenta is made by simmering coarsely ground cornmeal in water. When the water is drained off, the polenta will cool and firm. If you make your own polenta and want to substitute finely ground cornmeal, pour it slowly into boiling water; that way you will avoid lumps.

MAKES 8 SERVINGS

4 Tbsp (60 mL) coconut or avocado oil, divided

1½ cups (375 mL) finely chopped sweet onion

4 cloves garlic, finely chopped

1 eggplant, cut into ½-inch (1 cm) pieces

1 green bell pepper, cut into 1-inch (2.5 cm) pieces

1 red bell pepper, cut into 1-inch (2.5 cm) pieces

2 zucchini, cut into 1-inch (2.5 cm) pieces

1 can (28 oz/796 mL) diced tomatoes and juice

½ cup (125 mL) dry white wine

½ tsp (2 mL) sea salt

¼ tsp (1 mL) black pepper

2 Tbsp (30 mL) chopped fresh basil

1 lb (500 g) package ready-to-heat polenta, sliced in 8 (see Recipe Note)

1. Heat 2 Tbsp (30 mL) of the oil in a skillet over medium-high heat. Add the onion and cook, stirring constantly, for 5 minutes or until the onion is translucent. Add the garlic, eggplant, green and red peppers, zucchini, tomatoes, wine, salt and pepper. Bring to a boil. Cover, reduce the heat and simmer for 15 minutes. Uncover and cook for 10 minutes. Remove from the heat and stir in the basil.

2. Meanwhile, preheat the oven to broil (500°F/260°C) and move the oven rack to the top position.

3. Brush the polenta slices with the remaining 2 Tbsp (30 mL) oil and place in one layer on a parchment paper–lined, rimmed baking sheet. Broil for 3 minutes or until golden. Transfer to 8 serving dishes.

4. Spoon the ratatouille over the polenta pieces.

Smoked Tofu Skillet Supper

☐ FLEX APPEAL SAUSAGE

Satisfyingly simple, this easy skillet supper is exceptional because of the quality of the smoked tofu. —Pat

MAKES 4 SERVINGS

3 Tbsp (45 mL) apple cider vinegar

2 Tbsp (30 mL) granulated sugar

2 Tbsp (30 mL) coconut or avocado oil

1 onion, chopped

4 cups (1 L) shredded cabbage

3 potatoes, diced

1 apple, chopped

2 cups (500 mL) vegetable broth

1 cup (250 mL) cubed smoked tofu

½ tsp (2 mL) caraway seeds

1. In a bowl, combine the vinegar and sugar and set aside.

2. In a large skillet, heat the oil over medium-high heat. Sauté the onion for 5 minutes or until transparent and soft. Add the cabbage, potatoes, apple and broth. Bring to a boil. Stir in the vinegar mixture, reduce the heat and simmer for 5 to 7 minutes or until vegetables are crisp-tender.

3. Stir in the tofu and caraway seeds and warm through.

TIME-SAVING STRATEGIES

- Use an 8 oz (250 g) bag of pre-cut coleslaw mix to save time shredding the cabbage.

- Keep fat-free, no-salt-added, cubed hash brown potatoes in the freezer and substitute ½ cup (125 mL) for each fresh potato.

FLEX APPEAL

MAKES 2 SERVINGS

4 oz (125 g) precooked, low-fat smoked sausage, cut into ½-inch (1 cm) pieces

After step 2, transfer half of the vegetable mixture to a separate pan. Add tofu to one pan and sausage to the second pan. Add half the caraway seeds to each pan and warm through.

about tofu

Most people know that tofu is a high-protein bean curd made from soybeans. It may not be as widely known that tofu has an incredible ability to absorb the flavours of the spices, sauces or marinades it is cooked in.

Tofu and Broccoli Stir-Fry with Thai Flavours
☐ FLEX APPEAL TURKEY

Thai flavours add another dimension to this recipe. Lemongrass, lime juice and toasted sesame oil will become staples in your flex pantry. I like to serve this dish with rice noodles or quinoa. —Nettie

FLEX APPEAL

MAKES 2 SERVINGS

- 1 Tbsp (15 mL) coconut or avocado oil
- ½ cup (125 mL) chopped onion
- 6 oz (175 g) ground turkey

Heat the oil in a skillet over medium-high heat. Add the onion and cook, stirring frequently, for 5 minutes. Add the ground turkey and reduce the heat to medium. Stir constantly and break up any clumps with the back of a wooden spoon. Cook for 5 to 8 minutes or until the meat is browned with no pink inside. Drain off the fat. Add the turkey mixture to 2 of the bowls in step 4.

about broccoli

Broccoli is available year round, easy to cook and inexpensive. Always purchase stalks with tightly closed, dark green flowers. I have seen a cauliflower–broccoli cross called broccoflower, but it resembles and tastes like cauliflower.

Most people cook broccoli in a pot of boiling water. I prefer to steam it because it cooks quickly and does not lose its colour.

MAKES 6 SERVINGS

- 1 cup (250 mL) hot water or vegetable broth
- 2 trimmed stalks lemongrass, cut into 2-inch (5 cm) pieces (see Recipe Note)
- 3 cups (750 mL) broccoli florets, cut into 1½-inch/4 cm pieces
- 3 Tbsp (45 mL) toasted sesame oil
- 3 cloves garlic, minced
- 1 jalapeño, seeded and finely chopped
- 10 oz (300 g) firm tofu, cut into ½-inch (1 cm) cubes
- 1 red bell pepper, thinly sliced
- ½ cup (125 mL) finely chopped fresh cilantro
- 2 Tbsp (30 mL) freshly squeezed lime juice
- 4 green onions, finely diced
- 2 Tbsp (30 mL) tamari or soy sauce
- ¼ cup (60 mL) toasted pumpkin seeds (see page 49)

1. In a bowl, pour water or broth over lemongrass. Let steep for 5 minutes. Remove the lemongrass from the bowl and finely dice. Save the water and set aside.

2. Set a collapsible steamer in a saucepan. Add enough water to reach the bottom of the steamer basket. Bring to a boil over high heat. Place the broccoli in the steamer basket, cover and steam for 5 minutes, or until tender. Set aside.

3. Heat the oil in a wok or large skillet over medium-high heat. Add the garlic, jalapeño and tofu. Stir-fry for 2 minutes. Add the red pepper, steeped lemongrass and reserved lemongrass water. Cover and cook over medium heat for 5 minutes. Stir in the cilantro, lime juice, green onions, tamari and steamed broccoli. Cover and cook for 2 minutes.

4. Divide the broccoli mixture among 6 bowls. Garnish with toasted pumpkin seeds.

Sweet and Sour Tempeh and Rice Noodle Stir-Fry

☐ FLEX APPEAL SCALLOPS

MAKES 6 SERVINGS

10 oz (300 g) dried thin rice noodles

8 cups (2 L) boiling water

4 Tbsp (60 mL) toasted sesame oil, divided

8 oz (250 g) tempeh, room temperature, cut lengthwise into ¼-inch (6 mm) slices

½ cup (125 mL) pineapple juice

¼ cup (60 mL) white vinegar

4 Tbsp (60 mL) tamari or soy sauce

3 Tbsp (45 mL) granulated sugar

2 Tbsp (30 mL) cornstarch

2 tsp (10 mL) minced garlic

1 Tbsp (15 mL) finely chopped fresh ginger

1 cup (250 mL) fresh pineapple cubes

½ lb (250 g) snow peas, trimmed

2 Tbsp (30 mL) minced scallions

1 cup (250 mL) thinly sliced red bell pepper

2 Tbsp (30 mL) fresh lime juice

2 Tbsp (30 mL) chopped fresh basil

½ cup (125 mL) roasted cashews, for garnish

1. Place the rice noodles in a large bowl. Pour the boiling water over the noodles until totally covered. Let stand for 10 minutes to rehydrate. Drain and set aside.

2. In a skillet, heat 2 Tbsp (30 mL) of the oil over medium-high heat. Add the tempeh and cook for 5 to 8 minutes or until reddish brown on all sides. Set aside.

3. In a bowl, combine the pineapple juice, vinegar, tamari and sugar. Whisk in the cornstarch, mixing well. Transfer to a small saucepan and cook over medium heat until slightly thick, about 3 minutes. Set aside.

4. In a wok, heat the remaining 2 Tbsp (30 mL) oil over medium heat. Add the garlic and ginger. Cook, stirring frequently, for 1 minute. Add the cooked tempeh, pineapple cubes, snow peas, scallions, red pepper, lime juice and basil. Cook, stirring occasionally, for 3 minutes. Add the pineapple-vinegar sauce, stirring to mix well, and cook for 3 minutes.

5. Divide the rice noodles, heaping them in the centre of 6 soup bowls. Divide the tempeh mixture among the bowls.

6. Garnish with the cashews.

FLEX APPEAL

MAKES 2 SERVINGS

8 oz (250 g) scallops

1 Tbsp (15 mL) avocado oil

Preheat the oven to broil (500°F/260°C) and move oven rack to top position. While the tempeh mixture is cooking in step 4, arrange scallops in one layer on a lightly oiled, rimmed baking sheet and drizzle with oil. Broil on the top rack for 2 minutes each side, turning once. Scallops are done when they turn opaque.

After step 5, top 2 of the bowls with scallops, then continue with step 6.

RECIPE NOTE

Stir-fries are delicious hot or cold. My flat-bottomed wok allows me to cook everything quickly and evenly. Because the sides heat up more slowly than the base, I can sear the food and push it up the side away from direct heat. A well-seasoned, 14-inch carbon steel wok is an essential part of my working kitchen.

Vegetable Stir-Fry with Asian Flavours
☐ FLEX APPEAL PORK

One of the easiest and healthiest quick meals is one that is stir-fried. What keeps stir-fries simple is that you can slice some of the ingredients right into the pan without having to measure them. It's what I call a "look and cook" recipe: look at the amount in the wok and stop adding vegetables when you can see that you have enough to serve everyone. Trust me, with very little practice, you get very good at gauging amounts. We've used early summer vegetables like tender zucchini and snow peas, but you can make this technique your own with vegetables that are in season. —Pat

FLEX APPEAL

MAKES 2 SERVINGS

3 to 4 oz (90 to 125 g) pork loin

½ cup (125 mL) barbecue sauce

Cut the pork crosswise into thin strips. In a bowl, combine the pork strips with the barbecue sauce. Let marinate while preparing the vegetables for the stir-fry.

After step 2, transfer half of the vegetable mixture to a skillet and stir in the pork and marinade. Cook over medium-high heat, stirring constantly, for 2 to 3 minutes or until pork is browned with a trace of pink, then continue with step 3.

RECIPE NOTE

Asian flavours are clear, crisp and clean because of the use of flavourings like lime and lemon juice, tamari and ginger. Ginger gives a unique essence to the overall taste and for Asian-style recipes it is absolutely essential to use fresh ginger whenever possible. You can omit the lime juice if you don't have it, but ginger is part of what makes this recipe work.

MAKES 4 SERVINGS

2 Tbsp (30 mL) coconut or avocado oil

2 carrots, cut on the diagonal into 1-inch (2.5 cm) slices

½ red bell pepper, coarsely chopped

2 small zucchini, quartered lengthwise and sliced

1 handful of fresh snow peas, cut in half lengthwise

1 handful of fresh green beans, cut into 1-inch (2.5 cm) pieces

3 green onions, sliced

½ cup (125 mL) vegetable broth

2 Tbsp (30 mL) freshly squeezed lime juice

1 Tbsp (15 mL) tamari or soy sauce

1 Tbsp (15 mL) grated ginger

1 Tbsp (15 mL) cornstarch

1 or 2 baby bok choy, sliced (1 or 2 cups/250 or 500 mL)

¼ cup (60 mL) peanuts or cashews

1. In a wok, heat the oil over high heat. Reduce the heat to medium-high, slice the carrots into the wok and stir briskly for 2 minutes. Add the red pepper and stir briskly for 2 minutes. Add the zucchini, snow peas, green beans and green onions and stir briskly for 3 minutes.

2. In a bowl, combine the broth, lime juice, tamari and ginger. Whisk the cornstarch into broth mixture and stir into the vegetables. Increase the heat to high and cook, stirring constantly, for 3 minutes or until thickened (see image ❶).

3. Toss the bok choy into the mixture and cook for 1 minute or until wilted (see image ❷).

4. Spoon the stir-fry into 4 bowls and garnish with peanuts.

Vegetable
Stir-Fry
with Asian
Flavours

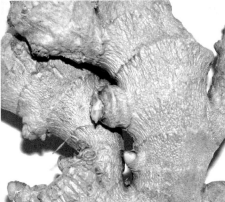

about ginger

Fresh ginger (*Zingiber officinale*) with its rich, warm citrus aroma and pungent flavour that is both hot and tangy adds a distinctly Asian tone to stir-fried dishes. It is fleshy and easily grated using a micro-grater.

There are several other forms of ginger, including one I often use: crystallized ginger. Dried or crystallized ginger has been sliced or cubed, boiled in syrup, dried and dusted with sugar. It keeps for up to 2 years and maintains most of the flavour properties of fresh ginger. Powdered ginger is bitter in comparison to either fresh or crystallized forms and is used mainly in baked products.

To buy fresh ginger: Look for plump, fleshy roots that are firm and unwrinkled.

To store fresh ginger: Wrap it in a damp dish towel or paper towel and keep in a plastic bag in the refrigerator for 1 or 2 weeks. For longer storage, peel and store in a zip-top freezer bag in the freezer for 2 to 3 months. To use frozen ginger, remove from the freezer, grate the desired amount immediately and return the frozen piece to the freezer.

1

2

Spicy Tempeh and Peach Stir-Fry
☐ FLEX APPEAL CHICKEN

It's the jalapeño that adds the zip, and the peaches that add the colour and zest to this fast and easy stir-fried dish. If you take advantage of our Plan-Ahead Strategy, you can have this great meal on the table in less than 30 minutes. This stir-fry is great on its own, or serve it over quinoa or other whole grain. —Pat

FLEX APPEAL

MAKES 2 SERVINGS

½ cup (125 mL) chopped cooked chicken

After step 3, divide the tempeh mixture in half. Stir chicken into one half and heat through.

PLAN-AHEAD STRATEGY

Clean, peel and chop or slice the vegetables up to 24 hours in advance. Store the cauliflower and broccoli in one zip-top bag and the onion, carrot and beans in separate zip-top bags in the refrigerator. Bring to room temperature before cooking.

MAKES 4 SERVINGS

⅓ cup (80 mL) orange juice

1 jalapeño, finely chopped (see Recipe Note)

2 Tbsp (30 mL) tamari or soy sauce

1 Tbsp (15 mL) grated fresh ginger

2 Tbsp (30 mL) coconut or avocado oil

1 onion, chopped

1 carrot, thinly sliced

½ cup (125 mL) cauliflower florets

½ cup (125 mL) broccoli florets

½ cup (125 mL) green beans, cut in 1-inch (2.5 cm) pieces

1 Tbsp (15 mL) cornstarch

3 fresh peaches, sliced, or 1½ cups (375 mL) frozen, sliced peaches (thawed)

1 cup (250 mL) cubed tempeh

1. In a bowl, combine the orange juice, jalapeño, tamari and ginger. Set aside.

2. In a wok, heat the oil over high heat. Add the onion and cook, stirring briskly, for 1 minute. Stir in the carrot and cook, stirring briskly, for 1 minute. Stir in the cauliflower and broccoli and cook, stirring briskly, for 2 minutes. Add the beans and cook, stirring briskly, for 2 minutes or until all the vegetables are tender-crisp. Push the vegetables to the sides of the wok.

3. Whisk the cornstarch into the orange juice–tamari mixture and pour into the centre of the wok. Reduce the heat to medium-high and cook, stirring constantly, for about 3 minutes or until the sauce is thickened. Add the peaches and tempeh and heat through, stirring to mix well.

oven and one-pot wonders

Vegetable-Stuffed Peppers
☐ FLEX APPEAL TURKEY

This is a great recipe for using up leftover or frozen cooked vegetables and grain. When I'm making both vegetarian and turkey-stuffed peppers, I use green bell peppers to identify the vegetarian peppers and red bell peppers to identify the turkey peppers, but any colour of bell pepper can be used. —Pat

FLEX APPEAL

MAKES 2 HALF PEPPERS

1 bell pepper

1 Tbsp (15 mL) coconut or avocado oil

6 oz (175 g) ground turkey

2 Tbsp (30 mL) shredded cheddar cheese

In step 3, use a second skillet and heat the oil over medium-high heat. Add the turkey and reduce the heat to medium. Cook, stirring constantly and breaking up the clumps, for 5 to 8 minutes or until the meat is browned with no pink on the inside.

After step 3, divide the cooked vegetable-grain mixture in half and add the cooked turkey to one half. Stuff the pepper halves with the turkey mixture and sprinkle with cheese. Continue with step 4 to stuff the remaining peppers and bake.

MAKES 4 HALF PEPPERS

2 bell peppers

2 Tbsp (30 mL) coconut or avocado oil

1 onion, chopped

2 cloves garlic, finely chopped

1 cup (250 mL) cooked adzuki beans (see Recipe Note)

1 cup (250 mL) chopped greens

1 cup (250 mL) cooked grains (see Recipe Note)

¼ cup (60 mL) shredded cheddar cheese

1. Preheat the oven to 375°F (190°C).

2. Cut the peppers in half and remove the stems, ribs and seeds. Place the halves cut side up on a parchment paper–lined, rimmed baking sheet.

3. In a skillet, heat the oil over medium-high heat. Sauté the onion for 5 minutes. Add the garlic and cook, stirring frequently, for 1 minute or until fragrant and soft. Stir in the adzuki beans, greens and cooked grains. Heat through, stirring constantly.

4. Using a 1-cup (250 mL) dry measure, scoop the filling mixture and pack into the pepper halves. Sprinkle 1 Tbsp (15) mL cheese over each stuffed pepper half.

5. Bake for 7 to 10 minutes or until the peppers are tender-crisp and the cheese is melted.

PLAN-AHEAD STRATEGY

Freezing cooked grains in 1- or 2-cup (250 or 500 mL) amounts is very convenient for recipes like this.

Vegetable-Stuffed Peppers

RECIPE NOTES

· If you can't find or don't have adzuki beans, you can substitute frozen or canned cooked lentils.

· Any cooked grain may be used in this recipe, such as short-grain brown rice, wheat berries, quinoa, buckwheat or bulgur.

Eggplant Parmesan with Tomato Spinach Sauce

☐ FLEX APPEAL CHICKEN

The key to saving time with this recipe is to make the tomato spinach sauce while the vegetables are roasting in the oven. It comes together quickly once the vegetables are roasted. I make the vegetarian version often and serve it with broccoli, Italian rapini or green beans, or a crisp green salad. If I happen to have cooked whole grains, I add them for their chewy texture and protein. If you want extra flavour but don't want the chicken option, try strips of tempeh instead. —Pat

FLEX APPEAL

MAKES 2 SERVINGS

1 boneless, skinless chicken breast (see Recipe Note)

1 Tbsp (15 mL) coconut or avocado oil

While the vegetables bake in step 2, slice the chicken crosswise into ½-inch (1 cm) strips. Transfer to a parchment paper–lined, rimmed baking sheet and drizzle with oil. Bake for 10 minutes or until done (it shows no pink).

In step 3, put one-third of the eggplant slices into a second casserole dish. Top with the cooked chicken. Pour one-third of the tomato-vegetable sauce over the chicken and top with one-third of the mozzarella and Parmesan. Bake both dishes as instructed.

RECIPE NOTE

The easiest way to cook the chicken strips is to add them to the baking sheet with the vegetables in step 2. Ask if your vegetarian diners are comfortable with having chicken baked on the same sheet as the vegetables.

MAKES 6 SERVINGS

1 eggplant, peeled and sliced into 1-inch (2.5 cm) slices (see Roasting Eggplant)

2 carrots, quartered lengthwise

1 parsnip, quartered lengthwise

3 Tbsp (45 mL) coconut or avocado oil

2½ cups (625 mL) Tomato Spinach Sauce (recipe follows)

½ cup (125 mL) shredded mozzarella cheese

¼ cup (60 mL) grated Parmesan cheese

1. Preheat the oven to 400°F (200°C).

2. Spread the eggplant, carrots and parsnip in one layer on a parchment paper–lined, rimmed baking sheet and drizzle with the oil. Bake for 15 minutes. Using tongs, turn vegetables. Bake 10 minutes more or until vegetables are tender.

3. Stack baked eggplant slices, cut into quarters and transfer to an 11- by 7-inch (2 L) casserole dish. Cut the baked carrots and parsnip into chunks and add to Tomato Spinach Sauce. Pour sauce mixture over eggplant in dish. Sprinkle mozzarella and Parmesan overtop and bake for 3 to 5 minutes or until the cheese is melted.

Eggplant Parmesan with Tomato Spinach Sauce

ROASTING EGGPLANT

Trim ends off eggplant and peel away lengthwise strips leaving alternating strips of peel on. Slice eggplant crosswise into 1-inch (2.5 cm) slices. See image ❶.

The slices should be the same thickness so that they cook evenly. Turn slices once during cooking and drizzle more oil over if they are dry. When roasted, eggplant is crisp on the outside and creamy on the inside. See image ❷.

For dips and other puréed eggplant dishes, charring whole, unpeeled eggplant over a gas flame or barbecue gives it a smoky taste and makes it very easy to peel away the skin. See image ❸.

continued on next page >

> Eggplant Parmesan with Tomato Spinach Sauce continued

Tomato Spinach Sauce

MAKES 2½ CUPS (625 mL)

2 Tbsp (30 mL) coconut or avocado oil

1 onion, chopped

½ leek, white and pale green parts only, sliced

4 cloves garlic, finely chopped

1 can (19 oz/540 mL) diced or whole tomatoes with juice

2 Tbsp (30 mL) chopped fresh rosemary

2 cups (500 mL) chopped fresh, or thawed and drained, frozen spinach

1. Heat the oil in a saucepan over medium-high heat. Add the onion and sauté for 5 minutes. Add the leek and garlic and cook, stirring frequently, for 2 minutes or until vegetables are soft. Stir in the tomatoes, rosemary and spinach. Reduce the heat to medium and simmer, stirring occasionally, for 15 minutes.

about eggplant

A member of the nightshade family (which includes tomatoes, sweet and hot peppers, tomatillos and potatoes), eggplant is called aubergine in England and Europe. Some recipes may call for eggplant to be salted and left to sit for up to an hour before rinsing and using, but the varieties grown today do not require salting because they aren't bitter.

For grilling and roasting, use meaty and firm-fleshed varieties of eggplant.

The most common varieties found in North America are the American or Sicilian types. These eggplants have a deep black-purple skin, are oblong or teardrop in shape and are fleshy with tiny, mild-tasting seeds.

Eggplant acts as a sponge for taking up oil when baked or grilled. To ensure that flavour and a delicious creamy texture are achieved, it is important to use enough oil to achieve the silky smooth interior and crispy outside.

Alsatian Vegetable Gratin
☐ FLEX APPEAL TURKEY

The turkey version of this delicious dish always appeared on the table after Thanksgiving and New Year's as I was growing up, and we loved it. My mother used canned cream of mushroom soup along with carrots and parsnips and, of course, leftover turkey. My version is filled with hearty winter vegetables and you have the option of adding cooked turkey or any leftover meat, but it is really tasty without. You can also add a cup of shredded sweet potato. This is one of those classic, comforting casseroles that are equally good reheated the next day. —Pat

MAKES 4 TO 6 SERVINGS

2 Tbsp (30 mL) olive or avocado oil

1 onion, chopped

1 leek, white and pale green parts only, chopped

3 carrots, chopped

2 parsnips, chopped

4 cloves garlic, finely chopped

3 Tbsp (45 mL) all-purpose or gluten-free flour

1 Tbsp (15 mL) chopped fresh rosemary

1 tsp (5 mL) sea salt

2 cups (500 mL) plain almond milk, rice milk or soy milk

1 cup (250 mL) chopped fresh, or thawed and drained, frozen kale or spinach

½ cup (125 mL) chopped almonds or walnuts

1½ cups (375 mL) torn whole wheat bread pieces

1 cup (250 mL) grated fontina or cheddar cheese

1. Preheat the oven to 425°F (220°C).

2. In a large saucepan, heat the oil over medium heat. Sauté the onion, leek, carrots and parsnips for 5 minutes or until onions are soft and translucent. Add the garlic and cook, stirring frequently, for 2 minutes.

3. In a bowl, whisk the flour, rosemary and salt into the almond milk. Stir the milk mixture into the vegetables. Cook, stirring constantly, for 5 minutes or until bubbling and thickened. Remove from the heat and stir in the kale and almonds. ←

4. Spoon into lightly oiled 8-cup (2 L) baking dish.

5. Spread bread pieces evenly overtop. Bake for 10 minutes. Sprinkle cheese over bread and bake for 3 to 5 minutes more or until the cheese is melted.

FLEX APPEAL

MAKES 3 SERVINGS

1 cup (250 mL) chopped cooked turkey, chicken, pork, ham or lamb

After step 3, spoon the vegetable mixture into 2 lightly oiled 4-cup (1 L) baking dishes. Add the turkey to one of the dishes and continue with step 5.

TIME-SAVING STRATEGY

Use a food processor to chop the onions, carrots, parsnips, garlic, rosemary and nuts.

MAKE-AHEAD STRATEGIES

• Make the vegetable mixture and spoon into a casserole dish, but do not add the bread pieces. Cover with plastic wrap. It will keep overnight or up to 2 days in the refrigerator if tightly wrapped. Bring to room temperature and continue with step 5.

• Double the recipe and freeze one casserole (without the bread and cheese topping) by wrapping it tightly and placing in a zip-top freezer bag. Use within 1 month. To cook: Thaw in the refrigerator and continue with step 5.

Roasted Vegetables over Spaghetti Squash with Tomato Sauce

☐ FLEX APPEAL CHICKEN

For this dish, root vegetables are roasted in a hot oven until browned, nutty-tasting and tender. The spaghetti squash is also roasted, and then topped with the vegetable tomato sauce just as you would do with regular spaghetti. —Pat

FLEX APPEAL

MAKES 2 SERVINGS

1 cup (250 mL) cooked chicken slivers or cubes

In step 6, ladle the tomato vegetable sauce over 4 servings of squash, reserving enough for 2 more servings. Set the plates in the oven to keep warm. Add the cooked chicken to the remaining tomato vegetable sauce. Heat over medium-high for 1 or 2 minutes. Ladle the tomato-vegetable-chicken sauce over the remaining 2 servings of squash and garnish with Parmesan and rosemary.

MAKES 6 SERVINGS

1 spaghetti squash, halved

1 head garlic

3 carrots, thickly sliced

2 parsnips, thickly sliced

2 onions, quartered

3 Tbsp (45 mL) coconut or avocado oil

1 can (19 oz/540 mL) tomato sauce (or Tomato Spinach Sauce, page 76)

1 Tbsp (15 mL) chopped fresh rosemary

½ cup (125 mL) grated Parmesan cheese, for garnish

4 to 6 fresh sprigs rosemary, for garnish

1. Preheat the oven to 475°F (240°C).

2. Scoop the seeds and fibre from the cavity of each squash half. See image ❶. Place on a parchment paper–lined, rimmed baking sheet, cut sides down. Rub the loose outer layers of skin away from the head of garlic. Slice ¼ inch (0.5 cm) off the top of the cloves in the head. Place on the baking sheet, root end down. Arrange the carrots, parsnips and onions around the squash and garlic head on the baking sheet. Drizzle the vegetables with oil. Roast for 25 minutes.

3. Remove the garlic, test the carrots, parsnips and onions and remove if tender-crisp. Continue to roast the squash and any firm vegetables for 5 to 10 minutes or until the vegetables are tender-crisp and the squash is soft when pierced with the tip of a knife.

Roasted Vegetables over Spaghetti Squash with Tomato Sauce

4. In a large saucepan, heat the tomato sauce over medium-high heat. Squeeze the soft roasted garlic into the sauce, mash with a fork and stir to mix well. Add the roasted carrots, parsnips and onions and the chopped rosemary, reduce the heat to low and simmer, stirring occasionally for 5 to 10 minutes or until the squash is ready to be served.

5. Using a fork, separate the strands of cooked squash (see image ❷) and scoop onto 6 plates. See image ❸.

6. Ladle the vegetable tomato sauce over the squash and garnish with Parmesan and rosemary.

continued on next page >

about winter squash

Many varieties of winter squash were given that name because they would keep well when stored in root cellars. Winter squash varieties include acorn, Ambercup (top left), banana, butternut, spaghetti (lower right), Carnival, Delicata, pumpkin, Hubbard and Black Futsu (lower left), and all of them are great when roasted. Summer squash are more tender and include zucchini varieties.

What makes them so nutritious?

Their deep, rich orange and yellow flesh is coloured by carotenoid pigments that are precursors to vitamin A, an antioxidant which boosts immune function, protects against infection and may help prevent certain cancers and heart disease.

What about roasting vegetables?

Roasting hearty root and winter vegetables (such as turnip or rutabaga, beets, squash, pumpkin, carrots, parsnips, onions and garlic) caramelizes their sugars and brings out a nutty sweet flavour.

To roast vegetables: Lay them flat in one layer on a parchment paper–lined, rimmed baking sheet. Drizzle with coconut or avocado oil and roast for 20 to 25 minutes in a 475°F (240°C) oven. When roasting onions, zucchini, or peppers, check them after 20 minutes and remove if browned or slightly charred and tender-crisp. Continue to roast root vegetables and squash until tender-crisp.

What about roasting garlic?

Roasted garlic is mellow and sweet and usually the whole head is roasted. Sugars seep to the outside of the skin and become caramelized. This makes the cloves of garlic soft, sticky and pleasant in taste.

To roast a whole head of garlic: Remove the loose outer papery skin by rubbing it between your palms. Using a French knife or kitchen scissors remove ¼ inch (0.5 cm) off the tips of the cloves. Set in a ceramic baking dish, drizzle with coconut or avocado oil and cover. Roast at 475°F (240°C) for 20 minutes or until tender when pierced with the tip of a knife. Let cool. Gently squeeze soft flesh out of the brittle skin from each clove.

about this recipe

What makes it great?

Roasting the vegetables renders them tender-crisp and gives them a nutty, sweet, mellow and complex flavour. You just can't get the professional finish to this recipe without roasting the veggies. While you can use canned tomato sauce to save time, making the garlicky tomato sauce with fresh rosemary sets it apart.

What makes it work?

Fresh rosemary gives ready-made tomato sauce an aromatic burst of nutmeg, pine and camphor added to the sweet-roasted garlic.

Black Bean Cheddar Squares

I often serve these squares with a tossed green salad and crusty whole-grain bread. They can be served on little buns as black bean sliders as well. There was a time when I did not have black beans in a can and used cannellini beans instead. The recipe still worked and next time I will use pinto. Serve steamed broccoli or cauliflower with toasted pumpkin seeds as an accompaniment to this dish. —Nettie

MAKES 6 SERVINGS

1 can (14 oz/398 mL) black beans, drained and rinsed (see Recipe Note)

1 large egg

3 Tbsp (45 mL) all-purpose flour

2 Tbsp (30 mL) olive or avocado oil

2 Tbsp (30 mL) freshly squeezed lemon juice

3 cloves garlic, minced

1 cup (250 mL) frozen peas

¾ cup (185 ml) breadcrumbs

½ cup (125 mL) shredded cheddar cheese

½ tsp (2 mL) sea salt

⅛ tsp (0.5 mL) black pepper

1½ cups (375 mL) warm tomato or spaghetti sauce

½ cup (125 mL) chopped fresh parsley

1. Preheat the oven to 350°F (180°C).

2. Combine the beans, egg, flour, oil, lemon juice and garlic in a food processor or blender and process for 3 minutes or until smooth and well combined.

3. Transfer the bean mixture to a bowl. Fold in the peas, breadcrumbs and cheese. Add salt and pepper. Mix well.

4. Transfer the mixture to an 8-inch (20 cm) Pyrex pan lined with parchment paper, patting down with a fork to form a smooth surface. Bake for 35 minutes. Let cool for 5 minutes.

5. Divide into 6 servings and garnish with warm tomato sauce and parsley.

RECIPE NOTE

My favourite pantry staple is organic canned beans. If you buy salt-free beans, you do not need to rinse them. I often use the liquid in the can to add flavour and moisture to recipes.

Quinoa Cheddar Casserole

When my family has a meal together, I need to please several palates. Crunch is essential, hence the pumpkin seeds. A creamy texture with a layer of well-cooked grain and seasoned sautéed vegetables touches all the bases. My 21-year-old daughter, Mackenzie, is my toughest critic. She should be. I have taught her everything I know! —Nettie

MAKES 6 SERVINGS

RECIPE NOTES

- For greens, you can use spinach, kale, Swiss chard, rapini or beet tops.

- Try toasted pine nuts instead of pumpkin seeds. Any toasted seed or nut will be fine. I believe in going to the pantry and using what is available, even combining different ingredients to meet the amount required.

MAKE-AHEAD STRATEGY

You can freeze the casserole without baking. Thaw in the refrigerator and bake at 350°F (180° C) as directed in step 5.

2 cups (500 mL) vegetable broth or water	4 cups (1 L) lightly packed greens, cut into 1-inch (2.5 cm) strips (see Recipe Note)
1 cup (250 mL) tan-coloured quinoa, rinsed for 3 to 5 minutes	¼ cup (60 mL) water
½ cup (125 mL) finely chopped fresh basil	1 tsp (2 mL) dried marjoram
1 can (5.5 oz/156 mL) tomato paste	½ tsp (black pepper)
3 Tbsp (45 mL) coconut or avocado oil	2 large eggs
2 sweet onions, finely chopped	2 cups (500 mL) cottage cheese
3 cloves garlic, minced	1¼ cups (310 mL) grated cheddar cheese
1 cup (250 mL) chopped red bell pepper	1 cup (250 mL) toasted pumpkin seeds (see Recipe Note)
1 can (6 oz/175 g) artichoke hearts, drained and coarsely chopped	

1. Preheat the oven to 350°F (180°C).

2. In a saucepan, bring the broth to a boil over high heat. Stir in the quinoa. Cover, reduce the heat to medium-low and simmer, stirring frequently, for 15 minutes or until the liquid is absorbed. Transfer to a bowl and stir in the basil and tomato paste.

3. Meanwhile, in a skillet, heat the oil over medium-high heat. Add the onions and garlic and cook, stirring constantly, for 5 minutes or until the onion is translucent. Add the red peppers, artichoke hearts, greens, water, marjoram and pepper. Cook for 5 to 8 minutes, or until the greens have wilted and the vegetables are soft.

4. In a bowl, lightly beat the eggs. Mix in the cottage cheese.

5. Cover the bottom of a 9- × 13-inch (3.5 L) casserole dish with the quinoa mixture. Spread the sautéed vegetables over the quinoa. Spread the cottage cheese mixture over the vegetables. Top with the grated cheese and pumpkin seeds. Bake, covered, for 25 minutes. Uncover and bake for 10 minutes more. Let stand for 5 minutes before serving.

Jalapeño and Pinto Bean Pie

I'm amazed at the flavour one jalapeño pepper can add to a recipe. Using the freshest paprika, cumin and chili powder, you can transform an ordinary can of beans into a taste sensation. Combining fresh and frozen vegetables with properly spiced beans baked against a crust is a new way to enjoy vegetarian cuisine. —Nettie

MAKES 6 SERVINGS

Pie Crust

1½ cups (375 mL) whole wheat pastry flour

1 tsp (5 mL) chili powder

1 tsp (5 mL) ground cumin

½ tsp (2 mL) paprika

½ tsp (2 mL) sea salt

½ cup (125 mL) unsalted cold butter

2 Tbsp (30 mL) ice water

Bean Filling

1 can (28 oz/796 mL) no-salt-added pinto beans, drained and rinsed

1 cup (250 mL) plain yogurt

½ tsp (2 mL) sea salt

¼ tsp (1 mL) black pepper

1 cup (250 mL) fresh or frozen corn kernels

1 red bell pepper, thinly sliced

1 green bell pepper, thinly sliced

1 cup (250 mL) grated cheddar cheese

½ cup (125 mL) breadcrumbs or nutritional yeast

1 jalapeño, seeded and minced

½ cup (125 mL) green onions, thinly sliced

½ cup (125 mL) chopped fresh cilantro

PLAN-AHEAD STRATEGY

Prepare the crust ahead of time or buy a 9-inch (23 cm) ready-to-use, frozen pie crust.

1. Preheat the oven to 350°F (180°C).

2. To make the pie crust, combine the flour, chili powder, cumin, paprika and salt in a food processor or blender and process for 1 minute or until well combined. Add the butter and process until the mixture resembles coarse meal. Add the ice water and pulse until the mixture forms a ball.

3. With floured hands, press the dough evenly onto the bottom and halfway up the side of a lightly oiled, 9-inch (2.5 L) springform pan. Chill for 5 minutes.

4. Bake for 15 minutes. Let cool.

5. To make the bean filling, purée 2 cups (500 mL) of the beans, yogurt, salt and pepper in a food processor or blender until smooth and well combined. Spread evenly onto the baked crust.

6. In a bowl, stir together the corn, red and green peppers, cheese, breadcrumbs, jalapeño, green onions, cilantro and remaining beans. Spread over the bean filling, pressing down gently.

7. Bake for 20 minutes. Let cool for 5 minutes before serving.

Mushroom Tagine

◻ FLEX APPEAL HAM

Delicious without any meat, this dish could become a staple because it is so easy and fast, and uses ingredients that a well-stocked pantry would have (such as canned beans and tomatoes, fresh or frozen greens, onions and carrots). The only item you need to buy fresh is the portobello mushrooms. —Pat

FLEX APPEAL

MAKES 2 SERVINGS

1 cup (250 mL) cooked chopped ham, chicken, pork or lamb

After adding the beans and greens in step 3, remove half of the mushrooms and sauce from the tagine and transfer to a separate saucepan. Add the ham to the saucepan. Continue with step 3, cooking the vegetarian option in the tagine and the meat option in the saucepan.

MAKES 4 SERVINGS

2 Tbsp (30 mL) coconut or avocado oil

1 onion, chopped

2 carrots, thinly sliced

1 cup (250 mL) diced turnip or rutabaga

1 can (28 oz/796 mL) whole tomatoes and juice

4 large portobello mushroom caps

1 can (19 oz/540 mL) white kidney beans, drained and rinsed

2 cups (500 mL) chopped greens

½ cup (125 mL) shredded cheddar cheese

1. In the bottom of a large tagine or Dutch oven, heat the oil over medium-high heat. Sauté the onion for 3 minutes. Add the carrots and turnip and cook, stirring frequently, for 5 minutes or until onions are translucent and vegetables are tender-crisp. Add the tomatoes with their juice and bring to a boil.

2. Nestle the mushrooms, cut side up, into the sauce so that the bottoms are touching the pan. Cover, reduce the heat to medium-low and cook for 10 minutes or until the mushrooms are tender when pierced with the tip of a knife.

3. Add the beans and greens and gently stir into the sauce without disturbing the mushrooms. Sprinkle 2 Tbsp (30 mL) cheese over each mushroom, cover and cook for 3 minutes or until the beans are heated, greens are wilted and cheese is melted.

Mushroom
Tagine

TIME-SAVING STRATEGY

You can use canned or frozen peas, corn or mixed vegetables
if you don't have fresh vegetables on hand.

MAKE-AHEAD STRATEGY

If you have a slow cooker and time in the morning, omit the
oil and combine the onion, carrots, turnip and tomatoes with
juice in a slow cooker. Cover and cook on low for 4 to 6 hours.
When ready to finish cooking, transfer the tomato sauce to a
tagine or Dutch oven and continue with step 2.

Pasta Shells with Kasha
☐ FLEX APPEAL BEEF

Buckwheat groats have a nutty texture and a distinctly earthy flavour. Love it or leave it, and leave it I did as a child. But as an adult, the sheer toastiness of the grain combined with onions, garlic and mushrooms have made me a fan. Kasha is roasted buckwheat groats. —Nettie

FLEX APPEAL

MAKES 2 SERVINGS

1 Tbsp (15 mL) coconut or avocado oil

6 oz (175 g) lean ground beef

Heat the oil in a skillet over medium-high. Add the ground beef and reduce the heat to medium. Cook, stirring constantly and breaking up any clumps, for 4 to 6 minutes or until the meat is browned with no pink inside. Drain off fat.

Divide into 2 portions and add to 2 bowls in step 5.

RECIPE NOTES

· For a vegan option, you can coat the kasha grains with olive or neutral grapeseed oil instead of using an egg. It keeps the grains separate.

· You can use other toasted nuts, such as pine nuts, almonds or cashews, instead of walnuts.

MAKE-AHEAD STRATEGIES

· The onion-mushroom mixture can be cooked ahead of time and stored in the refrigerator. Reheat before adding the pasta.

· The pasta can be cooked up to 1 hour ahead. Drain, rinse with water and keep at room temperature.

MAKES 6 SERVINGS

2 cups (500 mL) vegetable broth or water

¼ tsp (1 mL) sea salt

¼ tsp (1 mL) pepper

1 large egg

1 cup (250 mL) kasha (roasted buckwheat groats)

1 cup (250 mL) shell pasta

3 Tbsp (45 mL) coconut or avocado oil

1 cup (250 mL) diced onion

2 cloves garlic, finely chopped

1½ cups (375 mL) sliced button mushrooms

2 tsp (10 mL) soy sauce

2 Tbsp (30 mL) fresh chopped dill

½ cup (125 mL) walnuts, toasted (see Toasting Nuts and Seeds, page 95)

¼ cup (60 mL) chopped fresh parsley

1. In a saucepan bring the broth, salt and pepper to a boil.

2. Lightly beat egg in a bowl. Add the kasha and stir until well coated. Heat a dry, heavy-bottomed saucepan over medium-high heat. Add the egg-coated kasha and toast, stirring constantly, over medium-low heat for 3 to 4 minutes or until the grains begin to separate, darken and give off a toasted aroma. Add the boiled broth. Cover, reduce the heat and simmer for 8 to 10 minutes, or until most of the stock is absorbed. Remove from the heat and let stand for 5 minutes.

3. In a large pot, bring salted water to a boil. Stir in the pasta and boil for 8 to 10 minutes, or until al dente. Drain and rinse with cold water to stop the cooking. Set aside.

4. Heat the oil in a skillet over medium-high heat. Cook onion and garlic, stirring frequently, for 3 to 5 minutes or until softened. Add the mushrooms and cook, stirring frequently, for 3 to 5 minutes. Add the soy sauce and dill. Stir until combined.

5. Add the cooked pasta to onion mixture and cook over medium heat for 2 to 3 minutes or until the pasta is heated through. Add the cooked kasha and heat, stirring to avoid lumps. Add the toasted walnuts and parsley. Stir. Divide among 6 bowls.

express noodles

Angel Hair Pasta and Arugula Pesto
☐ FLEX APPEAL TURKEY

Angel hair is the perfect description for these long, thin and delicate strands of pasta. For people on the go who love pasta, angel hair is the solution to their need for quick, homemade meals because in less than 10 minutes, they are cooked. I use this pesto in the winter when fresh basil is a bit harder to find than arugula and parsley. By adding sour cream, it may be used as a dip or spread, so it is very versatile. —Pat

FLEX APPEAL

MAKES 2 SERVINGS

1 cup (250 mL) thinly sliced cooked turkey

In step 4, toss the turkey with noodles and pesto.

RECIPE NOTES

- Angel hair pasta is the thinnest of the different long, round pasta types. Called *capelli d'angelo* in Italy, it cooks quickly and is best served with a delicate sauce such as the creamy pesto in this recipe.

- One of the pleasures of making your own pesto is that you get to control not only the ingredients but the texture as well. I like my pesto coarsely chopped, but my husband prefers it smooth and spreadable, so when he makes it, he processes it longer than 1 minute in the food processor.

MAKES 4 SERVINGS

2 cloves garlic	¼ cup (60 mL) walnut oil
⅓ cup (80 mL) walnut pieces	1 Tbsp (15 mL) freshly squeezed lemon juice
2 cups (500 mL) lightly packed baby arugula leaves or spinach	½ cup (125 mL) sour cream
1 cup (250) lightly packed flat-leaf parsley leaves	1 lb (500 g) angel hair noodles (see Recipe Note)

1. To make the pesto, in a food processor, chop the garlic and walnuts. Add the arugula and parsley and pulse for about 30 seconds or until mixed with the garlic and walnuts.

2. With the motor running, drizzle walnut oil and lemon juice through the opening in the lid and pulse for about 1 minute. The mixture should be finely chopped and well mixed (see Recipe Note). Add more oil if the mixture is too dry.

3. Transfer to a bowl and combine with the sour cream.

4. Bring a large pot of salted water to a boil over high heat. Add the noodles and bring back to the boil. Reduce the heat and simmer for 3 to 5 minutes or until al dente. Drain and toss with the pesto.

MAKE-AHEAD STRATEGY

Make the pesto up to 5 days ahead and keep tightly covered in the refrigerator until ready to use. Bring to room temperature to toss with pasta or use as a spread.

Linguini with Leeks, Olive Oil and Garlic
☐ FLEX APPEAL ANCHOVY

I have chosen linguini for this recipe, but this garlicky combination would work well on any favourite pasta. Expanding your pasta repertoire doesn't mean making meals that are time-consuming or exotic; it simply means trying something new. I love to mix and match my pastas. Try different sizes and shapes of pasta for this recipe: spaghetti, rigatoni, ziti, penne, farfalle or orzo or shells. —Nettie

MAKES 6 SERVINGS

1 lb (500 g) linguini noodles	6 cloves garlic, minced
½ cup (125 mL) chopped fresh parsley	⅛ tsp (0.5 mL) black pepper
½ cup (125 mL) olive oil	2 cups (500 mL) lightly packed kale, spinach or Swiss chard, cut into 1-inch (2.5 cm) strips
1 cup (250 mL) sliced leeks, white and pale green parts only	½ cup (125 mL) grated Parmesan cheese

1. Bring a large pot of salted water to a boil over high heat. Add the noodles to the boiling water and cook according to package directions. Reserve about 1 cup (250 mL) of the cooking water. Rinse the noodles and drain well. Return the pasta to the empty pot, toss with the parsley and cover.

2. Meanwhile, heat the oil in a skillet over medium heat. Add the leeks, garlic and pepper. Sauté for 5 minutes or until soft. Stir in the kale and reserved cooking water and cook, stirring and tossing, for 2 minutes or just until wilted.

3. Divide cooked noodles among 6 bowls. Spoon the leek-kale mixture over noodles. Garnish each bowl with Parmesan.

MAKE-AHEAD STRATEGY

The leek-kale mixture can be prepared up to 1 day in advance, using plain water or vegetable stock instead of the reserved pasta cooking water. Cook the noodles just before your meal, reheat the vegetable mixture, toss with the pasta and serve.

FLEX APPEAL

MAKES 2 SERVINGS

2 oz (60 g) can anchovy fillets, drained and chopped
2 tsp (10 mL) freshly squeezed lemon juice

In a bowl, combine the anchovies and lemon juice. After step 2, toss with one-third of the leek-kale mixture. In step 3, top 2 of the bowls of noodles with the anchovy-leek-kale mixture and Parmesan.

Lemon
Tarragon
Linguine

FLEX
APPEAL
Chicken

Lemon Tarragon Linguini
□ FLEX APPEAL CHICKEN

The tart lemon and fragrant, licorice-tasting tarragon are a great taste combination, and also perfectly complement the chicken option. Pine nuts add a soft, almost creamy texture, and are also a good match for this dish. —Pat

MAKES 4 SERVINGS

1 lb (500 g) linguini noodles	2 buffalo mozzarella rounds, torn in half (see About Fresh Mozzarella, next page)
½ cup (125 mL) Lemon Tarragon Dressing (recipe follows)	4 sprigs fresh tarragon (optional)
4 heirloom tomatoes, sliced	

1. Bring a large pot of salted water to a boil over high heat. Add the noodles and bring back to the boil. Reduce the heat and simmer for 5 to 7 minutes or until al dente.

2. Drain and toss with Lemon Tarragon Dressing.

3. Divide the tomato slices evenly among 4 plates. Divide the pasta into 4 portions and swirl onto tomatoes. Garnish with mozzarella halves and a sprig of tarragon, if desired.

Lemon Tarragon Dressing

MAKES ½ CUP (125 mL)

¼ cup (60 mL) chopped fresh tarragon (see Working with Tarragon, next page)	5 Tbsp (75 mL) freshly squeezed lemon juice
¼ cup (60 mL) sunflower seeds or pine nuts	½ cup (125 mL) olive oil
2 Tbsp (30 mL) grated lemon rind	1 Tbsp (15 mL) granulated sugar or to taste

1. In a jar with a tight-fitting lid, combine the tarragon, sunflower seeds, lemon rind, lemon juice and olive oil. Shake to mix well. Taste and add sugar to desired sweetness.

FLEX APPEAL

MAKES 2 SERVINGS

2 cups (500 mL) chicken broth or water
1 piece (3 inches/7.5 cm) lemongrass (optional)
1 large (⅓ lb/170 g) skinless, boneless chicken breast

In a saucepan, bring the broth and lemongrass, if using, to a boil over high heat. Add the chicken, cover, reduce the heat to medium-low and simmer for 9 to 10 minutes or until the chicken turns opaque and there is no sign of pink on the inside. Chicken is cooked safely when a meat thermometer reads 165°F (74°C) when inserted into the meatiest part.

Let cool and slice into crosswise strips. Divide in half and add to 2 of the plates in step 3.

continued on next page >

> Lemon Tarragon Linguini continued

about fresh mozzarella

The mozzarella most widely used by North Americans (mostly for pizza) is the low-moisture variety, which is drier and somewhat harder than fresh mozzarella. Fresh mozzarella is high-moisture, soft and delicate. Fresh mozzarella, which is what we recommend for this recipe, is found in specialty food stores and has a shorter shelf life. We love it for this recipe because it can be easily broken or pulled apart and is the perfect texture to eat with the heritage tomatoes and tarragon linguini. Once the linguini is plated, we dredge the mozzarella halves in the Tarragon Dressing at the bottom of the bowl to coat them with the seeds and tarragon.

Our word mozzarella comes from the Italian *mozzare*, which means to cut, a technique used in the making of mozzarella. Fresh mozzarella may be made from buffalo or cow's milk, and in Italy raw milk is still used because of its flavour.

An Italian specialty, burrata (from the Italian word for buttered) would be a perfect cheese for this dish if you can find it—try Italian specialty or cheese shops. It's made by forming fresh mozzarella around a lump of sweet cream butter or by mixing mozzarella with cream and wrapping it in fresh mozzarella.

WORKING WITH TARRAGON

The first rule when working with this aromatic, anise-flavoured herb is to taste it to gauge the intensity of its fragrance and peppery, pine-licorice taste. Start with a small amount in recipes and add more if you like it. Cooking diminishes the aroma, but the flavour is sometimes intensified, especially if teamed with fats such as butter, oils or cream cheeses. In this recipe, you may wish to use less than ¼ cup (60 mL), or substitute chopped fresh basil if you prefer its milder, nutmeg-spiked taste.

Spiced Pappardelle Noodles with Feta

A rich, creamy sauce wants a wide and long pasta shape like pappardelle; otherwise, the sauce will overwhelm the pasta. This dish can be served hot or cold. The smoky, creamy, crunchy texture lends itself to a filling for half a cantaloupe (seeds removed) or against a bed of salad greens. Toasted pine nuts make a fine substitution for the pumpkin seeds. —Nettie

MAKES 6 SERVINGS

12 oz (375 g) dried pappardelle noodles	1 cup (250 mL) chopped fresh parsley or cilantro leaves
3 Tbsp (45 mL) pumpkin seeds	1 tsp (5 mL) lime zest
3 cloves garlic, minced	¼ cup (60 mL) freshly squeezed lime juice
½ tsp (2 mL) chipotle chili powder	¾ cup (185 mL) crumbled feta cheese
½ tsp (2 mL) salt	

1. Cook the pappardelle in a large pot of boiling salted water for 6 minutes, or until al dente. Drain and return to pot.

2. Toast the pumpkin seeds in a skillet over medium heat for 3 to 4 minutes until lightly browned, stirring often.

3. In a bowl, combine the garlic, chipotle and salt. Add the parsley, lime zest and juice. Fold in the cheese.

4. Toss the hot pasta with sauce in a serving bowl. Garnish bowls with the toasted pumpkin seeds.

COOKING PASTA

Whether fresh or dried, pasta should be cooked in a large pot of water so that it will cook more evenly and not stick together. I add 1 Tbsp (15 mL) of salt to every 4 quarts (4 L) of cold water. For long pasta, I add 1 Tbsp (15 mL) olive oil. Most of the salt will be drained away when you drain your pasta. Unsalted or insufficiently salted water will produce bland pasta.

Cashew Noodles with Purple Cabbage
☐ FLEX APPEAL BACON

This is an Asian Cobb salad and is delicious hot or cold. You can use any type of nut butter in the dressing, and many types of pasta will work. Open the cupboard and use what is available. Sesame seeds add calcium and crunch. Bacon is a good garnish for wilted cabbage. —Nettie

FLEX APPEAL

MAKES 2 SERVINGS

4 slices bacon

Arrange the bacon slices on a grill pan or skillet in one layer, making sure they don't touch. Cook, turning once or twice, over medium-high heat for 3 to 5 minutes or until the bacon is browned and crisp. Transfer to a paper towel–lined plate to drain.

Crumble into bite-sized pieces and add to 2 of the bowls in step 4.

MAKES 6 SERVINGS

1 lb (500 g) spaghetti noodles

4 cups (1 L) shredded red cabbage

4 green onions, thinly sliced

1 red bell pepper, cut into strips

¼ cup (60 mL) chopped fresh parsley

Cashew Dressing (recipe follows)

3 Tbsp (45 mL) toasted sesame seeds (see Toasting Nuts and Seeds)

1. Bring a large pot of salted water to a boil over high heat. Add the noodles and cook according to package directions.

2. Place shredded cabbage in a metal colander over the sink. Drain cooked noodles over the cabbage to wilt it.

3. Transfer the noodles and cabbage to a bowl. Add the green onions, bell pepper and parsley. Drizzle Cashew Dressing overtop and toss to combine.

4. Using tongs, divide noodle mixture among 6 bowls and garnish with sesame seeds.

Cashew Dressing

MAKES 1¼ CUPS (310 mL)

½ cup (125 mL) cashew nut butter

¼ cup (60 mL) tamari or soy sauce

⅓ cup (80 mL) water

2 Tbsp (30 mL) chopped fresh ginger

1 clove garlic, chopped

2 Tbsp (30 mL) red wine vinegar

2 Tbsp (30 mL) toasted sesame oil

2 tsp (10 mL) liquid honey

½ tsp (2 mL) dried red chili flakes

1. In a bowl, whisk together cashew nut butter, tamari, water, ginger, garlic, vinegar, sesame oil, honey and chili flakes. Set aside.

TOASTING NUTS AND SEEDS

Toasting nuts and seeds is a technique that intensifies their flavour and deepens their colour. Toasting may be done in the oven or toaster oven, or on the stovetop.

To toast nuts and seeds on the stove: Heat in a large, heavy-bottomed skillet over medium-high heat. Stir and toss for 3 to 4 minutes, or until lightly browned. If using this method for smaller nuts and seeds, reduce the cooking time to 2 to 3 minutes.

To toast nuts in the oven: Toast on a baking sheet lined with parchment paper. Place in a 350°F (180°C) oven for 4 to 6 minutes or until lightly coloured but not browned. Remove and cool.

Niçoise Noodles with Dijon Dressing
☐ FLEX APPEAL TUNA

I love it when traditional dishes are tweaked. This recipe is a new twist on the French salad of boiled new potatoes and green beans, olives, hard-boiled eggs, tuna and thinly sliced red onion over greens. With spaghetti swapped for the potatoes, it is delicious and simple, and with very little time . . . voilà. —Pat

FLEX APPEAL

MAKES 2 SERVINGS

1 can (6 oz/175 g) water-packed tuna, drained (see About Tuna, page 98)

In step 3, divide the noodles, vegetables and egg quarters between 2 platters. Break up the tuna and add it to one of the platters.

RECIPE NOTE

Try new greens, like Chinese broccoli for the snow peas. To cook Chinese broccoli, blanch in the salted boiling water for 1 minute before cooking the spaghetti. Rinse in cold water, drain and set aside until ready to assemble the platter.

MAKE IT SEASONAL

· In the spring, when new potatoes and fresh pod peas are in season, I always use them in place of the pasta and snow peas.

· In summer, I use summer greens instead of spinach, and garden peas and beans.

· In the fall, tomatoes, bell peppers, carrots and zucchini are good choices.

· In winter, tomatoes are lame because they come from faraway places, so I use roasted red pepper wedges in their place. It is easy to roast red peppers, but I always have a jar of them on my pantry shelves for convenience, especially in winter.

MAKES 4 SERVINGS

8 oz (250 g) spaghetti

¼ cup (60 mL) Dijon Dressing (recipe follows)

2 cups (500 mL) baby spinach (see Recipe Note)

1 lb (500 g) fresh snow peas, trimmed and halved lengthwise (see Recipe Note)

4 hard-boiled eggs, quartered

2 tomatoes, quartered (see Make It Seasonal)

¼ cup (60 mL) green or black olives

½ red onion, thinly sliced

1. In a large pot of boiling salted water, cook spaghetti for 7 minutes or until al dente. Using tongs, lift spaghetti into a colander, drain and rinse with cool water. Toss noodles to keep them from congealing and set aside to drain. See image ❶.

2. Transfer noodles to a bowl and toss with half of the Dijon Dressing.

3. To serve, pile noodles in the centre of a platter and surround with spinach, peas, egg quarters, tomatoes, olives and onion slices. Drizzle the remaining dressing over all or pass it separately.

Dijon Dressing

MAKES ¼ CUP (60 mL)

⅓ cup (80 mL) olive oil

2 Tbsp (30 mL) freshly squeezed lemon juice

2 Tbsp (30 mL) Dijon mustard

1. In a jar with a tight-fitting lid, combine the oil, lemon juice and mustard and shake well.

Niçoise Noodles
with Dijon
Dressing

①

about this recipe

What makes it great?

The visual appeal of the salad ingredients on the platter is dramatic and yet it is very easy to compile. Many of the ingredients may be in your pantry so that it can be prepared at the last minute for lunch or dinner, any time of year.

What about the noodles?

You can use any relatively thin noodle in this recipe, such as linguini, soba, spaghetti, rice vermicelli or cellophane noodles.

Cellophane noodles are long and transparent. To make them, bean or potato starch is spun into fine threads. These noodles only require about 15 minutes of soaking in warm water to soften them for adding to salads, stir-fries, soups or Asian-style recipes.

Vermicelli noodles are long and thin, and made from white or brown rice. These noodles are softened in water and used in stir-fries, soups or Asian-style dishes.

continued on next page >

> Niçoise Noodles with Dijon Dressing continued

Tuna Marinade

¼ cup (60 mL) tamari or soy sauce

2 Tbsp (30 mL) liquid honey

1 Tbsp (15 mL) toasted sesame oil

1 clove garlic, minced

1 Tbsp (15 mL) grated ginger

about tuna

What are the kinds of tuna we eat?

While there are several different species of tuna (*Thunnini*), we tend to see mostly albacore and some yellowfin or bluefin for sale, fresh and canned.

Can I use fresh tuna in this dish?

Yes, you can use fresh tuna. It's fast and easy to prepare, but you will need a cast iron grill pan or skillet or a barbecue. In the photo above, we rubbed a tuna steak with oil and coated the entire outside with sesame seeds before grilling.

To cook fresh tuna on the stovetop: Heat 2 Tbsp (30 mL) coconut or avocado oil in a cast iron grill pan or skillet over high heat. Rub the tuna with oil and sear for 2 minutes per side. Remove from the heat and let sit for several minutes. Fresh tuna prepared in this way will be white on the edges and pink in the centre. For extra flavour, you can marinate the seared tuna in the following sauce.

What about canned tuna?

The label on canned tuna should list the species (usually albacore) and the way it has been packed: "solid" means a piece of whole fish is packed into the can; "chunk" means a variety of large pieces; and "flaked" means smaller pieces of tuna.

In addition to the species, you need to pay attention to the medium used to pack canned tuna—oil or water. While water adds no calories, if the oil is pure olive oil it contains omega-3 fatty acids that are essential to healthy hearts.

How can I be sure that the tuna I buy is sustainable?

It is important to understand the methods used to catch tuna and to buy only tuna that has been caught using sustainable methods. Different brands of tuna have been ranked for their use of sustainable tuna (which does not include red-listed yellowfin tuna) and for their fishing methods. (See the Resources section for links to information on sustainable seafood and the current ranking list on Greenpeace's website.)

Classic Stovetop Macaroni

Macaroni and cheese is standard comfort food. You can mix and match your cheeses: replace cheddar easily with Parmesan and roquefort or use all three!
—Nettie

MAKES 6 SERVINGS

1 lb (500 g) elbow macaroni, whole wheat or gluten-free	1 cup (250 mL) grated cheddar cheese
3 Tbsp (45 mL) butter	½ cup (125 mL) grated Parmesan cheese
3 Tbsp (45 mL) all-purpose flour	¼ cup (60 mL) crumbled roquefort cheese
2 tsp (10 mL) dry mustard	½ cup (125 mL) breadcrumbs (see Recipe Note)
2 tsp (10 mL) curry powder	
1½ cups (375 mL) milk or alternative (rice, soy, almond)	

1. Preheat the oven to 350°F (180°C).

2. Bring a large pot of salted water to a boil. Add the macaroni and boil, uncovered, according to package directions until al dente. Drain and place in a lightly oiled 11- × 7-inch (2 L) casserole dish.

3. In a saucepan, melt butter over medium heat. Whisk in the flour and cook, whisking constantly, for 2 minutes or until thickened. Add the mustard and curry powder. Whisk together until blended. Gradually whisk in the milk. Cook, whisking constantly, for 5 minutes or until thickened. Stir in the cheeses. Cook, stirring constantly, for 1 or 2 minutes or until the cheese is melted.

4. Pour cheese sauce over the cooked macaroni and stir to mix well. Sprinkle breadcrumbs overtop.

5. Bake for 20 to 25 minutes or until lightly browned on top.

RECIPE NOTE

To make homemade breadcrumbs: For every cup (250 mL) of breadcrumbs required, use 3 medium-sized slices of white or whole-grain sandwich bread or a 5-inch (12 cm) piece of baguette with the bottom crust removed. Tear or coarsely chop the bread into 1-inch (2.5 cm) pieces. Toast the pieces if you want dry breadcrumbs. Pulse in a food processor until they are fine crumbs. Store in an airtight container in a cool, dry place for up to 2 weeks. Breadcrumbs also freeze well.

TIME-SAVING STRATEGY

Make the macaroni and cheese casserole a day ahead, tightly cover and refrigerate. Bring to room temperature, top with bread-crumbs and bake just before serving.

Vegetable Mac 'n' Cheese

Vegetable Mac 'n' Cheese
☐ FLEX APPEAL CHICKEN

Not your regular macaroni and cheese, this version adds vegetables to boost nutrients. For a variation, try broccoli or parsnips in place of cauliflower and carrots. —Pat

MAKES 4 TO 6 SERVINGS

½ head cauliflower, cut into florets	3 Tbsp (45 mL) all-purpose or gluten-free flour
2 cups (500 mL) elbow macaroni	1 Tbsp (15 mL) chopped fresh rosemary
2 Tbsp (30 mL) olive or avocado oil	1 tsp (5 mL) sea salt
1 onion, chopped	2 cups (500 mL) almond milk or rice milk or soy milk
1 leek, white and pale green parts only, chopped	1 cup (250 mL) grated fontina or cheddar cheese
3 carrots, chopped (see Recipe Note)	¼ cup (60 mL) grated Parmesan cheese
4 cloves garlic, finely chopped	

1. Preheat the oven to 425°F (220°C).

2. Bring a large pot of salted water to a boil over high heat. Add the cauliflower and macaroni and cook for 8 to 12 minutes or until the macaroni is al dente and cauliflower is tender-crisp. Drain, rinse with cool water and set aside.

3. In a saucepan, heat the oil over medium heat. Sauté the onion, leek and carrots for 5 minutes or until the onions are soft and translucent. Add the garlic and cook, stirring frequently, for 2 minutes.

4. In a bowl, whisk flour, rosemary and salt into milk. Stir milk mixture into vegetables in saucepan. Cook, stirring constantly, for 5 minutes or until the sauce is bubbling and thickened. Remove from the heat and stir in the cooked cauliflower and macaroni.

5. Spoon into lightly oiled 8-cup (2 L) casserole dish. Spread grated cheeses evenly overtop. Bake for 10 minutes or until the cheese is melted and mixture is bubbly.

FLEX APPEAL

MAKES 2 TO 3 SERVINGS

½ cup (125 mL) chopped cooked chicken

Spoon cauliflower and macaroni mixture into 2 prepared baking dishes. Add the chicken to one of the dishes and stir to combine. Top with cheese and bake as directed in step 5.

RECIPE NOTE

Try this variation: Add 1 cup (250 mL) shredded regular or sweet potato to the saucepan in step 3.

MAKE-AHEAD STRATEGIES

· Make this dish and spoon into baking dish but do not add the cheeses. Cover with plastic wrap and it will keep overnight or up to 2 days in the refrigerator if tightly wrapped. Bring to room temperature, spread cheeses overtop and bake as directed in step 5.

· Double the recipe and freeze one casserole (without the cheese topping) by wrapping tightly and placing in a zip-top freezer bag. Use within 1 month. To cook: Thaw overnight in the refrigerator, spread cheeses overtop and bake as directed in step 5.

FLEX
APPEAL
Lamb Chops

Moroccan Vermicelli with Lentils

☐ FLEX APPEAL LAMB CHOPS

Brown rice vermicelli noodles are used here because they are so easy to use, but you can substitute cooked udon or ramen. The Moroccan spices lend an exotic flavour to this hearty dish. —Pat

FLEX APPEAL

MAKES 2 SERVINGS

3 Tbsp (45 mL) coconut or avocado oil

1 Tbsp (15 mL) toasted sesame oil

2 Tbsp (30 mL) rice vinegar

2 Tbsp (30 mL) grated ginger

1 Tbsp (15 mL) tamari or soy sauce

2 to 4 lamb loin chops (about 2.5 oz/ 75 g each) (see Cooking Lamb)

In a shallow bowl, combine the coconut oil, sesame oil, vinegar, ginger and tamari. Add the lamb chops to the marinade and set aside until about 8 minutes before ready to grill. You can marinate the lamb, covered, in the refrigerator overnight if desired. Bring to room temperature before grilling.

Preheat the grill to high. Rub 2 to 4 metal skewers with oil and thread 1 lamb chop onto each skewer. Grill for about 3 minutes per side. Baste with marinade when you turn them. Use a meat thermometer to test for doneness: lamb is best cooked medium-rare (145°F/63°C).

Top 2 of the bowls in step 4 with lamb chops before adding the pumpkin seeds.

MAKES 4 SERVINGS

8 oz (250 g) brown rice vermicelli (see About Vermicelli, page 104)

2 Tbsp (30 mL) coconut or avocado oil

1 onion, chopped

1 leek, white and pale green parts only, chopped

1 carrot, chopped

2 cloves garlic, finely chopped

1 Tbsp (15 mL) Moroccan Spice Blend (page 181)

½ cup (125 mL) vegetable broth

2 cups (500 mL) chopped kale (see Recipe Note)

1 can (19 oz/540 mL) cooked red or brown lentils, rinsed and drained

¼ cup (60 mL) pumpkin seeds, for garnish

1. In a bowl, cover vermicelli with warm water and set aside for 15 minutes or until soft. Drain and set aside.

2. Meanwhile, in a flameproof tagine or skillet, heat the oil over medium-high heat. Add the onion and sauté for 5 minutes. Add the leek, carrot and garlic and cook, stirring frequently, for 2 minutes or until the onions and leeks are soft. Stir in the Moroccan Spice Blend. Add the broth and bring to a boil over high heat. Add the kale, cover, reduce the heat to low and simmer for 10 minutes.

3. Add the softened noodles and the lentils, mix and heat through.

4. Divide the mixture among 4 shallow bowls and garnish with the pumpkin seeds.

Moroccan
Vermicelli
with Lentils

continued on next page >

about vermicelli

You can buy white or brown rice vermicelli or Italian pasta vermicelli. The latter is larger in diameter than spaghetti and, like all pasta, requires cooking in boiling water. Rice vermicelli, which is used in this recipe, is easy to use in tagine, soup and stir-fry dishes because it softens in warm water while you prepare the rest of the ingredients.

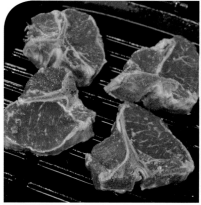

RECIPE NOTES

· For speed and convenience, we recommend using canned lentils, but you can cook dried lentils right in the tagine or skillet. Measure 1 cup (250 mL) dried red or brown lentils and 2½ cups (625 mL) broth (in place of the ½ cup/125 mL broth). Follow the directions for step 2, stirring the lentils in with the broth. Bring to a boil over high heat. Add the kale, cover, reduce the heat to low and simmer, stirring occasionally, for 35 to 40 minutes or until the lentils are tender and almost no liquid remains. Continue with step 3.

· Tagine dishes are the perfect place to use frozen chopped kale. There are many brands available, but we like the quality of a brand called Cookin' Greens.

cooking lamb

Of all the cuts you can use in this recipe, loin is the most tender and the best choice for the high-heat method of cooking utilized. Count on serving 1 or 2 chops per person.

Lamb chops are best cooked over a barbecue or cast iron grill. We rub the unheated grill with olive oil first.

The chops are grilled over high heat for about 3 minutes per side. For medium-rare, the temperature will be 145°F (63°C) and they should show some pink on the inside.

Sesame Honey Tofu and Soba Noodles
⬜ FLEX APPEAL PORK

We cook the soba noodles in a broth to add flavour. You can serve the broth in the bottom of the bowl. In a hurry? Use vegetable broth from a Tetra Pak. The sesame honey sauce can be used with tempeh as well. Always rinse your tofu with cold water before using it. —Nettie

FLEX APPEAL

MAKES 6 SERVINGS

MAKES 2 SERVINGS

Ginger Tamari Broth

10 cups (2.5 L) water

2½ inches (6 cm) fresh ginger, thinly sliced

3 garlic cloves, finely chopped

4 green onions, thinly sliced

5 Tbsp (75 mL) tamari or soy sauce

1 Tbsp (15 mL) rice vinegar

½ lb (250 g) soba noodles

3 cups (750 mL) thinly sliced baby bok choy

Sesame Honey Tofu

2 Tbsp (30 mL) toasted sesame oil

8 oz (250 g) extra firm tofu, rinsed and cut into ½-inch (1 cm) cubes

2 Tbsp (30 mL) honey

2 Tbsp (30 mL) soy sauce or tamari

1½ Tbsp (22.5 mL) water

1 tsp (5 mL) cornstarch

¼ cup (60 mL) chopped peanuts, for garnish

¼ cup (60 mL) chopped fresh cilantro, for garnish

3 to 4 oz (90 to 125 g) pork loin

½ cup (125 mL) barbecue sauce

1 Tbsp (15 mL) coconut or avocado oil

Cut the pork crosswise into thin strips. In a bowl, combine the pork strips with barbecue sauce. Let marinate while preparing the broth, noodles and tofu.

After step 3, transfer the tofu to a bowl. Wipe out skillet, add oil and heat over medium-high heat. Add the pork strips and marinade, reduce the heat to medium and cook, stirring constantly, for 2 to 3 minutes or until the pork is browned with a trace of pink.

In step 4, divide the tofu among 4 of the bowls and add pork to the other 2 bowls.

1. To make the broth, in a large saucepan, combine the water, ginger, garlic, green onions, tamari and vinegar. Bring to a boil over high heat. Cover, reduce the heat and simmer for 8 to 10 minutes. Remove the solids from broth with a slotted spoon and discard. Bring broth back to a boil and add soba noodles. Lightly boil for 6 to 8 minutes or until tender. Two minutes before the end of cooking, add bok choy. Remove the noodles and bok choy from broth and place in a covered bowl.

2. Meanwhile, to make the sesame honey tofu, heat the oil in a skillet over medium heat. Add the tofu cubes and cook, stirring frequently, until beginning to brown, 6 to 8 minutes.

3. In a small bowl, combine the honey, soy sauce, water and cornstarch and stir well. Add to skillet and cook, stirring, until the sauce has thickened and coats the tofu, about 2 minutes. ←

4. Divide the noodles, bok choy and broth among 6 bowls. Top with tofu and garnish with peanuts and cilantro. ←

Hot and Sour Tempeh Noodles
☐ FLEX APPEAL SCALLOPS

This is a quick and flavourful one-bowl dinner. Crumbling thawed tempeh between your fingers is a job worthy of any kid—5 years old and up. A new ingredient for many people, tempeh is a fermented soybean square, inoculated with an edible mold. It isn't very attractive, but cooked properly it is delicious and is high in protein and fibre. You can buy tempeh in health food stores and many supermarkets. It is available fresh and frozen, often vacuum sealed for a longer shelf life. —Nettie

FLEX APPEAL

MAKES 2 SERVINGS

8 oz (250 g) scallops

Preheat the oven to broil (500°F/260°C). While the cabbage is cooking in step 4, arrange scallops in one layer on a parchment paper–lined, rimmed baking sheet. Broil on the top rack of the oven, turning once, for 2 minutes each side or until the scallops turn opaque and are firm but not hard or rubbery. Remove and let drain on a paper towel–lined plate.

In step 5, top 2 of the bowls with scallops before garnishing with pistachios.

MAKES 6 SERVINGS

¼ cup (60 mL) coconut or avocado oil

8 oz (250 g) tempeh, finely crumbled

1 Tbsp (15 mL) finely chopped garlic

1 Tbsp (15 mL) finely chopped fresh ginger

1 Tbsp (15 mL) granulated sugar

½ tsp (2 mL) salt

¼ tsp (1 mL) pepper

1 Tbsp (15 mL) chili powder

4 cups (1 L) vegetable broth

¼ cup (60 mL) tamari or soy sauce

¼ cup (60 mL) rice wine vinegar

6 oz (175 g) dried thin rice noodles

2 cups (500 mL) chopped purple cabbage

½ cup (125 mL) chopped fresh cilantro

½ cup (125 mL) shelled pistachio nuts, for garnish

1. Heat the oil in a wok or skillet over medium-high heat. Add the tempeh and cook, stirring frequently for 6 to 8 minutes, or until reddish brown. Add the garlic, ginger, sugar, salt and pepper, stirring constantly for 1 minute or until the vegetables soften and tempeh is deeply coloured. Stir in the chili powder.

2. Add the broth, tamari and vinegar to wok. Bring to a boil over high heat. Lower heat to a simmer and cook, stirring frequently, for 10 minutes.

3. Meanwhile, in a bowl, pour 8 cups (2 L) boiling water over noodles until totally covered. Let stand for 8 to 10 minutes to rehydrate. Drain in colander.

4. Add the cabbage to wok and cook, stirring, for 2 minutes or until wilted. Add the rehydrated noodles and cilantro and heat through.

5. Divide the tempeh-noodle mixture among 6 bowls. Garnish with pistachios.

rapid wraps

Almond Butter Banana Rolls

These are delicious for breakfast. The cooked banana mixture tastes great on toast, in a sandwich or wrapped in a tortilla. If almond nut butter is not available, use cashew or peanut butter. —Nettie

MAKES 6 SERVINGS

3 bananas, sliced diagonally ½ inch (1 cm) thick

3 Tbsp (45 mL) dried cranberries

2 Tbsp (30 mL) freshly squeezed lime juice

1 tsp (5 mL) fresh grated ginger

1 tsp (5 mL) seeded, minced fresh green chili

¼ tsp (1 mL) ground allspice

six 6-inch (15 cm) corn or flour tortillas

½ cup (125 mL) smooth almond nut butter

¼ cup (60 mL) almonds or pecans, coarsely chopped

6 romaine lettuce leaves

1. Preheat the oven to 275°F (140°C).

2. In a bowl, toss together bananas, cranberries, lime juice, ginger, chili and allspice.

3. In a skillet, warm tortillas over medium-high heat for 2 minutes, turning once. Transfer to a heatproof platter and keep warm in the oven.

4. Working with 1 tortilla at a time, place 1½ Tbsp (22.5 mL) almond butter down centre of tortilla. Spoon ⅓ cup (80 mL) banana mixture overtop of nut butter. Sprinkle with 2 tsp (10 mL) almonds. Top with lettuce leaf. Fold bottom edge over filling and fold sides over.

Mango-Avocado Rice Paper Rolls
☐ FLEX APPEAL SHRIMP

I like to mix and match fresh herbs, especially with fruits and vegetables. The mint, basil and chives are a good combination in this dish. I was amazed how refreshing the addition of cream cheese was. Garnish anything with peanuts and I will come back for seconds! The rolls should be served immediately—the rice paper wrappers can dry out quickly and become a tough chew. —Nettie

FLEX APPEAL

MAKES 8 SERVINGS

1 avocado, diced

2 tsp (10 mL) grated lime zest

1 Tbsp (15 mL) freshly squeezed lime juice

1 red bell pepper, diced

½ cup (125 mL) shredded carrot

½ cup (125 mL) softened cream cheese

¼ cup (60 mL) chopped fresh chives

¼ cup (60 mL) chopped fresh mint

¼ cup (60 mL) chopped fresh basil

8 rice paper wrappers

2 cups (500 mL) chopped lettuce

2 cups (500 mL) fresh or frozen mango, thinly sliced

½ cup (125 mL) chopped peanuts

1 cup (250 mL) Sweet Thai Chili Sauce (page 184)

MAKES 4 SERVINGS

⅓ cup (80 mL) chopped cooked shrimp

After step 1, mix half of the avocado–cream cheese mixture with the shrimp. Continue with the remaining steps to prepare the rolls.

1. In a bowl, combine the avocado, lime zest and juice. Stir in the red pepper, carrot, cream cheese, chives, mint and basil.

2. Fill a shallow pan or bowl with warm water. Work with 1 rice paper wrapper at a time. Soak wrapper in warm water for 10 seconds or until softened. Place on a damp towel.

3. Spoon ¼ cup (60 mL) avocado–cream cheese mixture just below middle of rice paper wrapper, leaving 1-inch (2.5 cm) border on either side. Top with ¼ cup (60 mL) chopped lettuce, a few mango slices and 1 Tbsp (15 mL) peanuts.

4. Fold bottom of rice paper wrapper up over filling, pressing filling down as you go. Fold both sides of rice paper inward. Gently press to seal. Roll up wrapper to top edge. Brush water on top edge, if necessary, to seal.

5. Repeat steps 2 to 4 with the remaining rice paper wrappers. Serve with Sweet Thai Chili Sauce.

RECIPE NOTES

· Working with rice paper wrappers is easy. You only need to dip the individual sheets in hot water for 10 seconds to soften. Rice paper is a delicious, low-fat alternative to wheat-based wrappers. Made from rice flour and water, the translucent sheets are always sold dried. Store them in a cool, dark place.

· Many fillings are good in rice paper rolls. Steamed asparagus, julienned green papaya, spinach leaves and sticky rice are a few non-traditional, delicious ideas.

MAKE-AHEAD STRATEGY

If you do not serve immediately, wrap in a damp paper towel and plastic wrap, and serve within 1 hour.

Grilled Vegetable Shawarma with Tahini Dressing

☐ FLEX APPEAL LAMB

Lamb is the meat of choice for this Middle Eastern dish, but these hefty rolls are definitely good without the meat, so try the veggie version first. We used whole wheat pocketless pitas, but you could stuff this into a pita pocket and make it easier to eat. Either way, the taste is divine. —Pat

FLEX APPEAL

MAKES 2 SERVINGS

1 Tbsp (15 mL) coconut or avocado oil

2 bone-in lamb leg chops
(about 6 oz/175 g)

In a skillet or cast iron grill, heat the oil over medium-high heat. Cook the lamb chops for 3 minutes per side. They should show some pink on the inside (145°F/63° for medium-rare).

Cut into strips and spread over the vegetables on 2 of the pitas in step 2 above. If you have coloured toothpicks, use a different colour to secure the lamb shawarmas.

MAKES 4 SERVINGS

3 Tbsp (45 mL) coconut or avocado oil, divided	1 tsp (5 mL) ground cumin
1 onion, sliced	2 cups (500 mL) spinach leaves
2 cups (500 mL) cubed eggplant	4 pitas, warmed (see Warming Wraps)
1 cup (250 mL) sliced mushrooms	½ cup (125 mL) Tahini Dressing (recipe follows)
2 cloves garlic, finely chopped	tzatziki (optional)

1. In a tagine or a skillet with a lid, heat 2 Tbsp (30 mL) oil over medium-high heat. Sauté the onion for 4 minutes. Add the remaining oil and the eggplant and mushrooms and stir to mix well. Cover, reduce the heat to low and cook, stirring occasionally, for 12 minutes or until the eggplant is soft. Stir in the garlic, cumin and spinach. Cover and cook, stirring occasionally, for 2 minutes or until the spinach has wilted.

2. On a work surface, lay out pitas. Spread Tahini Dressing over each pita, leaving a 1-inch (2.5 cm) border around the edges. Spread onion-eggplant mixture down the centre of each pita. Fold sides of the pita around the filling and secure with toothpicks. Serve with tzatziki, if desired.

Tahini Dressing

MAKES ½ CUP (125 mL)

¼ cup (60 mL) mayonnaise	1 clove garlic, minced
2 Tbsp (30 mL) tahini (see About Tahini, page 17)	2 Tbsp (30 mL) freshly squeezed lemon juice

1. In a bowl, combine the mayonnaise, tahini, garlic and lemon juice.

Grilled
Vegetable
Shawarma with
Tahini Dressing

FLEX
APPEAL
Lamb

WARMING WRAPS

It is essential that you work out an easy way to warm tortillas, tacos, pita and other wrap breads if you want to fully enjoy them. If you have a flameproof clay tortilla warmer as pictured here, you can heat them over a stovetop flame just before filling and rolling.

To warm wrap breads using an oven, cover them with a dampened tea towel and seal in foil or place in a casserole dish with lid. Heat for up to 20 minutes in an oven preheated to 300°F (175°C). If using a microwave oven, cover with a dampened tea towel and microwave on high for 30 seconds to 1 minute.

Caramelized Squash and Farro Wraps

The squash is a treat on its own. Salted and warm from the oven, the caramelized slices make a great after-school snack. The key here is to have some whole grain already cooked because it is so easy to thaw and adds extra texture and protein to the wrap ingredients. —Pat

MAKES 4 WRAPS

1 small squash, halved and seeded (see About Squash)	½ cup (125 mL) green sprouts (see About Sprouts)
2 Tbsp (30 mL) olive or avocado oil	¼ cup (60 mL) Lemon Dressing (recipe follows)
4 slices red onion, ¼-inch (60 mm) thick	½ cup (125 mL) farro or other cooked grain (see About Grains)
4 slices goat cheese, ¼-inch (60 mm) thick	sea salt and pepper
4 large tortillas	

1. Preheat the oven to 400°F (200°C).

2. Slice squash into ½-inch (125 mm) slices, arrange in one layer on parchment paper–lined, rimmed baking sheet, and drizzle with oil. See image ❶. Roast for 25 to 30 minutes or until soft and golden.

3. Transfer the squash to a plate (leave the oven on), grind salt over and let sit until cool enough to handle. See image ❷. Remove the peel.

4. Arrange the onion slices on the baking sheet and top each with a slice of goat cheese. See image ❸. Bake for 3 to 5 minutes or until the cheese is golden and soft. Watch carefully and remove before cheese is completely melted. Cut each slice into quarters.

5. Meanwhile, warm the tortillas on the stovetop or wrap them in foil and warm them in the oven.

6. On a work surface, lay out warm tortillas. Lay roasted squash slices down the centre of each tortilla. Spread sprouts over squash. Drizzle ½ Tbsp (7.5 mL) Lemon Dressing over each tortilla. Sprinkle grain over the sprouts and top with onion-cheese quarters. Drizzle the remaining dressing over each and season to taste with salt and pepper. See image ❹. Fold in the top and bottom of tortillas and roll up.

Caramelized
Squash and
Farro Wraps

Lemon Dressing

MAKES ¼ CUP (60 mL)

2 Tbsp (30 mL) olive or avocado oil	1 Tbsp (15 mL) freshly squeezed lemon juice
1 Tbsp (15 mL) toasted sesame oil	2 tsp (10 mL) grated lemon rind

1. In a jar with a tight-fitting lid, combine the oils, lemon juice and lemon rind. Shake well to combine.

continued on next page >

MAKE-AHEAD STRATEGIES

· Measure dressing ingredients into a clear jar, cap it and keep in the refrigerator for up to 10 days. Bring to room temperature and shake well before using.

· Roast the squash and keep, tightly wrapped, in the refrigerator for up to 2 days. Bring to room temperature before using in wraps.

about grains

Grains add texture and extra plant protein to wraps and sandwich fillings. Try brown or black rice, quinoa, pot barley, amaranth, spelt, wheat berries or other whole grains in wraps.

We've used Italian farro (*Triticum dicoccum*) in this recipe but you can choose any ancient or whole grain. If you're cooking the grain for this recipe, you will need to start it before roasting the squash in step 2. One cup (250 mL) farro cooks in 2 cups (500 mL) boiling salted water to the chewy stage in about 30 minutes and makes 2 cups (500 mL) cooked grain. Drain and rinse before using. Cool and freeze leftover grain in zip-top freezer bags in 1-cup (250 mL) amounts. For food safety, cool and thaw cooked grain in the refrigerator. You can store freshly cooked, chilled rice or other grains for up to 2 days in the refrigerator.

about squash

There are more than 500 different cultivars of pumpkins and squashes. Some are ornamental, but the edible varieties fall into what we call summer or winter varieties. The winter varieties have a thicker skin and store better than the summer squashes, which include zucchini. Butternut and acorn are great winter squash varieties, but we tend to rely exclusively on these two types because they are widely available in supermarkets. Like most fruits and vegetables, many heritage types or varieties are not grown for the convenience of the distributor. You can find interesting varieties at farm stands and farmers' markets. Some are sweet, some are mealy-fleshed, some are creamy-fleshed, some are dry and others are nutty and smooth-textured. Try any of the smaller-sized squash (Corresponding images: Carnival ❶, Futsu ❷, Heart 'o Gold ❸, Sweet Potato ❹) in this recipe.

about sprouts

Green sprouts from nuts, legumes, beans, grains and peas are power-houses because they're packed with all the vitamins, minerals and enzymes necessary for growing the mature plant. They're easy to grow from seeds and make a great sandwich or wrap ingredient.

While bean sprouts are widely available, farmers' markets and some specialty food shops carry many different sprouts, including:

· Sunflower sprouts, not surprisingly, have a slightly nutty flavour. See image **1**.

· Pea sprouts offer up a taste reminiscent of raw peas right out of the pod. See image **2**.

· The bright yellow of butternut squash sprouts adds colour to wraps and sandwiches. See image **3**.

about this recipe

What makes it great?

Roasting the squash gives it a sweet, nutty flavour that is delicious, but when combined with the roasted onion and goat's cheese, the combination is bistro quality.

Can I use other ingredients?

The onion with goat's cheese is essential, but you can use any grain or add legumes such as pinto beans or chickpeas. While I also think the roasted squash is essential, I understand that some people just don't care for squash, so try any of the following:

· roasted beets, carrots or parsnips

· roasted red bell peppers

· shredded raw cabbage or coleslaw

Thinly sliced lettuce is a great addition as well.

Romaine Boats

☐ FLEX APPEAL CRAB

I enjoy mixing fresh herbs with noodles and nuts. It is a delicious combination. I have also used angel hair pasta in place of the soba noodles. This recipe is a great balance of salty, sour and sweet. —Nettie

FLEX APPEAL

MAKES 2 SERVINGS

1 can (6 oz/175 g) lump crabmeat, rinsed and drained

After step 3, spoon the crabmeat over 2 of the romaine boats.

about soba noodles

Soba noodles are long, thin Japanese noodles made from either 100% buckwheat flour or a combination of buckwheat and unbleached or whole wheat flours. Nutty in flavour, soba noodles are eaten in soups, in broths or cold on their own with a dipping sauce.

MAKES 8 SERVINGS

¼ lb (125 g) soba noodles

2 cups (500 mL) dry-roasted peanuts, plus ½ cup (125 mL) for garnish

2 garlic cloves

2 Tbsp (30 mL) freshly squeezed lime juice

2 Tbsp (30 mL) granulated sugar

1 Tbsp (15 mL) tamari or soy sauce

½ cup (125 mL) water

8 romaine lettuce leaves

2 cups (500 mL) mixed greens

½ cup (125 mL) chopped fresh cilantro

½ cup (125 mL) chopped fresh basil

1. In a pot over high heat, bring 6 cups (1.5 L) of salted water to a boil. Add the soba noodles and bring the water back to a boil. Reduce the heat and simmer for 6 to 8 minutes or until tender. Drain and rinse with warm water.

2. In a food processor, purée 2 cups (500 mL) peanuts and garlic until smooth. Add the lime juice, sugar, tamari and water. Purée for an additional 30 seconds.

3. Place romaine leaves on a large platter. Layer each with ¼ cup (60 mL) mixed greens, ¼ cup (60 mL) cooked noodles, and 1 Tbsp (15 mL) each cilantro and basil.

4. Spoon 3 Tbsp (45 mL) of the peanut mixture over each romaine boat. Garnish with extra peanuts.

Roasted Vegetable and Bean Wraps

This recipe is all about time management. While the vegetables are roasting, reheat the canned beans. Using canned beans (or cooked frozen beans) is a huge time-saver, and beans from a can are so easy to flavour. I like to put a cup of the chili garlic beans aside for breakfast the next morning. —Nettie

MAKES 6 SERVINGS

Oven-Roasted Vegetables

3 Tbsp (45 mL) coconut or avocado oil

1 Tbsp (15 mL) rice vinegar

2 tsp (10 mL) tamari or soy sauce

salt and pepper

15 asparagus spears, trimmed and cut into 2-inch (5 cm) lengths

5 potatoes, cut into ¼-inch (6 mm) slices

2 zucchini, cut into ½-inch (1 cm) rounds

1 onion, thinly sliced

1 cup (250 mL) cherry tomatoes

Chili Garlic Beans

1 Tbsp (15 mL) coconut or avocado oil

2 cloves garlic, finely chopped

1 Tbsp (15 mL) chili powder

½ tsp (2 mL) ground cumin

1 can (19 oz/540 mL) black or pinto beans, drained and rinsed

2 Tbsp (30 mL) water, or as needed

2 Tbsp (30 mL) fresh chopped dill

six 10-inch (25 cm) flour tortillas (see Recipe Note)

1 cup (250 mL) tomato salsa

RECIPE NOTE

Supermarkets sell plain, whole wheat and vegetable-flavoured tortillas, and can be made with vegetable short-ening or lard. Vegetarians should be aware that tortillas sold in Latin or Mexican stores often contain lard. Read your labels.

1. Preheat the oven to 450°F (230°C).

2. To roast the vegetables, in a large bowl, whisk together oil, vinegar and tamari. Add salt and pepper to taste. Add the asparagus, potatoes, zucchini, onion and tomatoes. Toss to coat.

3. Spread vegetables in single layer on a parchment paper–lined, rimmed baking sheet. Cover with heavy-duty foil, crimping edges to seal. Reduce oven to 400°F (200°C) and bake for 20 to 25 minutes or until the vegetables are tender. Remove from oven and place in a bowl.

4. To prepare the beans, heat the oil in a saucepan over medium-high heat. Add the garlic and cook, stirring frequently, for 1 minute. Add the chili and cumin, stirring constantly for 1 minute. Add the beans and cook for 3 to 5 minutes or until heated through. Remove from the heat and mash to desired consistency with a potato masher. Add the water if mixture is too thick. Add the dill and mix well.

5. In a skillet over medium heat, warm tortillas for 2 minutes, turning once. Place ½ cup (125 mL) roasted vegetables and ½ cup (125 mL) reheated beans down the centre of each tortilla, leaving 1-inch (2.5 cm) border at bottom and top. Fold bottom edge over filling and fold sides over. Roll up from bottom. Serve with salsa.

Chickpea and Halloumi on Naan

The combination of grilled asparagus and halloumi gives this open-faced sandwich a roasted taste and chewy texture. We used watercress as the topping greens, but any sprout or baby green such as arugula or spinach would be great. Served right on a pizza stone, this is a great sharing dish at lunch or for a light dinner. —Pat

MAKES 4 SERVINGS

1 can (19 oz/540 g) chickpeas, drained and rinsed

4 Tbsp (60 mL) coconut or avocado oil, divided

1 clove garlic, minced

1 Tbsp (15 mL) Garam Masala (page 179)

24 asparagus spears, trimmed (about 10 oz/300 g)

8 oz (250 g) naan bread

½ cup (125 mL) tzatziki

6 oz/175 g halloumi cheese, thinly sliced

1 cup (250 mL) green sprouts (see About Sprouts, page 115)

2 green onions, sliced

1. Preheat the oven to 400°F (200°C).

2. Using a potato masher, coarsely mash chickpeas until about half are crumbled.

3. In a skillet, heat 2 Tbsp (30 mL) oil over medium-high heat. Add the chickpeas, garlic and garam masala. Cook, stirring frequently, for 6 minutes or until the chickpeas are crisp. Set aside. See image ❶.

4. Meanwhile, arrange asparagus on a barbecue or stovetop grill, drizzle with remaining oil and grill for 4 or 5 minutes, or until tender-crisp. Set aside. See image ❷.

5. Place naan bread on a pizza stone or baking sheet and spread tzatziki overtop. Spread chickpea mixture over the tzatziki and top with halloumi slices. Bake for 6 to 8 minutes or until the halloumi is golden.

6. Lay the asparagus over halloumi and top with sprouts and green onions.

Chickpea and Halloumi on Naan

1

2

3

RECIPE NOTE

Garam masala (page 179) is a mild blend of spices including cardamom, coriander, cumin, allspice or cloves. See image ❸. It usually contains cinnamon, which makes it pleasantly sweet tasting. If you don't have time to make your own, you can find it in specialty stores.

Scrambled Tofu with Kale

▢ FLEX APPEAL BACON

Because wraps can be stuffed, or folded and rolled, they can contain ingredients that would fall out of an ordinary sandwich. Wraps can hold beans, grains, vegetables and sauces without turning into a soggy mess. This recipe is an excellent example of an ordinary filling that is transformed by a wrap and can be easily transported. —Nettie

FLEX APPEAL

MAKES 2 SERVINGS

4 strips side bacon, chopped

In a skillet, cook chopped bacon over medium-high heat, stirring frequently, for 4 minutes or until browned and crisp. Using a slotted spoon or lifter, transfer bacon bits to a paper-lined plate and let drain.

Add to 2 pitas in step 5.

MAKES 6 SERVINGS

3 Tbsp (45 mL) coconut or avocado oil

1 red onion, chopped

2 cloves garlic, finely chopped

1 Tbsp (15 mL) curry powder

1 tsp (5 mL) finely chopped fresh ginger

2 cups (500 mL) sliced kale leaves

½ cup (125 mL) vegetable broth or water

10 oz (300 g) extra firm tofu, drained, rinsed and crumbled

sea salt and pepper

six 4-inch (10 cm) pita pocket rounds

1 cup (250 mL) mixed sprouts

½ cup (125 mL) halved cherry tomatoes

1 cup (250 mL) shredded lettuce

1. Preheat the oven to 350°F (180°C).

2. In a skillet, heat the oil over medium-high heat. Add the onion and garlic and sauté for 5 minutes or until soft. Add the curry powder, ginger, kale and broth. Cook, stirring frequently, for 5 to 7 minutes or until the kale is bright green and tender.

3. Add the tofu and cook, stirring, until heated through, about 3 or 4 minutes. Season with salt and pepper to taste.

4. Cut a thin slice off the top of each pita. Heat pitas for 3 to 5 minutes or until warm.

5. Stuff each pita with an equal amount of curried tofu mixture and top with sprouts, tomatoes and lettuce.

Vegetable Tacos

☐ FLEX APPEAL CHICKEN

Soft tortillas can accommodate almost any filling. Broccoli slaw is available at supermarkets and can be added instantly to any stir-fry to save time. The vegetables are sliced razor thin, and are delicious raw when added to salads. —Nettie

MAKES 6 SERVINGS

six 10-inch (25 cm) corn or flour tortillas

3 Tbsp (45 mL) coconut or avocado oil

2 cups (500 mL) shiitake mushrooms, stems removed and caps thinly sliced

1 cup (250 mL) cooked black beans

½ cup (125 mL) frozen corn kernels

½ cup (125 mL) frozen peas

¼ tsp (1 mL) ground cayenne

3 Tbsp (45 mL) white miso

2 Tbsp (30 mL) orange juice

2 tsp (10 mL) rice vinegar

1 cup (500 mL) broccoli slaw (store-bought or use Thai Slaw, page 147)

2 Tbsp (30 mL) sliced green onions

1. Preheat the oven to 300°F (150°C).

2. Stack tortillas on a parchment paper–lined, rimmed baking sheet. Cover with foil and place in the oven to warm while filling is being prepared.

3. Heat the oil in a skillet over medium-high heat. Add the mushrooms, black beans, corn, peas and cayenne and cook, stirring occasionally, for 8 minutes or until the vegetables start to turn golden brown. Transfer to a bowl.

4. In a separate bowl, whisk together miso, orange juice and rice vinegar. Drizzle over mushroom mixture. Stir in the broccoli slaw.

5. Remove the warmed tortillas from oven one at a time. Spread ¾ cup (185 mL) of vegetable mixture over half of each tortilla, leaving a 1-inch (2.5 cm) border at the edges.

6. Top with green onions and fold tortillas in half to serve.

FLEX APPEAL

MAKES 2 SERVINGS

1½ cups (375 mL) chicken broth

1 skinless, boneless chicken breast (6 oz/175 g)

In a saucepan, heat chicken broth over high heat until boiling. Add the chicken breast and reduce the heat to keep broth gently simmering. Poach, turning the breast once, for 8 to 10 minutes or until the chicken is cooked through. Chicken is cooked safely when a meat thermometer reads 165°F (74°C) when inserted into the meatiest part.

Remove the pan from heat and leave chicken in the broth until it is cool enough to handle. Cut the chicken crosswise into thin strips and add to 2 of the tortillas in step 5.

TIME-SAVING STRATEGY

If you don't have cooked beans on hand or time to prepare them, buy frozen or canned cooked beans and measure out what you need.

Pinto Bean and Corn Salsa Tacos

☐ FLEX APPEAL FISH

If you're not planning to add fish to two of these tasty tacos, you can still chop the nutty topping from the non-vegetarian recipe and sprinkle over the ingredients for an extra nutty garlic hit. —Pat

FLEX APPEAL

MAKES 2 SERVINGS

- 6 oz (175 g) whitefish or trout fillets, deboned
- ½ lemon
- ¼ cup (60 mL) natural almonds
- 1 clove garlic
- 1 slice whole wheat bread, torn into pieces
- 1 Tbsp (15 mL) avocado oil

Preheat the oven to 375°F (190°C). Lay fish, skin side down, on parchment paper–lined, rimmed baking sheet and squeeze lemon juice over.

In a blender or food processor, combine the almonds, garlic and bread pieces. Process for 30 seconds or until chopped. Add the oil and process until well mixed.

Spread topping evenly over the fish, pressing it onto each fillet. Bake for 5 minutes or until the fish is opaque and flakes easily when tested with a fork. Cut the fish into 1-inch (2.5 cm) wide slices and top 2 of the tortillas in step 2.

MAKES 4 SERVINGS

- ½ can (7 oz/200 g) pinto beans, drained and rinsed
- 1 clove garlic
- 1 Tbsp (15 mL) cashew butter or tahini (see About Tahini, page 17)
- 1 Tbsp (15 mL) freshly squeezed lemon juice
- 3 Tbsp (45 mL) olive or avocado oil
- sea salt and pepper
- 4 large tortillas
- 3 cups (750 mL) Corn Salsa (recipe follows)
- 1 cup (250 mL) spinach leaves
- ¼ cup (60 mL) shredded cheddar cheese
- ¼ cup (60 mL) chopped fresh cilantro (optional)

1. In a blender or food processor, combine the beans, garlic, cashew butter and lemon juice. Process for 15 seconds or until chopped. With the motor running, drizzle oil through the opening in the lid and process until smooth. Season to taste with salt and pepper.

2. On a work surface, lay out tortillas. Spread bean and garlic mixture over each tortilla, leaving a 1-inch (2.5 cm) border around the edges. Spoon Corn Salsa down the centre of each tortilla. Distribute spinach over the salsa. Sprinkle 1 Tbsp (15 mL) cheddar and cilantro, if desired, over all.

3. Fold the top and bottom of each tortilla towards the centre, then fold each side towards the centre.

Corn Salsa

MAKES 3 CUPS (750 mL)

1 can (12 oz/355 mL) corn kernels, drained	½ can (7 oz/200 g) pinto beans, drained and rinsed
1 cup (250 mL) chopped tomato	1 Tbsp (15 mL) freshly squeezed lemon juice
3 Tbsp (45 mL) chopped red onion	

1. In a bowl, combine the corn, tomato and onion with beans. Toss with lemon juice.

TIME-SAVING STRATEGY

Use a store-bought salsa instead of the Corn Salsa. With the hundreds of prepared salsas available, it is fun to find favourite brands to keep on hand as pantry staples.

MAKE-AHEAD STRATEGIES

- Make the Corn Salsa up to 2 days in advance. Wrap tightly and refrigerate but bring to room temperature before assembling the tacos.
- Cook the fish a day in advance and store tightly wrapped in the refrigerator, or use leftover fish or other cooked meat. Reheat in an ovenproof dish in a 350°F (180°C) oven or in a microwave oven.

short-order soups and stews

about heirloom beets

What sets heirloom beets (and other heirloom plants) apart is that they are not genetically modified and they are open-pollinated, meaning they rely on bees and other insects, birds, bats and wind to come to fruit. These plants have been around for generations and are important varieties for cooking because they are usually very tasty and may have different colours or textures than varieties that have been bred to facilitate mechanical harvesting, transportation and long shelf-life.

Here are a few of the many different and interesting beets that you can try in this soup.

- Dating from around 1840, the Bull's Blood variety is sweet and the leaves are delicious in salads and soups. See image ❶.

- Chioggia, also called Candy Cane, has its origins in the Italian coastal town of Chioggia, near Venice. I like to slice them paper-thin and use with a vinegar brine because the beautiful stripes fade when cooked, but their taste and texture are great in the soup recipe above. See image ❷.

- Beautiful in soups, salads and with pasta, this orange variety is often teamed with oranges or orange juice or blood oranges in salads. See image ❸.

- The flavour of white beets is sweet and milder than the red varieties. Use in soups or stews, or steam them when they're picked before they mature, as in the photograph here. See image ❹.

Beet Soup

Roasting the beets brings out their natural sweetness and lends a bistro quality to this soup. It's incredibly easy to make so I often double the recipe and freeze the extra. For added appeal, float Parmesan Quinoa Sliders (page 62) on top as you would croutons. —Pat

MAKES 4 TO 6 SERVINGS

3 lb (1.5 kg) beets, quartered (see Recipe Note)	8 cups (2 L) vegetable broth
3 onions, peeled and quartered	2 Tbsp (30 mL) fresh chopped rosemary
6 cloves garlic	sea salt and pepper
2 Tbsp (30 mL) coconut or avocado oil	¼ to ⅓ cup (60 to 80 mL) plain yogurt, for garnish

1. Preheat the oven to 400°F (200°C).

2. Spread beets, onions and garlic in one layer on a rimmed baking sheet and drizzle with oil. Roast for 35 to 40 minutes or until al dente when pierced with the tip of a knife. Let vegetables cool enough to handle.

3. In a soup pot or large saucepan, bring the broth to a boil over high heat. Add the roasted vegetables and the rosemary. Simmer for 5 minutes or until the beets are soft.

4. Ladle ½ cup (125 mL) broth and some of the vegetables into a blender, purée and empty the blender contents into a bowl. Repeat until all vegetables have been puréed. Return the puréed soup to the pot, stir and heat through over medium heat. Add salt and pepper to taste.

5. Garnish bowls with a tablespoon (15 mL) of yogurt.

RECIPE NOTE

For a different texture, instead of puréeing the vegetables , try coarsely chopping them in a food processor after roasting. Add the chopped vegetables to the broth and simmer for 5 minutes or until soft.

Beet
Soup

1

2

3

4

Minute Tuscan Minestrone

Commonly referred to as *fazool* in American-Italian communities and made famous by the line in the song "Amore" ("when the stars make you drool just like pasta fazool . . . "), this hearty, traditional meatless Italian dish is made with pasta and beans or in Italian, *pasta e fagioli*. —Pat

MAKES 4 TO 6 SERVINGS

2 Tbsp (30 mL) coconut or avocado oil	1 can (19 oz/540 mL) cannellini or white kidney beans, drained and rinsed
1 onion, chopped	1 cup (250 mL) chopped fresh, or thawed and drained, frozen spinach or kale
3 cloves garlic, finely chopped	
1 carrot, chopped	2 Tbsp (30 mL) chopped fresh rosemary
1 can (28 oz/796 mL) diced or whole tomatoes with juice	
2 cups (500 mL) vegetable or chicken broth	1 Tbsp (15 mL) chopped fresh oregano
½ cup (125 mL) elbow macaroni (see Recipe Note)	grated fresh Parmesan (optional)

COOKING DRIED BEANS

For convenience, you can use cooked canned beans in recipes, but it's more economical to cook your own dried beans. See image ❶. It just takes some time because the beans must be rehydrated by soaking them overnight. (Dried navy beans, dried white kidney beans and dried cannellini beans are cooked in exactly the same way.)

Here's how to make 3 to 5 cups (750 mL to 1.25 L) of cooked beans:

Measure 1 or 2 cups (250 or 500 mL) of dried beans. In a soup pot or large saucepan, cover the beans with 4 or 6 cups (1 or 1.5 L) cool water. Set aside to soak overnight. Next day, drain off the soaking water and pour 4 or 6 cups (1 or 1.5 L) fresh water over beans. Bring to a boil over high heat. Cover, reduce the heat and simmer for 40 minutes to 1 hour or until the beans are tender. Drain and rinse well.

Store cooked beans in a covered container in the refrigerator for up to 3 days or freeze in 1- or 2-cup (250 or 500 mL) amounts for up to 3 months. See image ❷.

1. In a soup pot or large saucepan, heat the oil over medium-high heat. Sauté the onion for 4 minutes. Add the garlic and carrot and cook, stirring constantly, for 1 minute. Add the tomatoes, their juices and the broth and bring to a boil.

2. Add the macaroni, reduce the heat to medium and simmer for 12 to 15 minutes or until the pasta and vegetables are soft. Stir in the beans, spinach, rosemary and oregano and simmer for a minute or until the greens are wilted.

3. Top with freshly grated Parmesan, if desired.

RECIPE NOTE

We've used elbow macaroni, but you can use any small pasta such as orecchiette, ziti, orzo or fusilli.

MAKE-AHEAD STRATEGY

To make up to 2 days ahead, cook the soup to the end of step 1, let it cool, cover tightly and refrigerate until an hour before serving. Bring the soup to room temperature. Bring to a boil over medium-high heat, add pasta and continue with step 2.

Minute
Tuscan
Minestrone

1

2

Artichoke Zucchini Chowder

☐ FLEX APPEAL LAMB

This recipe allows you to empty your pantry or refrigerator of ingredients you forgot you still had! Olives, capers, chickpeas, zucchini and celery—use them up to create a delicious meal. Chowders can be as thick as you like. Always have more stock or water on hand to reach your desired texture. —Nettie

FLEX APPEAL

MAKES 2 SERVINGS

1 Tbsp (15 mL) coconut or avocado oil

1 clove garlic, finely chopped

6 oz (175 g) ground lamb

In a skillet over medium-high heat, heat the oil. Add the garlic, stirring frequently, for 1 minute. Add the ground lamb and reduce the heat to medium. Cook, stirring constantly and breaking up the lumps, for 5 to 8 minutes or until the meat is browned with no pink on the inside. Using a slotted spoon, transfer to a bowl.

In step 3, stir the lamb mixture into 2 of the bowls of chowder.

MAKES 6 SERVINGS

¼ cup (60 mL) coconut or avocado oil

1 red onion, chopped

4 cloves garlic, finely chopped

2 Japanese eggplants, cut crosswise into ½-inch (1 cm) slices

4 stalks celery, sliced

2 zucchini, sliced

1 carrot, grated

6 cups (1.5 L) vegetable broth or water

1 can (14oz/398 mL) chickpeas, drained and rinsed

½ cup (125 mL) chopped pitted black olives

1 Tbsp (15 mL) drained capers

1 can (14 oz/398 mL) artichoke hearts, drained and quartered

½ cup (125 mL) chopped fresh parsley

sea salt and pepper

1. In a soup pot or large saucepan, heat the oil over medium-high heat. Cook the onion for 5 minutes or until softened. Add the garlic, eggplants, celery, zucchini and carrot. Cook for 8 minutes, stirring occasionally.

2. Add the broth, chickpeas, olives and capers and bring to a boil. Reduce the heat and simmer for 10 minutes. Add the artichokes, parsley, salt and pepper. Simmer, stirring often, for 5 minutes.

3. Ladle chowder into 6 bowls.

Squash and Celery Cheddar Soup
◻ FLEX APPEAL BACON

In order to prepare this hearty soup within 30 minutes, you need to purchase squash that has already been peeled and cut into pieces or squares. —Nettie

MAKES 4 SERVINGS

6 cups (1.5 L) vegetable broth

4 cups (1 L) diced squash (1-inch/2.5 cm dice) (see Recipe Note)

1 cup (250 mL) chopped onions

1 clove garlic, finely chopped

1 cup (250 mL) thinly sliced celery

½ tsp (2 mL) sea salt

¼ cup (60 mL) butter

¼ cup (60 mL) unbleached white flour

1½ cups (375 mL) milk or alternative milk (almond, rice or soy)

1 cup (250 mL) grated cheddar cheese

⅛ tsp (0.5 mL) ground black pepper

¼ cup (60 mL) chopped fresh parsley, for garnish

1. In a soup pot or large saucepan, bring the broth to boil over medium-high heat. Add the squash, onions, garlic, celery and salt. Cover, reduce the heat to medium and cook, stirring occasionally, for 15 minutes. Transfer to a food processor or use a wand mixer to process until smooth. Return to pot and keep warm over low heat.

2. In a separate saucepan, melt butter over medium heat. Whisk in the flour and cook, whisking constantly, for 2 minutes or until thickened. Gradually whisk in the milk. Cook, whisking constantly, for 3 to 5 minutes or until thickened. Stir in the cheese and pepper and cook, stirring constantly, for 2 minutes or until the cheese is melted.

3. Add the cheese sauce to puréed soup and heat through, stirring often.

4. Ladle soup into 4 bowls and garnish with parsley.

RECIPE NOTE

I am amazed at the variety of squash available: acorn, buttercup, butternut, Delicata, Hubbard, kabocha, spaghetti and turban (right). Each variety has its own flavour, sweetness and unique texture. Make sure the squash does not have any soft spots, which are often the sign of improper storage.

FLEX APPEAL

MAKES 2 SERVINGS

4 slices bacon

Arrange the bacon slices on a grill pan or skillet in one layer, making sure they don't touch. Cook, turning once or twice, over medium-high heat for 3 to 5 minutes or until the bacon is browned and crisp. Transfer to a paper towel–lined plate to drain.

Crumble when crisp and add to 2 of the bowls in step 4.

Cauliflower and Coconut Curry Chowder
☐ FLEX APPEAL FISH

A good curry paste or powder is essential for this dish. We used coconut water as the liquid, but you can use coconut milk for a thicker soup. You can customize this soup according to the season: potatoes and carrots in winter, asparagus and peas in spring. —Pat

FLEX APPEAL

MAKES 2 SERVINGS

1 Tbsp (15 mL) coconut or avocado oil

1 Tbsp (15 mL) butter

6 oz (175 g) whitefish or cod fillet

In a skillet, heat the oil and melt butter over medium-high heat. Add the fish and cook for 3 to 5 minutes on each side (10 minutes total per inch/2.5 cm of thickness) or until the fish turns opaque and flakes easily with a fork.

After step 2, divide the fillet in half and add to 2 of the bowls.

MAKES 4 SERVINGS

2 Tbsp (30 mL) coconut or avocado oil	1 cup (250 mL) vegetable broth or water
1 onion, chopped	½ cauliflower, divided into florets
1 Tbsp (15 mL) curry powder or paste	1 potato, diced
2 cups (500 mL) coconut water	2 carrots, shredded

1. In a soup pot or large saucepan, heat the oil over medium-high heat. Sauté the onion for 4 minutes. Add the curry powder and cook, stirring constantly, for 1 minute. Add the coconut water and vegetable broth and bring to a boil. Add the cauliflower, potato and carrots. Reduce the heat to medium and simmer for 15 to 17 minutes or until the vegetables are tender-crisp.

2. Ladle into 4 bowls.

Cauliflower and Coconut Curry Chowder

about coconut water

Pure coconut water is the clear liquid found inside young, green coconuts. As a refreshing drink, it tastes nutty sweet with a hint of toasted coconut, and it has a wide range of uses in recipes. With 730 mg potassium, 32 mg calcium and 18 mg magnesium, it's a healthful substitute for water. I use it in stir-fry dishes and to cook rice for savoury or dessert dishes.

Look for pure, plain coconut water (the ingredient on the label should read simply "coconut water") and avoid brands with added juice, sugar or flavourings, which make them virtually the same as soda or other sugary beverages.

Summer
Bean
Stew

Summer Bean Stew

This summer bean medley is just the kind of light summer meal we crave when the oven is the last thing we want to turn on. It relies on fresh fava beans (canned are okay, but if you can find fresh beans, they add so much extra flavour) and fresh green or yellow wax summer beans. We've teamed our stew with oversized, pesto-topped whole wheat croutons, making it a meal in itself. —Pat

MAKES 6 TO 8 SERVINGS

2 Tbsp (30 mL) coconut or avocado oil

1 onion, chopped

2 cloves garlic

3 sprigs rosemary, leaves only (see About the Ingredients)

6 cups (1.5 L) vegetable broth

2 cups (500 mL) cooked, peeled fava beans (see About the Ingredients)

1 cup (250 mL) fresh green or yellow wax beans, cut in 1-inch (2.5 cm) pieces

1 cup (250 mL) coarsely chopped carrots

1 cup (250 mL) chopped fresh sorrel or spinach

Pesto Croutons (recipe follows)

1. In a soup pot or large saucepan, heat the oil over medium-high heat. Sauté the onion for 4 to 5 minutes or until soft and fragrant.

2. Meanwhile, chop the garlic and rosemary together. Add to onions and cook, stirring constantly, for 1 minute. Add the broth, fava beans, green beans, carrots and sorrel. Cook for 15 to 20 minutes or until the vegetables are tender.

3. Ladle into bowls and top each bowl with a crouton or serve the croutons on the side.

MAKE-AHEAD STRATEGIES

- Blanch and shell the fava beans up to 1 day in advance. Keep tightly covered in the refrigerator and bring to room temperature just before adding to the stew.

- Freshly made pesto will store in a capped jar or tightly wrapped container in the refrigerator for up to 10 days.

Pesto Croutons

Makes 6 to 8 large croutons

three to four 1-inch (2.5 cm) slices whole wheat bread

⅓ cup (80 mL) Mediterranean Herb Pesto (page 183)

1. Preheat the oven to 375°F (190°C) with oven rack on top shelf. Lay out bread slices on a baking sheet. Toast in the oven for 2 to 3 minutes or until lightly toasted on top. Using tongs, flip slices over and spread pesto evenly over untoasted side. Bake for 2 to 3 minutes or until the bread is browned around the edges. Cut in half and serve with stew.

continued on next page ›

about the ingredients

What are fava beans?

Fresh fava beans (*Vicia faba*), also known as broad beans, are native to northern Africa and are used extensively in Mediterranean dishes. The Egyptian dish *ful medames* is a good example of a dish that relies on the fresh fava.

Fava beans are grown in North America and are available at farmers' markets early in the summer. Their texture is creamy, the flavour is buttery and somewhat nutty and worth the effort to cook them. See image ❶.

How do I cook fava beans?

First, you have to remove the beans from the pod. This is easy to do if you squeeze the pod along the lengthwise seams so that it splits open. Scoop out the beans and discard the pods. See image ❷.

Simmer the shelled beans in boiling salted water for 6 minutes or until tender. Let cool. See image ❸.

When the beans are cool enough to handle, remove the tough outer skin by squeezing the bean out through the bottom end. Discard the tough skins. See image ❹.

For our summer stew, we left the beans whole. You can mash them with garlic and oil for an incredible purée to use as a dip or for crudités, or to act as a base for baked fish or roasted vegetables.

Can I use other beans?

In this recipe, you can use other fresh beans such as lima beans or edamame (fresh soybeans) in place of the fava beans.

Edamame cook faster and do not have a tough outer skin, so they're easier to use than fava beans. See image ❺.

What is sorrel?

Sorrel (*Rumex acetosa*) is a perennial herb that was considered a "pot herb" of medieval times. Sorrel is best eaten in spring when the leaves are small and the amount of naturally occurring oxalic acid is not enough to cause problems for people with kidney disorders, gout or rheumatoid arthritis. See image ❻.

Chopping the garlic and rosemary

A razor-sharp vegetable knife is used in this recipe to finely chop the garlic and the rosemary at the same time. I prefer to use either a French or vegetable knife for this kind of task because both herbs will be uniformly chopped and fine. See image ❼.

Using a blender or a mortar and pestle pulverizes or mashes the herbs, especially the softer garlic. Careful use of a small food processor—pulsing in short bursts—will achieve almost the same results as using a vegetable or French knife.

about this recipe

What makes it great?

The fresh flavours of the fava and green beans along with the fresh spring greens and rosemary make this a delicate and exceptionally tasty summer stew.

What other ingredients would be great in this recipe?

Any other spring green, legume or grain can be added to this summer stew. For variety, you could substitute any of the following in place of the sorrel or spinach:

· dandelion greens (See image ❽), asparagus, bok choy or fresh fiddleheads in the spring.

· chopped wild leeks (See image ❾), snow peas or fresh summer peas.

· chopped spring turnips and their greens. See image ❿.

How to clean wild leeks

Be sure to correctly identify all wild plants and to observe conservation principles. But if you are lucky enough to know where to look for wild leeks in the spring, dig only a small amount, leaving the patch to propagate and grow larger. Knock off the dirt that clings to the roots and follow these steps for easy removal of the dirty outer layer and rootlets at the end of the small bulb.

Leaving the green leaves attached to the stem, grasp a leek with your left hand (if right-handed, or with the right hand if left-handed) on the stem just above the point where the white bulb starts. See image ⓫.

With your right hand, pull the loose outer skin back over the rootlets. See image ⓬.

Snap off the end. This takes away the loose outer skin and the rootlets at the base of the bulb. Now swish the leaves and trimmed bulbs in cool water and pat dry. See image ⓭.

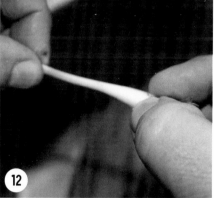

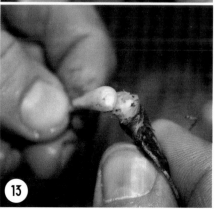

Apricot Bok Choy Stew
☐ FLEX APPEAL SHRIMP

Delicious hot or cold, the sauce alone is worth preparing. We always use organic tofu made from soybeans grown locally by Harro Wehrmann (from Ripley, Ontario) for Sol Cuisine, a handcrafted, artisanal soy foods distributor who sell an excellent brand of tofu. Serve this stew with quinoa or rice. —Nettie

FLEX APPEAL

MAKES 2 SERVINGS

6 oz (175 g) shrimp, peeled and deveined

2 Tbsp (30 mL) coconut or avocado oil

1 Tbsp (15 mL) fresh lime juice

Rinse the shrimp under cool water, drain and pat dry.

Heat the oil in a heavy-bottomed skillet over medium-high heat. Reduce the heat to medium-low and add the rinsed shrimp to the pan. Cook for 2 to 3 minutes or until the bottom edges start to turn bright pink. Using tongs, turn shrimp and cook for 2 minutes on flip side or until the undersides are bright pink. Remove the shrimp to a bowl and stir in the lime juice.

In step 4, add shrimp to 2 of the bowls.

MAKES 6 SERVINGS

¼ cup (60 mL) coconut or avocado oil

1 lb (500 g) extra-firm tofu, rinsed and sliced into 1 inch (2.5 cm) cubes

1 cup (250 mL) mango chutney

2 Tbsp (30 mL) apple cider vinegar

2 Tbsp (30 mL) grated fresh ginger

1 Tbsp (15 mL) Dijon mustard

1 tsp (5 mL) sea salt

¼ cup (60 mL) butter

1 cup (250 mL) grated carrots

2 cups (500 mL) chopped baby bok choy (see About Bok Choy)

1 cup (250 mL) sliced dried apricots

½ cup (125 mL) thinly sliced green onions

½ cup (125 mL) chopped almonds

2 Tbsp (30 mL) freshly squeezed lime juice

1. In a skillet, heat the oil over medium-high heat. Sauté the tofu for 5 to 7 minutes or until lightly browned. Using a slotted spoon, transfer to a bowl and set aside.

2. In a bowl, mix together chutney, vinegar, ginger, mustard and salt. Set aside.

3. In the skillet used to brown the tofu, heat butter over medium heat. Sauté the carrots and bok choy for 3 minutes. Add the sautéed tofu and the apricots. Cook over medium heat for 3 to 5 minutes. Add the chutney mixture and cook for 2 minutes more. Add the green onions, almonds and lime juice.

4. Divide the mixture among 6 bowls.

about bok choy

Often referred to as Chinese cabbage, this popular vegetable in Asian dishes is in fact a member of the Brassica family. Its advantage in cooking is that it adds crunchy texture as well as leafy greens to stir-fry, skillet and casserole dishes. The term bok choy means "white vegetable" in Cantonese. With many different varieties and names, the importance of this vegetable is that it contributes high levels of vitamins A and C as well as some of the same anti-cancer phytonutrients found in cabbage and other plants in the Brassica family.

In this recipe, we've used baby bok choy (above left), a small version of the regular type, because it is tender and the greens are mild in flavour.

Vegetable Stroganoff
☐ FLEX APPEAL BEEF

FLEX APPEAL

For a faster, high-heat cooking method using a grill or skillet, you will need a good-quality cut of beef such as sirloin or NY strip fillet.

MAKES 2 SERVINGS

6 oz (175 g) boneless beef loin

1 Tbsp (15 mL) coconut or avocado oil

Preheat a barbecue grill, or use a cast iron grill pan or skillet on the stovetop.

Rub beef all over with oil. Grill on preheated barbecue or in a heated grill or skillet over high heat for about 5 minutes per side. Medium-rare beef should register 160°F (71°C). Let rest until ready to serve the stroganoff in step 4. Cut into thin strips and top 2 of the plates with beef before garnishing with parsley.

MAKE-AHEAD STRATEGY

The noodles must be cooked just before serving, but you can make the vegetable stroganoff up to 2 days in advance if you don't add the sour cream. Store tightly covered in the refrigerator and warm in a saucepan over medium-low heat or in a microwave oven. Add the sour cream and continue with step 4.

Stroganoff is made from mushrooms sautéed in butter with some onion and broth added. Ours retains the mushrooms but adds more vegetables for diversity. You can serve this stew over wide egg noodles, rice or potatoes. I like it over baked sweet potatoes. Cornstarch and sour cream thicken the stew, but if you wish, you can omit them and serve the vegetables in broth over cooked soba or udon noodles as you would an Asian soup. —Pat

MAKES 6 SERVINGS

1 lb (500 g) wide egg noodles

1 Tbsp (15 mL) butter

2 Tbsp (30 mL) coconut or avocado oil

1 onion, chopped

1 cup (250 mL) sliced mushrooms

2 cups (500 mL) vegetable broth

2 Tbsp (30 mL) Dijon mustard

¼ cabbage, thinly sliced

1 cup (250 mL) diced turnip, rutabaga or carrots

2 tsp (10 mL) cornstarch

2 Tbsp (30 mL) fresh thyme leaves

⅓ cup (80 mL) sour cream

sea salt and pepper

¼ cup (60 mL) chopped fresh parsley, for garnish

1. Bring a pot of salted water to a boil over high heat. Add the noodles and cook according to package directions. Drain and toss with butter.

2. Meanwhile, in a soup pot or large saucepan, heat the oil over medium-high heat. Sauté the onion for 5 minutes. Add the mushrooms and cook, stirring constantly, for 2 minutes or until golden and soft. Stir in the broth and mustard and bring to a boil. Add the cabbage and turnip, reduce the heat to medium-low and simmer for 12 to 15 minutes or until the vegetables are tender-crisp.

3. In a bowl, mix cornstarch with enough cool water to make a smooth paste. Stir into broth and cook, stirring frequently, for 2 minutes or until the sauce thickens. Remove from the heat and stir in the thyme and sour cream. Add the salt and pepper to taste.

4. Serve over cooked noodles. Garnish with parsley.

Cabbage Kale Goulash

⬚ FLEX APPEAL CHORIZO

What is a goulash? In Hungary it is prepared as a soup, but in our recipe it resembles a stew. Cabbage is available year round and the smooth-leaf purple variety offers great colour and texture. —Nettie

MAKES 6 SERVINGS

- 2 Tbsp (30 mL) olive or avocado oil
- 1 cup (250 mL) chopped onion
- ½ tsp (2 mL) caraway seeds
- 1 Tbsp (15 mL) paprika
- 3 Tbsp (45 mL) chopped fresh dill, divided
- ½ tsp (2 mL) sea salt
- 4 cups (1 L) shredded purple cabbage
- 2 cups (500 mL) chopped kale
- 1 cup (250 mL) vegetable broth or water
- 2 cans (28 oz/796 mL) whole peeled tomatoes
- ⅛ tsp (0.5 mL) black pepper
- 1½ cups (375 mL) plain yogurt or sour cream

1. Heat the oil in a large pot or Dutch oven over medium heat. Add the onion and cook, stirring frequently, for 5 minutes or until softened. Stir in the caraway seeds, paprika, 1 Tbsp (15 mL) dill and salt and cook, stirring constantly, for 1 minute. Add the cabbage and cook, stirring constantly, for 5 minutes.

2. Add the kale, broth, tomatoes and pepper and bring to a simmer. Cover, reduce the heat and simmer for 15 minutes.

3. Ladle into 6 bowls. Garnish bowls with yogurt and remaining dill.

RECIPE NOTE

To prepare cabbage, always remove the first layers of exterior leaves and then the core. To shred, cut cabbage into quarters and cut crosswise into thin strips or use a mandoline.

FLEX APPEAL

MAKES 2 SERVINGS

- 1 Tbsp (15 mL) coconut or avocado oil
- 4 oz (125 g) fresh chorizo sausage, chopped into ½-inch (1 cm) pieces

In a skillet, heat the oil over medium-high heat. Add the chorizo and cook, stirring constantly, for 8 minutes or until browned and crisp. Keep heat high enough to brown the meat but reduce the heat if chorizo begins to burn. Transfer to a paper towel-lined plate and let drain.

In step 3, add chorizo to 2 bowls of goulash before garnishing with yogurt and dill.

Curried Black Lentil Stew
☐ FLEX APPEAL BEEF

In India, lentil-based stews are served with vegetables and spices. Using turmeric, garlic, ginger and coconut milk, this entrée is full of flavour. Best of all, the stew improves with time, so you can make it ahead for an evening when you require a quick meal. I often eat it cold when the weather is hot. —Nettie

FLEX APPEAL

MAKES 2 SERVINGS

6 oz (175 g) sirloin tip steak

1 clove garlic, crushed

1 tsp (5 mL) smoked paprika

1 Tbsp (15 mL) coconut or avocado oil

sea salt and pepper

While the onions are cooking in step 2, spread both sides of steak with garlic and sprinkle with paprika. Heat the oil in a skillet or ridged grill pan over medium-high heat. Add the steak and cook for 6 to 8 minutes, turning once. Beef is cooked to medium-rare when a meat thermometer registers 145°F (63°C) and is cooked to medium when a meat thermometer resisters 160°F (71°C).

Remove from the heat and season with salt and pepper. Let rest for 8 minutes and thinly slice. Divide the steak slices into 2 portions and add to 2 of the bowls in step 4.

MAKES 8 SERVINGS

1 cup (250 mL) vegetable broth or water

2 cans (28 oz/796 mL) diced tomatoes and juice

2 cups (500 mL) black lentils, rinsed

1 Tbsp (15 mL) olive or avocado oil

1 tsp (5 mL) sea salt

2 cups (500 mL) coconut milk

2 Tbsp (30 mL) unsalted butter or olive oil

1½ cups (375 mL) finely chopped sweet onions

4 cloves garlic, minced

1¼ cup (300 mL) button mushrooms, thinly sliced

1 tsp (5 mL) finely diced fresh ginger root

1 tsp (5 mL) ground turmeric

1 tsp (5 mL) ground coriander

1 tsp (5 mL) ground cumin

½ tsp (2 mL) ground cardamom

1. In a large pot or Dutch oven, combine the broth, tomatoes, lentils, oil and salt. Bring to a boil, stirring often. Cover, reduce the heat and simmer for 20 minutes, stirring often. Add the coconut milk and simmer for 10 minutes.

2. In a skillet over medium heat, melt butter. Add the onions and cook for 5 minutes or until softened. Stir in the garlic, mushrooms, ginger, turmeric, coriander, cumin and cardamom and sauté for 5 minutes.

3. Stir into the lentil mixture and cook over medium-low heat for 5 minutes or until heated through.

4. Ladle stew into 8 bowls.

Pinto Bean Stew

Thank goodness for canned beans and tomatoes. Serve this recipe with basmati rice, quinoa or any cooked leftover grain in the refrigerator. Satisfying and quick, this ragout can easily be doubled. —Nettie

MAKES 4 TO 6 SERVINGS

2 Tbsp (30 mL) coconut or avocado oil

1 onion, chopped

2 cloves garlic, finely chopped

1½ Tbsp (22.5 mL) chili powder

2 tsp (10 mL) ground cumin

1 tsp (5 mL) dried oregano

1 can (28oz/796 mL) diced tomatoes and juice

½ cup (125 mL) frozen corn kernels

1 cup (250 mL) chopped red bell pepper (see Recipe Note)

2 zucchini, chopped

½ tsp (2 mL) sea salt

⅛ tsp (0.5 mL) black pepper

1 can (19 oz/540 mL) pinto beans, drained and rinsed (see Recipe Note)

½ cup (125 mL) sour cream or Greek yogurt, for garnish

4 to 6 sprigs fresh cilantro, for garnish

1. Heat the oil in skillet over medium-high heat. Add the onion and cook, stirring frequently, for 5 minutes or until soft. Add the garlic, chili powder, cumin and oregano. Cook, stirring frequently, for 1 minute.

2. Add the tomatoes, corn, red pepper, zucchini, salt and pepper. Bring to a boil over medium heat. Reduce the heat and simmer for 15 minutes, stirring often. Add the beans and simmer, stirring often, for 5 minutes.

3. Ladle the stew into 4 to 6 bowls. Garnish each bowl with sour cream and a sprig of cilantro.

RECIPE NOTES

- You can use roasted red peppers in place of red bell peppers in this recipe.

- Like all beans, pinto beans are high in fibre and make a great addition to soups and stews.

- When there are no frozen beans in my freezer, I go to my pantry and am so grateful for my canned beans. Canned beans come in a variety of sizes: 14 oz (398 mL), 19 oz (540 mL) and 28 oz (796 mL).

Stovetop Chili
☐ FLEX APPEAL BEEF

I love this chili's texture; it is so robust and filling. Serve with lots of garnishes: sour cream, yogurt, toasted pumpkin seeds and grated cheddar. It's also great on an open-faced sandwich, in a tortilla wrap or as stuffing for a cabbage roll. Try it with spaghetti or other pasta. This is a versatile recipe that pleases everyone. —Nettie

FLEX APPEAL

MAKES 2 SERVINGS

1 Tbsp (15 mL) coconut or avocado oil

6 oz (175 g) lean ground beef

While the chili is simmering, heat the oil in a skillet over medium-high. Add the ground beef and reduce the heat to medium. Cook, stirring constantly and breaking up any clumps, for 4 to 6 minutes or until the meat is browned with no pink inside. Drain off fat.

After step 2, stir into 2 of the bowls.

MAKES 6 SERVINGS

2 Tbsp (30 mL) olive or avocado oil

1 red onion, chopped

4 cloves garlic, chopped

1 zucchini, cut into ½-inch (1 cm) pieces

½ cup (125 mL) frozen or canned, drained corn kernels

1 Tbsp (15 mL) chili powder

1 tsp (5 mL) ground cumin

one 2-inch (5 cm) cinnamon stick

5 oz (150 g) tomato paste

2 cans (14 oz/398 mL) black beans, drained and rinsed

1 can (28 oz/796 mL) diced tomatoes with juice

2 cups (500 mL) vegetable broth or water

½ cup (125 mL) freshly brewed coffee

2 Tbsp (30 mL) molasses

½ tsp (2 mL) sea salt

1. Heat the oil in a large saucepan or Dutch oven over medium heat. Add the onion and garlic and cook, stirring frequently, for 5 minutes. Add the zucchini and corn, reduce the heat and cook for 2 minutes. Add the chili powder, cumin, cinnamon stick and tomato paste. Stir together. Add the beans, tomatoes, broth, coffee, molasses and salt. Bring the mixture to a boil. Reduce to a simmer and cook until the zucchini is tender, about 20 minutes.

2. Remove the cinnamon stick and ladle chili into 6 bowls.

MAKE-AHEAD STRATEGY

This chili is equally good when it's made ahead of time and reheated. It also freezes very well in an airtight container, for up to 6 months.

warm and cold salads

Thai Slaw

Thai Slaw

Cabbage and daikon radish are combined with flavours of Asia for new tastes for a winter vegetable salad. Add an exotic fruit for an extra boost of the Orient. —Pat

MAKES 4 SERVINGS

3 cups (750 mL) shredded green cabbage	¼ cup (60 mL) shredded rutabaga
1 cup (250 mL) shredded daikon radish	¾ cup (185 mL) Thai Vinaigrette (recipe follows)
1 carrot, shredded	¼ cup (60 mL) pumpkin seeds, for garnish

1. In a salad bowl, combine the cabbage, daikon, carrot and rutabaga. Drizzle the vinaigrette over and toss to combine.

2. Divide among 4 salad plates or bowls and garnish with pumpkin seeds.

Thai Vinaigrette

MAKES ¾ CUP (185 mL)

½ cup (125 mL) extra virgin olive oil or grapeseed oil	1 Tbsp (15 mL) chopped fresh oregano
2 tsp (10 mL) toasted sesame oil	¼ tsp (1 mL) red chili flakes
3 Tbsp (45 mL) freshly squeezed lime juice	

1. In a bowl, whisk together olive oil, sesame oil, lime juice, oregano and chili flakes until well combined.

about oregano

Often referred to as "the pizza herb," oregano is a powerful anti-oxidant with potent antibacterial, antifungal and anti-parasitic properties. As part of the mint family of plants, oregano adds a peppery, spicy taste to tomato dishes and hearty sauces, as well as salad dressings, especially vinaigrettes such as the one above.

Caesar Salad

☐ FLEX APPEAL CRAB

Contrasting cool and warm, soft and crunchy, this salad will both be familiar and have a twist. Grill the romaine. Its leaves will char slightly but remain crisp. Another twist to the recipe is the addition of silken tofu to the dressing instead of egg. The tofu will bind the ingredients together and add texture. An essential caesar salad dressing ingredient is Worcestershire sauce. Read your labels carefully because if it contains anchovies it isn't vegetarian. —Nettie

FLEX APPEAL

MAKES 2 SERVINGS

1 can (6 oz/175 g) lump crabmeat, rinsed and drained

In step 4, spoon crabmeat over 2 of the salads before topping with croutons.

RECIPE NOTE

Use leftover Caesar Dressing for drizzling over baked potatoes or other cooked vegetables, as a dressing for potato salad, or for tossing with leftover grains or pasta.

TIME-SAVING STRATEGY

Some very good, ready-made croutons are available to buy, for days when you have no time to make your own.

MAKES 4 SERVINGS

4 hearts of romaine lettuce, halved lengthwise	1½ cups (375 mL) Croutons (recipe follows)
½ recipe Caesar Dressing (recipe follows)	

1. Preheat gas grill to medium-high.

2. On preheated grill, grill romaine, cut side down, covered, for 2 minutes or until grill marks appear.

3. Cut the romaine crosswise into 2-inch (5 cm) strips and place in a large bowl. Toss the romaine with half of the dressing to coat.

4. Divide the salad among 4 salad plates and top with Croutons.

Caesar Dressing

MAKES 1 CUP (250 mL)

6 oz (175 g) extra-firm silken tofu	1 Tbsp (15 mL) vegetarian Worcestershire sauce
¼ cup (60 mL) extra virgin olive oil or grapeseed oil	¼ tsp (1 mL) sea salt
1 clove garlic, minced	¼ tsp (1 mL) black pepper
2 Tbsp (30 mL) freshly squeezed lemon juice	¼ cup (60 mL) finely grated Parmesan cheese
1 Tbsp (15 mL) Dijon mustard	

1. Using a food processor or blender, combine the tofu, oil, garlic, lemon juice, mustard, Worcestershire sauce, salt, pepper and cheese. Blend for 2 minutes. Scrape down the sides of the bowl and process for 2 to 3 minutes or until very smooth.

2. Refrigerate the remaining dressing in an airtight container for up to 2 days (see Recipe Note).

Croutons

MAKES 1½ CUPS (375 mL)

2 Tbsp (30 mL) coconut or avocado oil	12 thin slices baguette bread
⅛ tsp (0.5 mL) sea salt	1 garlic clove, halved

1. Mix oil with salt. Brush over both sides of bread slices. In a skillet, grill for 1 to 2 minutes, turning occasionally, until golden. Rub cut side of garlic over both sides of toasted slices. Cut into 1-inch (2.5 cm) cubes.

Little Black Salad

☐ FLEX APPEAL BEEF SIRLOIN

FLEX APPEAL

MAKES 2 SERVINGS

For a faster, high-heat cooking method using a grill or skillet, you will need a good-quality cut of beef such as sirloin or New York strip fillet, but you can use any cooked, thinly sliced cut of boneless beef (or pork or lamb) in this recipe.

---

6 oz (175 g) boneless beef sirloin

1 Tbsp (15 mL) coconut or avocado oil

Preheat a barbecue grill, cast iron grill pan or skillet.

Brush beef on all sides with oil. Grill over high heat for about 5 minutes per side. Medium-rare beef should register 160°F (71°C). Let rest until ready to serve salad.

Cut into thin strips and top 2 of the bowls in step 3 with beef.

MAKE-AHEAD STRATEGIES

· Make the dressing up to 5 days in advance. Store in covered jar in refrigerator.

· Prepare all of the salad ingredients up to 2 days in advance and store in a zip-top bag in the refrigerator. Bring the dressing and salad ingredients to room temperature before combining to serve.

In celebration of the healthy dark side of nature, I've developed this delicious black salad—dress it up or down ... It will take you anywhere. —Pat

MAKES 4 SERVINGS

½ cup (125 mL) arame (see About the Ingredients)

2 cups (500 mL) cooked black rice (see About the Ingredients)

1 cup (250 mL) thinly sliced red cabbage

1 cup (250 mL) cooked beluga lentils or black beans

1 beet, shredded

½ red onion, thinly sliced

½ cup (125 mL) dried cherries or cranberries

freshly ground black peppercorns and black salt (optional)

1 cup (250 mL) Sour Cherry Dressing (recipe follows)

---

1. In a bowl, cover arame with warm water and set aside for 10 minutes. Drain well.

2. In a large bowl, combine the rice, cabbage, lentils, beet, onion, cherries and drained arame. Grind black pepper and salt over salad, if desired. Drizzle the dressing over the salad and toss well.

3. Divide the salad among 6 bowls.

Sour Cherry Dressing

MAKES 1 CUP (250 mL)

½ cup (125 mL) avocado or olive oil

¼ cup (60 mL) chopped dried cherries or cranberries

2 Tbsp (30 mL) pomegranate molasses or corn syrup

¼ cup (60 mL) sherry or red wine vinegar

---

1. In a jar with lid, combine the oil, cherries, molasses and vinegar. Secure lid on jar and shake to mix well.

Little
Black
Salad

about this recipe

What makes it great?

The stunning black colour is very dramatic, as you can see in the photograph. You can have fun with the ingredients by adding shredded raw purple carrots or blue, purple or black fruits such as blueberries, plums, prunes, Concord or Muscat grapes, or blackberries.

What makes it so healthy?

The power nutrients in blue, black, purple and dark red fruits and vegetables are high in antioxidant compounds called anthocyanins. These compounds help to neutralize free radicals, which damage cells and contribute to causing diseases as well as the symptoms of aging.

What is black salt?

Salt that is black or brown gets its dark colour from roasting or smoking or by the addition of activated charcoal (as in the Hawaiian black salt called Hiwa Kai, which is solar-evaporated sea water that is combined with activated charcoal in black lava pans).

continued on next page >

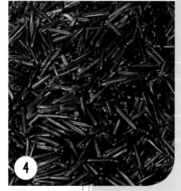

about the ingredients

What is arame?

It is one of many different dried, edible sea herbs (or seaweed) that are becoming widely available in North America. Arame is easy to add to salad, soup and stew because it rehydrates quickly in warm water. Look for a brand (such as Eden) that is wild harvested, shredded, cooked and sun-dried. See image ❶.

Arame's thin black strands are high in fibre, iron and vitamin A and contain 100 to 500 times the iodine found in shellfish. They also have a whopping 10 times the amount of calcium found in milk.

How do I use arame in recipes?

To add to salads, measure dried arame into a bowl. Cover with warm water and let stand for at least 10 minutes. Drain and add directly to salads. See image ❷.

You can add arame directly to soups or stews without soaking by stirring it into the simmering dish about 10 minutes before you plan to serve.

Can I use other sea herbs?

The only other sea herb that may be used in recipes in exactly the same way as arame is wakame. You can use other dried sea herbs such as kombu or kelp or dulce, but follow the directions on the package for soaking and adding to recipes.

What is black rice?

Like most plants, there are many varieties of rice. Many are white but others are brown or red or black in colour. We now have access to the once "forbidden," highly treasured and protected black rice of China's emperors, which is high in antioxidants, iron and amino acids. In fact, black rice bran may contain higher amounts of antho-cyanin antioxidants than do blueberries. Red, black, mahogany, short brown and black Thai jasmine rice are some of the darker rice varieties becoming available in whole food and health food stores and the organic sections of some supermarkets.

Can I use wild rice in place of black rice in this recipe?

Yes you can!

What is wild rice?

The product we know as wild rice is actually not a rice—it's the seed heads of a type of grass which grows in the freshwater lakes of central North America. See image ❸.

Much of it is now paddy cultivated, so unless labelled "hand harvested from the wild" it may not be grown in the wild. (For information about Canadian wild rice, see Resources.)

How do I cook black, brown, red and wild rice?

To make 2 cups (500 mL) of cooked rice, bring 2 cups (500 mL) of salted water or broth to a boil over high heat. Stir in 1 cup (250 mL) of rice. Cover, bring back to a boil and reduce to keep the water simmering for 40 minutes or until all of the liquid has been absorbed. Fluff with a fork and let sit, uncovered, for 2 minutes. See image ❹.

Bulgur and Pomegranate Salad

Because it reconstitutes easily with hot water, using bulgur makes quick work of the preparation for this colourful salad. —Pat

MAKES 4 SERVINGS

2 Tbsp (30 mL) coconut or avocado oil

1 onion, chopped

2 cups (500 mL) vegetable broth

2 tsp (10 mL) pomegranate molasses

1 cup (250 mL) bulgur

1 cup (250 mL) finely diced broccoli stems (see Recipe Note)

1 cup (250 mL) pomegranate seeds

½ cup (125 mL) chopped fresh parsley or mint

sea salt and pepper

1. In a skillet, heat the oil over medium-high heat. Sauté the onion for 5 minutes or until soft. Add the broth and molasses and bring to a boil. Stir in the bulgur, cover, remove from the heat and let sit for 2 minutes or until all the liquid has been absorbed.

2. Stir in the broccoli, pomegranate seeds and parsley. Season to taste with salt and pepper. Serve warm or at room temperature.

RECIPE NOTE

Most recipes call for broccoli spears or florets, which means using the top third or the very tip of the broccoli head, respectively. Except for the leaves, which are delicious edible greens, these are the tenderest parts of the plant and perfect for a showy side dish, stir-fry or salad. But why waste the goodness in the stems?

By peeling away the tough outer skin of the broccoli stem, you can access all the taste and nutrients in the tender inner flesh. Using the stems also allows you to dice the flesh as called for in this recipe or shred it for a slaw or other raw salad.

MAKE-AHEAD STRATEGY

You can cover this salad and refrigerate for up to 24 hours in advance. Bring to room temperature before serving.

Marinated Radish and Fennel Salad
☐ FLEX APPEAL SALMON

FLEX APPEAL

A mandoline is important to this recipe for slicing the ingredients into thin wafers. The fresh fennel and radish make this salad a delight for spring meals. —Pat

MAKES 2 SERVINGS

MAKES 4 SERVINGS

6 oz (175 g) smoked salmon

Top 2 of the salads in step 3 with smoked salmon.

Orange Chili Marinade

½ cup (125 mL) olive or avocado oil

⅓ cup (80 mL) freshly squeezed orange juice

3 Tbsp (45 mL) rice vinegar

1 tsp (5 mL) grated orange zest

1 tsp (5 mL) chili pepper flakes

½ tsp (2 mL) sea salt or to taste

Radish and Fennel Salad

2 watermelon radishes or daikon, thinly sliced (see About Radishes)

1 fennel bulb, thinly sliced (see Using Fennel)

½ English cucumber, thinly sliced

½ red onion, thinly sliced

1. To make the marinade, in a salad bowl, whisk together oil, orange juice, vinegar, orange zest and chili pepper seeds. Taste and add sea salt as required.

2. Add the radish, fennel, cucumber and onion to the marinade and toss to mix well. Let stand for 1 hour, or cover and place in the refrigerator for up to 4 hours.

3. Divide the salad among 4 plates using tongs or a slotted spoon.

USING FENNEL

Fennel is a bulb that is similar to celery in appearance but its stems have wispy, feathery leaves. The whole plant has an anise flavour that blends well with citrus ingredients. Use fennel raw in salads, braise or grill it, or cook it in stir-fry dishes, soups and casseroles. See image ❶.

Cut the green stems off and set aside to use for flavouring soups or stews. Cut the bulb in half and cut the core out and discard. See image ❷.

Lay each half cut side down on a cutting board. Using a French knife or mandoline, slice crosswise into thin strips. See image ❸.

Strip the feathery green leaves from the stems and dry on a drying rack or colander in a dark, warm place. Transfer to a dark jar and store in a cool place for up to 10 months. See image ❹.

about radishes

The root vegetables known as radish (*Raphanus sativus*) are in the same family—
Brassicaceae—as Brussels sprouts, broccoli and cabbage, and offer some of the same
anti-cancer and antioxidant health benefits as their cousins. There are many different varieties of radish available to the vegetable gardener and any of them will work in this salad.

· The long, large, mild-flavoured, white radish that is most prevalent in Asia is usually shredded and pickled or used with other vegetables in salads and stir-fry dishes. See image **5**.

· French Breakfast radish is an elongated red radish with a circle of white at the tip. It is a
  heritage variety that has been sold at Paris markets since 1879. The mild flavour and crisp
  texture make it a popular garnish for salads and egg dishes. See image **6**.

· The watermelon radish, a large, sweet radish with a white or green skin and brilliant, mild,
  sweet-tasting rose flesh, is actually an heirloom Chinese daikon radish. It is best when
  eaten raw as in this recipe, but you can cook this radish as you would turnip. See image **7**.

· The long, thin, white radish is the young daikon radish. Slice, shred or chop it into stir-fry
  dishes or other cooked casseroles and use raw in salads. See image **8**.

Caramelized Beet and Halloumi Salad
⬜ FLEX APPEAL CHICKEN

FLEX APPEAL

Grilling the ingredients separately means that they will be cooked to perfection. You will need several metal skewers so that the longer-cooking beets are added to the grill first and the onions are added last and removed before they char or burn. —Pat

MAKES 2 SERVINGS

MAKES 4 SERVINGS

6 oz (175 g) skinless, boneless chicken breast, cut into 1½-inch (4 cm) pieces

2 beets, quartered

2 red onions, quartered

1 lb (500 g) halloumi cheese, cut into 8 squares

½ cup (125 mL) Ginger Coconut Dressing (recipe follows)

2 cups (500 mL) baby arugula

In step 2, thread chicken onto a separate skewer and brush with dressing.

In step 3, grill at the same time as the beets, turning frequently, for 6 to 8 minutes or until done. Chicken is cooked when a meat thermometer reaches 165°F (74°C) when inserted into the centre of the piece.

In step 4, add chicken to 2 of the bowls.

1. Heat barbecue grill to medium-high.

2. Thread beet quarters onto one skewer, onion quarters onto a second skewer and cheese cubes onto a third skewer. Brush dressing over ingredients on skewers.

3. Grill beet skewers over a hot grill, turning frequently, for 6 to 8 minutes or until tender-crisp. Add the onion and halloumi skewers to the grill and cook, turning frequently, for 2 to 4 minutes. Test and remove each skewer as its contents are done.

4. Divide the arugula among 4 salad bowls. Top each bowl with 2 beet quarters, 2 onion quarters and 2 cheese squares. Drizzle with the remaining dressing or pass separately.

Ginger Coconut Dressing

MAKES ½ CUP (125 mL)

¼ cup (60 mL) coconut cream or milk

2 Tbsp (30 mL) lime juice

2 Tbsp (30 mL) coconut or avocado oil

1 Tbsp (15 mL) grated fresh ginger

1 tsp (5 mL) sea salt or to taste

1. In a jar, combine the coconut cream, lime juice, oil, ginger and salt. Shake to mix well.

Asparagus and Orzo Salad
☐ FLEX APPEAL CHICKEN

Orzo is a small, rice-shaped pasta. It doesn't become soggy when marinated and is terrific in a salad. This is a great warm or cold salad that can be served right away or the next day. —Nettie

MAKES 6 SERVINGS

3 Tbsp (45 mL) red wine vinegar

2 Tbsp (30 mL) extra virgin olive oil or grapeseed oil

1 Tbsp (15 mL) Dijon mustard

1 tsp (5 mL) brown sugar

½ lb (250 g) orzo pasta

1 Tbsp (15 mL) butter

½ cup (125 mL) finely chopped shallots

½ lb (250 g) sliced shiitake mushrooms

⅔ lb (350 g) fresh asparagus, cut into ½-inch (1 cm) pieces

1 cup (250 mL) cherry tomatoes, halved

sea salt and pepper

½ cup (125 mL) tamari-roasted almonds, or pistachio nuts, for garnish

1. To prepare the vinaigrette, in a bowl, whisk together vinegar, oil, mustard and sugar until well combined. Set aside.

2. In a pot, bring salted water to a boil. Stir in the orzo and boil for 10 to 13 minutes, or until al dente. Drain and rinse with cold water, and set aside.

3. Heat butter in a skillet over medium heat. Add the shallots and cook, stirring frequently, for 3 minutes or until soft. Stir in the mushrooms and cook, stirring occasionally, for 5 minutes. Add the asparagus. Cover and reduce the heat. Cook, stirring occasionally, for 5 minutes or until the asparagus is tender-crisp. Stir in the tomatoes and season to taste with salt and pepper. Remove from the heat.

4. In the skillet or a bowl, combine the cooked orzo and vegetables. Pour prepared vinaigrette over and toss to mix.

5. Divide the salad among 6 bowls. Garnish with tamari-roasted almonds.

FLEX APPEAL

MAKES 2 SERVINGS

2 cups (500 mL) chicken broth or water

1 piece (3 inches/7.5 cm) lemongrass (optional)

1 large (⅓ lb/170 g) skinless, boneless chicken breast

In a saucepan, bring the broth and lemongrass, if desired, to a boil over high heat. Add the chicken, cover, reduce the heat to medium-low and simmer for 9 to 10 minutes or until the chicken turns opaque and there is no sign of pink on the inside.

Let cool and slice into crosswise strips. Top 2 of the salads in step 5 with chicken before garnishing with almonds.

Quinoa Taco Salad

⬜ FLEX APPEAL BEEF SIRLOIN

My endless supply of wraps was used up and I needed a base for this salad, so I used tortilla chips. I always have a few bags in the pantry made from organic corn. I prefer the blue tortilla chips for ingredient colour contrast, but you can mix and match. I have been known to use an occasional potato chip or two. Crunchy lettuce, organic beans from a can and red quinoa will make this salad a favourite recipe in your repertoire. —Nettie

FLEX APPEAL

MAKES 2 SERVINGS

6 oz (175 g) sirloin tip steak

1 clove garlic, crushed

1 Tbsp (15 mL) coconut or avocado oil

salt and pepper

Heat the oil in a skillet or ridged grill pan over medium-high heat. Spread both sides of steak with garlic. Cook for 6 to 8 minutes, turning once.

Remove from the heat and season with salt and pepper. Let rest for 8 minutes and slice into thin slices. In step 4, top 2 of the bowls with sirloin before garnishing with tortilla chips, cheese, salsa and limes.

MAKES 6 SERVINGS

3 Tbsp (45 mL) coconut or avocado oil

1 large onion, chopped

1 cup (250 mL) fresh or frozen corn kernels

2 cups (500 mL) grape tomatoes, halved

2 cups (500 mL) cooked Red Inca quinoa (see About Quinoa, page 63)

1 can (14 oz/398 mL) kidney or black beans, drained and rinsed

1 Tbsp (15 mL) ancho chili powder

1 tsp (5 mL) dried oregano

½ tsp (2 mL) sea salt

½ cup (125 mL) chopped fresh cilantro or basil

1 cup (250 mL) prepared tomato salsa

3 cups (750 mL) shredded iceberg lettuce

2 cups (500 mL) grated cheddar cheese

3 cups (750 mL) coarsely crumbled tortilla chips, for garnish

1 lime, sliced in 6 wedges, for garnish

---

1. Heat the oil in a skillet or saucepan over medium-high heat. Add the onion and cook, stirring frequently, for 5 minutes or until the onion begins to brown and soften. Add the corn and 1 cup (250 mL) of the tomatoes. Cook for 2 minutes. Add the quinoa, beans, chili powder, oregano and salt. Cook, stirring frequently, for 5 minutes.

2. In a bowl, combine the remaining tomatoes, the cilantro and the salsa. Mix well.

3. In a large bowl, toss lettuce with bean mixture, half of the cilantro-salsa mixture and 1 cup (250 mL) of the cheese.

4. Divide the salad among 6 bowls. Garnish with tortilla chips, remaining cheese, remaining salsa and lime slices.

Avocado and Olive Salad
🔲 FLEX APPEAL TROUT

Avocado oil is used in the vinaigrette to complement the sliced avocado in the salad, but you can substitute any polyunsaturated or nut oil. —Pat

MAKES 6 SERVINGS

4 cups (1 L) mixed greens, torn into bite-sized pieces

1 avocado, thinly sliced

½ cup (125 mL) thinly sliced red onion

½ cup (125 mL) pitted black olives

½ cup (125 mL) cherry tomatoes, halved

1 cup (250 mL) cooked lentils or beans

¾ cup (185 mL) Dijon Vinaigrette (recipe follows)

1. In a salad bowl, toss together greens, avocado, onion, olives, tomatoes and lentils.

2. Serve dressing on the side or drizzle over salad and toss well. Divide the salad among 6 bowls. ←

Dijon Vinaigrette

MAKES ¾ CUP (185 mL)

½ cup (125 mL) avocado oil

¼ cup (60 mL) balsamic vinegar

2 tsp (10 mL) Dijon mustard

2 cloves garlic, minced

sea salt and pepper

1. In a jar with a lid, combine the oil, vinegar, mustard and garlic. Secure the lid and shake to mix well. Taste and add salt and pepper as desired.

FLEX APPEAL

MAKES 2 SERVINGS

6 oz (175 g) smoked trout

In step 2, top 2 of the salad bowls with smoked trout.

FLEX APPEAL Trout

Spicy Tofu Salad with Basmati Rice

This is a delicious one-bowl recipe that is colourful, easy to prepare, and great to eat before a workout. The basmati rice absorbs the chili garlic sauce well and makes a natural canvas for the cucumber, carrot and salad greens. —Nettie

MAKES 6 SERVINGS

¼ cup (60 mL) tamari or soy sauce

¼ cup (60 mL) chili garlic sauce (see Recipe Note)

2 Tbsp (30 mL) toasted sesame oil

2 Tbsp (30 mL) olive or avocado oil

1 lb (500 g) extra-firm tofu, rinsed and cut into ½-inch (1 cm) cubes

4 green onions, white parts minced and green parts coarsely chopped

½ cup (125 mL) plain yogurt

2 Tbsp (30 mL) freshly squeezed lemon juice

2 cups (500 mL) cooked basmati rice

4 cups (1 L) mixed salad greens

1 carrot, grated

2 cups (500 mL) sliced cucumber

1 avocado, diced

¼ cup (60 mL) shelled pistachio nuts, for garnish

1. To make the dressing, in a bowl, whisk together tamari, chili garlic sauce and sesame oil. Set aside.

2. Heat olive oil in a skillet over medium heat. Add the tofu cubes to the skillet and stir-fry for 8 to 10 minutes or until golden, stirring often.

3. Transfer the tofu to the tamari dressing bowl. Add the green onions, yogurt and lemon juice and stir well.

4. Mound rice into 6 bowls. Top with mixed greens and carrot, and then add stir-fried tofu and prepared dressing. Arrange the cucumber and avocado on top and garnish with pistachio nuts.

RECIPE NOTE

If you can't find chili garlic sauce, any spicy chili sauce can be used. I always take into account to whom I will be serving my meals: adults who enjoy spice versus young kids who either dislike or have not developed a taste for spicy ingredients. You can also add to the level of heat by increasing the amount of chili sauce.

MAKE-AHEAD STRATEGY

You can cook the rice ahead of time and refrigerate for up to 2 days.

weekend flexing:
unhurried fare and meat mains

When your schedule allows extra time in the kitchen, cooking can be a more relaxed activity. All of the recipes in this section will take more than an hour to prepare. The non-vegetarian recipes that we've included are perfect for special dinners when you're preparing main dishes for both meat-eaters and vegetarians, and when you want to plan your flexitarian meals for the coming week. Having non-vegetarian guests gives you an opportunity to cook larger cuts such as roasts and freeze the leftovers or use them during the week in many of the recipes in this book.

Tofu Cutlets with Red Quinoa

Crispy-crunchy tofu with a citrus-pepper marinade. The longer you marinate the tofu, the more pronounced the flavour will be. If you want a centre-of-the-plate meat substitute, cut your tofu in thicker, larger pieces. Stir-fried or baked, these tofu cutlets are delicious. —Nettie

MAKES 6 SERVINGS

Citrus-Pepper Marinade

2 Tbsp (30 mL) freshly squeezed lime juice

3 Tbsp (45 mL) freshly squeezed orange juice

½ inch (1 cm) fresh ginger, minced

2 cloves garlic, minced

2 tsp (10 mL) white miso

1 tsp (5 mL) rice vinegar

1 tsp (5 mL) tamari or soy sauce

1 tsp (5 mL) brown sugar

½ tsp (2 mL) black pepper

Tofu Cutlets

1 lb (500 g) extra-firm tofu, cut into 6 pieces

½ cup (125 mL) all-purpose flour

½ cup (125 mL) dried breadcrumbs

½ tsp (2 mL) sea salt

⅓ cup (80 mL) olive oil

Kale Quinoa Stir-Fry

1 Tbsp (15 mL) coconut or avocado oil

1 onion, chopped

4 cups (1 L) chopped kale

2 cups cooked red quinoa (see page 63)

1 Tbsp (15 mL) fresh lemon juice

1. To make the marinade, in a medium-sized bowl, mix together lime juice, orange juice, ginger, garlic, miso, vinegar, tamari, sugar and pepper. Set aside.

2. To prepare the tofu cutlets, arrange tofu in a single layer in an 8- × 10-inch (20 to 25 cm) baking dish. Pour marinade over tofu. Cover with plastic wrap and marinate tofu in the refrigerator for 6 hours or overnight. Bring to room temperature.

3. Place flour and breadcrumbs in separate bowls. Add salt to breadcrumbs.

4. Lift the tofu pieces from the marinade and coat them with flour. Dip the tofu pieces in the marinade once more and coat with breadcrumbs. Set aside on a large plate.

5. In a skillet, heat the olive oil over medium heat. Fry the tofu, turning once, until browned, about 1 to 2 minutes on each side. Set aside.

6. To make the stir-fry, heat the coconut oil in a wok or large skillet over medium-high heat. Add the onion and cook, stirring frequently, for 5 minutes or until soft and lightly coloured. Reduce the heat to medium and add half of the kale. Stir for about 1 minute and, as kale begins to shrink, add the remaining kale along with a small amount of water (about 2 Tbsp/30 mL) to keep the kale from sticking as it cooks. Cook, stirring and tossing, for 5 minutes or until tender. Add the quinoa and lemon juice and heat through.

7. Divide the kale-quinoa mixture among 6 plates. Top each plate with a tofu cutlet.

Split Pea and Cashew Loaf

This is a vegetarian "meat" loaf using split peas. It's savoury and can be served hot or cold. Try leftover slices on toasted rye bread coated with honey mustard. —Nettie

MAKES 6 SERVINGS

1 cup (250 mL) green split peas, rinsed (see Recipe Note)

3 cups (750 mL) vegetable broth

2 Tbsp (30 mL) olive or avocado oil

¼ cup (60 mL) dry breadcrumbs

1 onion, finely chopped

2 cloves garlic, minced

1 cup (250 mL) sliced button mushrooms

1 stalk celery, chopped

1 small carrot, grated

½ cup (125 mL) coarsely ground roasted cashews

3 Tbsp (45 mL) chopped fresh basil

3 large eggs

1 cup (250 mL) shredded cheddar cheese

½ tsp (2 mL) sea salt

⅛ tsp (0.5 mL) ground black pepper

1. Preheat the oven to 350°F (180°C).

2. In a saucepan, combine the split peas and broth. Bring to a boil over high heat. Reduce the heat to medium and simmer for 20 minutes or until tender. Drain and set aside.

3. Heat the oil in a saucepan over medium heat. Add the onion and garlic and sauté for 5 minutes or until soft. Stir in the mushrooms, celery and carrot. Cook, stirring occasionally, for 5 minutes or until soft. Add the cashews, basil and drained split peas. Reduce the heat to medium-low and cook for 2 to 3 minutes.

4. In a bowl, beat the eggs. Stir into the split pea mixture. Add the cheese, salt and pepper. Stir until well combined.

5. Transfer the mixture to an 8- × 4-inch (1.5 L) loaf pan lined with parchment paper, packing it down to form a smooth surface. Cover with foil and bake for 45 minutes. Uncover and bake for 10 minutes more or until browned. Let cool in pan for 5 minutes before serving.

RECIPE NOTE

You can use yellow split peas or lentils in this recipe instead of green split peas. Once, in the fall, I cooked the split peas in freshly pressed apple cider and it was very refreshing.

MAKE-AHEAD STRATEGY

Cook split peas up to 2 days ahead of time and refrigerate.

about split peas

Ancient Romans and Greeks shelled peas for drying. Nowadays, two types of green peas are grown: wrinkly-skinned sweet peas for eating and smooth-skinned starchy peas for drying. The dried peas are split in half to cook quickly. Available in yellow and green, they can be used in many dishes, to thicken sauces and in soups.

Zucchini Mushroom Moussaka
🔲 FLEX APPEAL LAMB

I am replacing eggplant with green and yellow summer zucchini in this recipe because it's very colourful. If yellow zucchini are difficult to obtain, one colour will be fine. The sweet spices add an extra flavour dimension, a delicate touch to a savoury dish without a lot of unnecessary fat. —Nettie

FLEX APPEAL

MAKES 4 SERVINGS

2 Tbsp (30 mL) coconut or avocado oil

½ lb (250 g) ground lamb

In step 2, remove ¾ cup (185 mL) of the white sauce to a bowl.

MAKES 10 SERVINGS

White Sauce

½ cup (125 mL) butter

½ cup (125 mL) unbleached flour

3 cups (725 mL) milk or plain soy milk

1 cup (250 mL) finely grated Parmesan cheese

¼ tsp (1 mL) ground nutmeg

Moussaka

2 lb (1 kg) potatoes, sliced crosswise, (¼ inch/6 mm thick)

4 to 5 Tbsp (60 to 75 mL) coconut or avocado oil, divided

2½ lb (1.25 kg) green and yellow zucchini, sliced lengthwise

2 onions, thinly sliced

3 cloves garlic, minced

2 cups (500 mL) sliced button mushrooms

1 can (28 oz/798 mL) crushed tomatoes and juice

¼ cup (60 mL) red wine

½ tsp (2 mL) sea salt

½ tsp (2 mL) paprika

¼ tsp (1 mL) ground cinnamon

⅛ tsp (0.5 mL) black pepper

½ cup (125 mL) chopped fresh basil

1. Preheat the oven to 425°F (220°C).

2. To make the white sauce, melt butter in a saucepan over medium heat. Whisk in the flour and cook, whisking constantly, for 2 minutes or until thickened. Gradually whisk in the milk. Cook, whisking constantly, for 5 minutes or until thickened. Stir in the Parmesan and nutmeg. Cook, stirring constantly, for 1 or 2 minutes or until the cheese is melted. Set white sauce aside.

3. Meanwhile, to prepare the moussaka, place potato slices on lightly oiled or parchment paper–lined, rimmed baking sheets. Bake for 15 minutes or until browned and easily pierced by a fork. Let cool on a wire rack. Lower oven temperature to 350°F (180°C).

4. Heat 1 Tbsp (15 mL) oil in a skillet over medium heat. In batches, add the zucchini in a single layer. Cook for 3 minutes, until lightly browned, then flip over and cook for 3 minutes. Transfer to a platter lined with paper towels. Continue cooking zucchini, adding 1 Tbsp (15 mL) oil for each new batch, until all the zucchini has been cooked. Wipe out pan.

5. In the same skillet, heat 2 Tbsp (30 mL) of the oil over medium heat. Add the onions and garlic and sauté for 5 minutes, or until soft. Stir in the mushrooms, 1 cup (250 mL) at a time. Cook, stirring constantly, for 3 to 5 minutes or until soft. Add the tomatoes, wine, salt, paprika, cinnamon and pepper. Reduce the heat to low, cover and simmer for 30 minutes, stirring occasionally. Remove from the heat. Stir in the basil. ←

6. Cover the bottom of a lightly oiled, 9- × 13-inch (3.5 L) baking pan with a layer of baked potato slices. Top with a layer of cooked zucchini. Pour half of the tomato sauce over the zucchini. Add a final layer of potatoes and zucchini and the remaining tomato sauce.

7. Spread white sauce smoothly over the top. Cover with foil and bake for 15 minutes. Remove the foil and bake for 15 minutes more or until the moussaka is golden and bubbling.

In step 5, while the tomato sauce is simmering, heat the oil in a skillet over medium-high heat. Add the ground lamb and reduce the heat to medium. Cook, stirring constantly and breaking up the clumps, for 5 to 8 minutes or until the meat is browned with no pink on the inside. Using a slotted spoon, lift the meat into a bowl.

Before beginning step 6, lightly oil an 8-inch (20 cm) square pan. Cover the bottom of both pans with a layer of potatoes and zucchini. Spread the lamb over the zucchini slices. Pour 1½ cups (375 mL) of the tomato sauce over the zucchini in the larger pan and 1 cup (250 mL) tomato sauce over the lamb in the smaller pan. Add another layer of potatoes and zucchini and top with the remaining tomato sauce, dividing it between the 2 pans. Continue with step 7.

Fresh Herb Lasagna

Who doesn't enjoy lasagna? The quality of the canned tomatoes, grated cheese and noodles will affect the flavour because these are the essential ingredients. —Nettie

MAKES 8 SERVINGS

RECIPE NOTE

You can interchange the parsley with other leafy fresh herbs in your refrigerator. Basil, dill, cilantro or tarragon would be suitable substitutes for the parsley. Once, in a remote location, I combined my precious assortment of fresh herbs and the results were delicious and provided a lot of conversation. Each guest was convinced their piece of lasagna was the best!

MAKE-AHEAD STRATEGY

The lasagna can be assembled up to 1 day ahead and refrigerated, covered. Bring to room temperature before baking.

Tomato Sauce

3 Tbsp (45 mL) olive or avocado oil

1 onion, chopped

4 cloves garlic, minced

1 green bell pepper, chopped

1 can (28 oz/796 mL) crushed tomatoes with juice

1 can (5½ oz/156 mL) tomato paste

⅓ cup (80 mL) dry red wine

1 tsp (5 mL) tamari or soy sauce

1 Tbsp (15 mL) fresh chopped oregano

¼ tsp (1 mL) black pepper

2 bay leaves

½ cup (125 mL) chopped fresh basil

Ricotta Filling

1½ lb (750 g) whole milk ricotta (store-bought or see recipe, page 187)

1 large egg, lightly beaten

1 cup (250 mL) grated Parmesan cheese, divided

¼ cup (60 mL) chopped fresh parsley (see Recipe Note)

½ tsp (2 mL) sea salt

½ tsp (2 mL) black pepper

⅛ tsp (0.5 mL) ground nutmeg

9 lasagna noodles, cooked and drained (according to package directions)

1 lb (500 g) mozzarella cheese, shredded and divided into 3

1. Prepare the tomato sauce by heating oil in a large saucepan over medium heat. Add the onion and garlic and cook, stirring frequently, for 5 minutes or until soft. Add the green pepper, tomatoes, tomato paste, wine, tamari, oregano, pepper and bay leaves. Cover, lower heat to medium-low and simmer, stirring often, for 30 minutes. Remove and discard the bay leaves. Stir in the basil and set aside.

2. Preheat the oven to 375°F (190°C).

3. To prepare the filling, in a bowl, combine the ricotta, egg, ½ cup (125 mL) of the Parmesan cheese, parsley, salt, pepper and nutmeg.

4. Assemble lasagna by spreading ½ cup (125 mL) of tomato sauce over the bottom of a 9- × 13-inch (3.5 L) casserole dish. Cover with 3 noodles in one layer. Spread half of the ricotta filling evenly over the noodles. Cover filling with one-third of the remaining tomato sauce. Sprinkle one-third of the mozzarella over sauce. Cover with 3 more noodles, the remaining filling, one-third of the tomato sauce and one-third of the mozzarella. Cover with remaining noodles and remaining tomato sauce. Sprinkle the remaining ½ cup (125 mL) Parmesan and mozzarella evenly over the top.

5. Cover and bake for 20 minutes. Uncover and bake for 10 minutes more, or until the sauce is bubbling and cheese is browned. Let stand for 5 minutes before serving.

about fresh pasta

In my opinion, not all fresh pastas are superior to dried pastas. Fresh pasta is made from all-purpose flour and eggs. It is more porous than dried and best used with creamy sauces that are meant to be absorbed. Because it is perishable, it needs to be used as soon as possible. The so-called "fresh refrigerated pastas" at most supermarkets are pasteurized, containing additives for an extended shelf life.

Preparing fresh pasta at home is the best of both worlds. For those of us who do not have the time, good-quality dried pasta (when cooked properly) has a wonderful firmness that goes best with tomato-based sauces, as in lasagna.

Easy Baked Whitefish

A whole whitefish (or salmon or trout) fillet is baked on a bed of diced vegetables. This dish cooks in less than 30 minutes for a delicious non-vegetarian main course. Serve with a warm or cold salad or a side of noodles. Leftover cooked fish keeps for up to 2 days if tightly covered and stored in the refrigerator. —Pat

MAKES 6 SERVINGS

2 potatoes, coarsely chopped

2 turnips, coarsely chopped (see About Turnips)

1 onion, coarsely chopped

1 large carrot, shredded

1 fillet (2½ lb/1.25 kg) whitefish

10 basil leaves

sea salt and pepper

2 Tbsp (30 mL) olive or avocado oil

Dijon Mustard Paste (page 182) (optional)

1. Preheat the oven to 350°F (180°C).

2. In a lightly oiled 9- × 13-inch (3.5 L) casserole dish, combine the potatoes, turnips, onion and carrot. Lay fish over vegetables and spread basil leaves overtop. Season with salt and pepper and drizzle oil over all. Bake for 15 minutes or until the fish turns opaque and flakes easily with a fork.

3. Let rest for 5 minutes before serving. Serve with mustard paste, if desired.

about turnips

The vegetable we call turnip (*Brassica rapa*) is often confused with another root vegetable, the larger and more common rutabaga. Tender white turnips are in season in the spring, when they appear at farmers' markets around the country. See image **1**. The taste is mild and almost sweet when they are young.

Rutabaga (*Brassica napobrassica*), often called Swede, is a larger root vegetable with yellow flesh. See image **2**. It may be substituted for turnip in most recipes, including this one. Many are waxed in order to preserve them, so be sure to pare the skin away when this is the case.

Easy Baked
Whitefish

Chicken: Two Ways

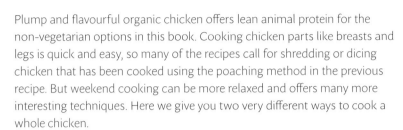

Plump and flavourful organic chicken offers lean animal protein for the non-vegetarian options in this book. Cooking chicken parts like breasts and legs is quick and easy, so many of the recipes call for shredding or dicing chicken that has been cooked using the poaching method in the previous recipe. But weekend cooking can be more relaxed and offers many more interesting techniques. Here we give you two very different ways to cook a whole chicken.

Roast Chicken with Sage Stuffing

Crispy skin, savoury stuffing and moist, tender flesh combine to make this a special, celebratory way to cook whole chicken. It's a virtual make-ahead recipe because once the chicken is prepared for the oven, you can enjoy your guests as it cooks with no fussing needed. —Pat

MAKES 6 SERVINGS

3 Tbsp (45 mL) olive or avocado oil, divided	¼ cup (60 mL) chopped fresh parsley
1 Tbsp (15 mL) butter	3 Tbsp (45 mL) chopped fresh sage (see About Sage)
1 onion, chopped	sea salt and pepper
3 cloves garlic, finely chopped	1 whole chicken (3 to 4 lb/1.5 to 1.8 kg)
3 pears, chopped	
4 cups (1 L) whole wheat or gluten-free bread cubes	

1. Preheat the oven to 350°F (180°C).

2. In a skillet, heat 2 Tbsp (30 mL) of the oil and melt butter over medium heat. Add the onion and cook for 5 minutes, stirring occasionally. Add the garlic and pears and cook, stirring occasionally, for 3 to 5 minutes or until soft and golden.

3. In a bowl, combine the bread cubes, parsley, sage, salt and pepper. Toss to mix well. Add the onion mixture, scraping the skillet to include the browned bits.

about sage

Sage has traditionally been used as an herb for enhancing the taste of chicken and turkey. In fact, it's the main ingredient in the blend of herbs known as "poultry seasoning."

I like to use chopped fresh sage from the garden in dressing, but if that is not available, substitute 4 tsp (20 mL) of dried ground sage or store-bought poultry seasoning. To chop sage, use a French knife or a double-handled mezzaluna.

As an interesting change from chopped sage, you can stack the leaves and cut fine strips using kitchen shears or a French knife. Any medium-sized herb leaf, such as sage or mint, may be shredded in this way.

Roast
Chicken
with Sage
Stuffing

Chicken Tagine
with Morrocan
Spice Blend

4. Fill cavity of chicken with stuffing mixture. Cover opening with a small piece of foil to prevent exposed stuffing from charring. Brush remaining oil over chicken skin and grind more salt and pepper overtop.

5. Place chicken, breast side up, in roasting pan. Bake for 1 hour or until a digital thermometer registers 185°F (85°C) when inserted into the centre of both thigh and breast.

6. Transfer to a cutting board and cover with foil. Let rest for 15 minutes before carving.

continued on next page >

> Chicken: Two Ways continued

Chicken Tagine with Moroccan Spice Blend

You can make this recipe using a Dutch oven if you do not have a tagine. Because the vegetables and whole chicken are constantly basted with steam in the tagine, the skin is not crispy as in the roast chicken recipe. Instead, the North African flavours infuse the ingredients for a meltingly delicious dish. —Pat

MAKES 4 TO 6 SERVINGS

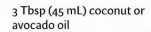

3 Tbsp (45 mL) coconut or avocado oil	4 cloves garlic, finely chopped
1 onion, coarsely chopped	12 cremini mushrooms, cut in half
1 leek, white and pale green parts only, coarsely chopped	½ cauliflower, cut into pieces
1 Tbsp (15 mL) Moroccan Spice Blend (recipe follows)	1 whole chicken (3 lb/1.5 kg)
	1 cup (250 mL) chicken broth

1. In the bottom of a tagine designed for stove-top use, heat the oil over medium-high heat. Add the onion and leek and cook, stirring frequently, for 5 minutes. Add the spice blend, garlic, mushrooms and cauliflower and cook, stirring occasionally, for 3 minutes.

2. Add the chicken to the pan, breast side down. Slide it around so that the spices coat the skin. Turn chicken breast side up and slide it around, moving the vegetables out of the way so that the skin is in direct contact with the bottom of the pan.

3. Add the broth and bring to a boil over medium-high heat. Cover with tagine lid, reduce the heat to low and simmer for 30 to 40 minutes or until a digital thermometer registers 185°F (85°C) when inserted into the centre of both thigh and breast. Remove from the heat, replace lid and let rest for 15 minutes before carving.

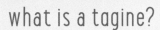

what is a tagine?

The two-piece cooking utensil called a tagine originated in the northwestern African region known as the Maghreb. There, roaming tribes of indigenous people coped with life on the move through desert and barren lands, and they devised a cooking pot made from local material that can be used in portable braziers. The word tagine is used for both the cooking utensil as well as the type of dish, usually a stew, that is made in the pot.

Why use a tagine?

Foods cooked in a tagine are tender and delicious, richly flavoured, usually with fruit or Moroccan-spiced savoury sauces. The tall, tapered lid allows moisture and steam to circulate up and around the food so it steams as it cooks, and this moist cooking method makes it very tender.

Sticky Pomegranate Pork with Red Spice Paste

This recipe is great for a weekend dish because it is cooked in the oven or slow cooker, it can be used for pulled pork additions to many of the vegetarian dishes in this book, and it's just a pure and simple meat dish that is versatile and easy on the cook. You can cook ribs using this recipe, but the amount of meat for future meals will be significantly reduced. For a non-vegetarian meal, team the roast with baked potatoes and a slaw or green salad. —Pat

MAKES 10 SERVINGS

3 Tbsp (45 mL) Red Spice Paste (recipe follows)

3 lb (1.5 kg) boneless, whole pork loin roast

2 onions, thinly sliced

1 cup (250 mL) pomegranate juice

1 cup (250 mL) lightly packed brown sugar

¼ cup (60 mL) liquid honey

seeds of 1 pomegranate (optional)

1. Rub spice paste over pork. Place onions in a slow cooker (see Recipe Note) and position pork on top of onions.

2. In a bowl, whisk together pomegranate juice, sugar and honey. Drizzle over pork.

3. Cover and cook on low for 4 to 5 hours (see Recipe Note). Pork is done when a digital meat thermometer reads 160°F (71°C).

4. Meanwhile, remove the seeds from the pomegranate, if using, and set aside for garnishing the meat.

Red Spice Paste

MAKES 3 TBSP (45 mL)

4 cloves garlic

2 tsp (10 mL) coriander seeds

2 tsp (10 mL) cumin seeds

1 tsp (5 mL) brown mustard seeds

1 (2-inch/5 cm) stick cinnamon, crushed

2 tsp (10 mL) ground cayenne pepper

1. Using a mortar and pestle or small spice grinder, crush the garlic. Add the coriander, cumin, mustard and cinnamon. Grind spices into a rough powder. Add the cayenne pepper and mix well.

RECIPE NOTE

A slow cooker is the easiest and most convenient tool for long, slow cooking but you can use a casserole dish or Dutch oven as long as it has a lid. If not using a slow cooker, you will need to preheat the oven to 350°F (180°C) and reduce cooking time to 3 hours.

MAKE-AHEAD STRATEGY

The cooked roast will keep, tightly covered in the refrigerator, for up to 3 days.

To freeze, pull the strands of meat apart. Measure 1- or 2-cup (250 or 500 mL) amounts and transfer to freezer bags. Label and keep frozen for up to 3 months. Thaw in a refrigerator for 4 to 6 hours or overnight before using in a recipe.

Maple-Roasted Lamb

Locally raised, organic lamb is available frozen all year, but if you can get a fresh bone-in leg in the late spring or early summer, you (or your non-vegetarian friends) will delight in the mild taste and meltingly tender texture. This recipe serves a lot of people, so it provides plenty of cooked meat for future flex options or for a feast. —Pat

MAKES 8 TO 10 SERVINGS

4 lb (1.8 kg) bone-in lamb leg	1 cup (250 mL) brown sugar
1 head garlic (8 to 12 cloves), peeled	2 Tbsp (30 mL) balsamic vinegar
1 cup (250 mL) freshly squeezed orange juice	2 Tbsp (30 mL) fresh chopped rosemary
	sea salt and pepper
1 cup (250 mL) pure maple syrup (see About Maple Syrup)	

1. Preheat the oven to 350°F (180°C).

2. Trim excess fat from lamb, leaving a ¼-inch (5 mm) thick layer. Using a carving fork or the tip of a paring knife, make slits into the flesh, evenly spaced all over the roast. Insert a clove of garlic into each slit. Place lamb, fat side up, into a roasting pan.

3. In a saucepan, combine the orange juice and maple syrup and bring to a boil over high heat. Add the brown sugar and cook, stirring constantly, for 2 minutes or until the sugar is dissolved and mixture is thick. Remove from the heat and add vinegar, rosemary, salt and pepper. Drizzle half of the maple glaze over prepared lamb.

4. Roast in the oven for 30 minutes. Drizzle the remaining maple glaze over lamb and roast for 30 minutes more. Test for doneness using a meat thermometer inserted into the centre of the meat (not touching the bone). We recommend cooking lamb to either rare 140°F (60°C) or medium-rare 150°F (65°C).

5. Transfer the lamb to a cutting board, tent with foil and let rest for 20 minutes before carving.

MAKE-AHEAD STRATEGIES

- If you are roasting lamb for later use, you can cut slices from the bone, cover tightly and keep them in the refrigerator for up to 4 days. Use the bone for soup broth or freeze it to use in soup or stew.

- To keep cooked lamb longer than a few days, cut slices into ½-inch (1 cm) wide strips or medium (½-inch/1 cm) dice. Measure 1- or 2-cup (250 or 500 mL) amounts and transfer to freezer bags. Label and keep frozen for up to 3 months. Thaw in a refrigerator for 4 to 6 hours or overnight before using in a recipe.

about maple syrup

In the spring when daytime temperatures rise above freezing, the sap on many deciduous trees begins to be converted from stored starch. This clear, slightly sweet and sticky liquid flows throughout the trunk and limbs. A good sap year depends on nighttime temperatures dipping below freezing and daytime temperatures inching above freezing, because this causes pressure to build up in the trees, triggering the movement of sap.

Sugar maple (*Acer saccharinum*) is the most widely used tree for collecting sap for maple syrup. See image ❶.

Modern methods of sap collection rely on an intricate network of plastic lines that funnel the sap directly to the boiler without the extra work of emptying buckets and trucking the valuable liquid by hand. See image ❷.

The sap is boiled until the water content is reduced and the sugars are concentrated into a syrup-thick liquid. See image ❸.

Syrup from the first sap run of the season is light amber and mild in taste, labeled No. 1 Extra Light in Canada and Grade A Light Amber or Fancy in the US. Subsequent "runs" result in syrup that gets progressively stronger in taste and colour, so that by the end of the season it is a rich, full-bodied, dark amber colour. I prefer the dark amber maple syrup for both cooking and drizzling on pancakes because of its deep maple flavour. See image ❹.

The process of collecting and boiling sap to make pure maple syrup is still intensely time-consuming, which affects the cost. Be aware of inexpensive maple syrup imitations that are made from corn, beet or cane sugars and artificial flavouring. Real maple syrup is made from maple sap with nothing added. See image ❺.

Poached Turkey Breast

You can also cook boneless chicken breasts using this method, but test for doneness after 30 to 40 minutes. This is a moist and gentle method of cooking lean, tender white turkey or chicken breast meat so the meat is meltingly tender, never rubbery. —Pat

MAKES 6 TO 8 SERVINGS

MAKE-AHEAD STRATEGIES

- To store cooked turkey or chicken breast, cover tightly and store in the refrigerator for up to 3 days.

- To freeze, cut into crosswise slices and cut slices into ½-inch (1 cm) strips or chop into medium (½-inch/1 cm) dice, or use a mandoline to finely slice or shred. Measure 1- or 2-cup (250 or 500 mL) amounts and transfer to freezer bags. Label and keep frozen for up to 3 months. Thaw in a refrigerator for 4 to 6 hours or overnight before using in a recipe.

2 lb (1 kg) boneless, skinless turkey breast	1 cup (250 mL) white wine
¼ fresh lemon	2 bay leaves
3 cups (750 mL) chicken broth	3 sprigs fresh sage
	Wine Gravy (recipe follows)

1. Preheat the oven to 350°F (180°C).

2. Rub turkey with lemon, squeezing the juice as you rub.

3. Combine the broth, wine, bay leaves and sage in a baking dish or roasting pan. Add the turkey and the squeezed lemon quarter. Cover with lid or wrap tightly with lightly oiled aluminum foil. Bake for 1 hour, turning breast over once or twice. Check for doneness using a meat thermometer. Poultry pieces are safely cooked when a meat thermometer inserted into the centre of the breast reaches 160°F (74°C).

4. Carve and serve with Wine Gravy, if desired.

Wine Gravy

Use the strained poaching liquids from the recipe above for light-coloured, wine-flavoured gravy. To make extra for freezing, double the ingredients.

MAKES 2 CUPS (500 mL)

2 Tbsp (30 mL) butter	2 cups (500 mL) strained poaching liquid
2 Tbsp (30 mL) all-purpose or gluten-free flour	

1. In the roasting pan or a saucepan, melt butter over medium-high heat. Stir in the flour until a paste forms. Whisk in the liquid and bring to a boil, whisking constantly over high heat. Reduce the heat to medium-low and cook, whisking constantly, for 3 to 4 minutes or until the sauce thickens.

speedy seasonings and sauces

A Trio of Spice Blends

Mixing your own spice blends is fun and allows you to customize the blend to your taste. Almost all large, ethnically diverse urban centres have a few stores that sell dried whole spices in bulk. Until you know your consumption habits, purchase bulk spices in small amounts for making spice blends.

Ethiopian Berbere

The legendary spice route brought exotic tea, silks and ginger from China and cinnamon and turmeric from India into North African ports. At the same time, the Spice Islands were shipping their pungent cloves and nutmeg to Arabia and the eastern coast of Africa, where Ethiopia lies. All of these goods eventually made their way to Europe across the Mediterranean Sea or overland through Istanbul (Constantinople) to Venice. And so it was that the cuisine of the port countries was enriched by the flavours of faraway places. While many of the spice blends of the region are mild, this spice adds heat to a dish. —Pat

MAKES ¼ CUP (60 mL)

Ethiopian Berebere

1 Tbsp (15 mL) black peppercorns	6 whole cloves
1 Tbsp (15 mL) allspice berries	1 piece (1-inch/2.5 cm) cinnamon, crushed
1 tsp (5 mL) cumin seeds	6 whole dried cayenne (chili) peppers
1 tsp (5 mL) fenugreek seeds	

1. Combine the peppercorns, allspice, cumin, fenugreek, cloves and cinnamon in a small cast iron pan or spice wok (see Spice Equipment). Toast over medium-low heat, stirring frequently, for 3 to 5 minutes or until fragrant and the smaller seeds begin to pop or jump. Watch carefully and remove from the heat before the spices begin to burn or smoke. Let cool.

2. Using scissors, cut cayenne pepper pods into thin crosswise strips, allowing the seeds to fall into the blend.

3. Using an electric grinder or a mortar and pestle, grind the spices to the texture you wish. Store in a dark container in a cool, dark place for up to 8 months.

Garam
Masala

Tandoori
Masala

Garam Masala

In Hindi, *masala* is the word for spices. Garam masala is a blend of "hot" spices widely used in Indian, Nepalese and other Asian cuisines. This combination is not spicy hot in my opinion, but you can always add cayenne pepper for heat. Good-quality brands can now be found in natural food stores and Indian markets, but it is so easy to make. —Pat

MAKES ¼ CUP (60 mL)

2 Tbsp (30 mL) green cardamom pods	2 tsp (10 mL) fenugreek seeds
1 Tbsp (15 mL) coriander seeds	1 tsp (5 mL) allspice berries
2 tsp (10 mL) cumin seeds	1 tsp (5 mL) black peppercorns
2 tsp (10 mL) fennel seeds	1 piece (2-inches (5 cm) cinnamon, crushed

1. Combine all the spices in a small cast iron pan or spice wok (see Spice-Grinding Equipment, next page). Toast over medium-low heat, stirring frequently, for 3 to 5 minutes or until fragrant and the smaller seeds begin to pop or jump. Watch carefully and remove from the heat before the spices begin to burn or smoke. Let cool.

2. Using an electric grinder or a mortar and pestle, grind the spices to the texture you wish. Store in a dark container in a cool, dark place for up to 8 months.

Tandoori Masala

A tandoor is a tall, oval, clay, pot-like oven used mainly in northern India, Pakistan and Afghanistan. While the amounts and ingredients in tandoori masala vary, they tend to include some fresh ingredients like garlic, onion or shallot, ginger and lemon juice mixed with a garam masala spice blend. For this reason, a homemade tandoori blend is made in smaller amounts and used within a short period. —Pat

MAKES ¼ CUP (60 mL)

2 cloves garlic	2 Tbsp (30 mL) Garam Masala (recipe this page)
1 piece (1-inch/2.5 cm) fresh ginger	
½ tsp (2 mL) sea salt	1 Tbsp (15 mL) freshly squeezed lemon juice

1. In a mortar, using a pestle, pound the garlic and ginger with the salt until it forms a paste. Add the garam masala and enough lemon juice to form a thick paste.

2. Use immediately or store, covered, in the refrigerator for up to 8 days.

RECIPE NOTE

If you're short on time to prepare your own garam masala, small artisanal spice shops are popping up in urban centres across North America, so very good, small-batch spice blends without chemical preservatives and additives are available.

continued on next page ›

SPICE-GRINDING EQUIPMENT

Hand Grinders

For roasting whole spice bark, pods and seeds, a cast iron spice wok (top left) is ideal. You can find these at Indian spice emporiums or specialty food stores. You can also use a small cast iron or stainless steel skillet in place of a spice wok.

The traditional mortar and pestle is a simple way to grind herbs. It grinds roughly and unevenly, so the resulting blend is rustic and not finely powdered.

A wide variety of shapes, sizes and materials for mortars and pestles is available. Of the three in image ❶, I use the tall metal mortar (top right) to grind toasted spices for blends such as the three here. The small cast iron mortar (bottom right) works well to pound cardamom pods (shown) so that they split and their tiny black seeds may be removed easily. The porcelain mortar (bottom left) works best for pounding garlic and mashing fresh herbs for pesto or salsa verde.

Electric Grinders

Using an electric spice grinder (see image ❷) dedicated to grinding spices will result in a more uniform and finer spice blend than you can achieve with a mortar and pestle. You can stop grinding at any time and check the texture, ensuring just the right degree of grind. A medium-ground blend takes under a minute in an electric grinder.

I have used coffee grinders, spice grinders (virtually the same thing) and small-capacity food processors, but the very best electric mixer and the one I use now for grinding spices is the Bamix chopping attachment used with the wand (see page 6). Unlike coffee/spice grinders that only process small amounts (under ¼ cup/60 mL), its capacity is larger—up to about 1 cup (250 mL) whole spices. The flat-sided bowl facilitates even grinding.

Moroccan Spice Blend

1 piece (2-inch/5 cm) cinnamon	1 tsp (5 mL) cardamom seeds
2 Tbsp (30 mL) coriander seeds	5 whole cloves
1 Tbsp (15 mL) cumin seeds	1 whole star anise

1. In a mortar, using a pestle, crush cinnamon into coarse pieces. In a spice wok (see top left in image ❶) or skillet, toast the crushed cinnamon with the rest of the spices over medium heat until lightly coloured and fragrant, about 3 to 4 minutes. Do not let the spices smoke and burn.

2. Remove from the heat and let cool. Grind using a mortar and pestle or spice grinder. Store in a dark-coloured glass jar in a cool place.

Apple Butter

Apple butter can be used to replace fat in cake and cookie recipes. I prefer it to applesauce, which can be too watery. My favourite recipes to use it in are oatmeal cookies, apple cakes and pies. When you substitute apple butter for fat, use an equal amount of fruit purée for the shortening or butter. Apple butter makes baked goods moist and flavourful, but does not extend their shelf life—eat them within two days before they are past their prime. —Nettie

MAKES 2 CUPS (500 mL)

4 lb (1.8 kg) tart apples (Rome, Granny Smith, Matsu), thinly sliced	⅛ tsp (0.5 mL) ground cinnamon
½ cup (125 mL) apple juice	⅛ tsp (0.5 mL) ground nutmeg
1 cup (250 mL) brown sugar	⅛ tsp (0.5 mL) ground ginger
1 Tbsp (15 mL) pure vanilla extract	⅛ tsp (0.5 mL) ground cloves
1 Tbsp (15 mL) freshly squeezed lemon juice	

1. Combine all ingredients in a large stockpot. Bring to a boil over medium-high heat. Cover, reduce the heat to low and simmer, stirring frequently, for 20 to 25 minutes or until the apples are very soft.

2. Transfer the ingredients to a blender or food processor or use your immersion wand in the pot. Pulse until smooth.

Dijon Mustard Paste

I've been making my own mustard ever since I discovered how easy it is. Each time I make a new batch, I tinker with the ingredients (like adding honey and tarragon and champagne . . .) and I now have a variety of combinations. Here is my easy, basic recipe—it's pretty mild in flavour. You can substitute champagne for the wine, or add herbs or other spices. This recipe makes a whole-seed paste. —Pat

MAKES 1½ CUPS (375 mL)

1 cup (250 mL) brown or yellow mustard seeds (see Recipe Note)	1 tsp (5 mL) ground sea salt
1 cup (250 mL) white wine or unsweetened grape juice	¾ tsp (3 mL) ground allspice
	½ tsp (2 mL) ground ginger
1 Tbsp (15 mL) wine vinegar	½ tsp (2 mL) ground cinnamon
1 Tbsp (15 mL) liquid honey	¼ tsp (1 mL) ground nutmeg
	¼ tsp (1 mL) ground cloves

1. In a bowl, cover mustard seeds with wine and vinegar. Stir in the honey and cover loosely with a cloth. Let sit in a cool place (but not the refrigerator) for 48 hours.

2. Transfer to the bowl of a food processor and add salt, allspice, ginger, cinnamon, nutmeg and cloves. Process on high for 3 minutes. Let stand for 4 hours. Process on high for 5 minutes.

3. Spoon the mustard into small jars and store in a cool, dark place for a minimum of 2 weeks before using in order to bring out the flavours of the ingredients. After 2 weeks, store in the refrigerator for up to 6 months.

RECIPE NOTE

Dried mustard seeds are so brittle, they cannot be ground at home in a food processor, but must be pulverized in a mortar and pestle. However, once soaked, the seeds absorb the liquid and become softer and more easily ground using a food processor. It's important to keep the soaking seeds covered with the liquid, so you may have to top up the liquid once or twice. Fresher mustard seeds will absorb less liquid than older, drier seeds and it is hard to predict the exact yield of this recipe.

Even with soaking and grinding in the food processor, the seeds are not uniformly ground to a very fine paste. To make smoother mustard, you will need to press the mixture through 2 conical metal sieves. After processing, press the paste through a 15 per inch/ 6 per cm mesh and then through a sieve with a 30 per inch/12 per cm mesh.

Mediterranean Herb Pesto

Food processors were invented to make pesto quickly. When I think back to all the time I wasted using a mortar and pestle! I am embracing modernity the older I become. My favourite way to eat pesto is with corn on the cob. There is always pesto in my freezer. It can last for up to 2 months. My secret is to leave out the Parmesan and stir it into the thawed sauce as I reheat it. —Nettie

MAKES 1½ CUPS (375 mL)

3 cloves garlic

½ cup (125 mL) pine nuts

1 cup (250 mL) grated Parmesan cheese

1 tsp (5 mL) sea salt

½ tsp (2 mL) black pepper

3 cups (750 mL) fresh basil leaves

⅔ cup (160 mL) olive oil

1. In a food processor, process garlic for 30 seconds or until finely chopped. Add the pine nuts, Parmesan, salt, pepper and basil. Pulse until finely chopped. With the motor running, add oil, blending until smooth.

2. Cover tightly and refrigerate. Pesto will keep in refrigerator for 1 week, covered.

French Herb Mix

Creating a blend of herbs specific to one country is rather personal and has more to do with our experiences or perceptions of food and flavours from other countries. As a culinary herbalist, I know that many herbs common to one area are also easily grown in another. But that aside, the herbs I associate with French cooking are garlic, chervil, rosemary, lavender, thyme and bay—the herbs I turn to for classic French dishes. Use dried herbs for this mix. —Pat

MAKES ⅓ CUP (80 mL)

1 bay leaf

3 Tbsp (45 mL) dried chervil

2 Tbsp (30 mL) dried thyme

2 Tbsp (30 mL) dried rosemary

1 tsp (5 mL) dried lavender

1. Using scissors, cut thin crosswise strips of the bay leaf into a bowl. Add the chervil, thyme, rosemary and lavender and mix well.

2. Store in a dark container in a cool, dark place for up to 8 months.

Sweet Thai Chili Sauce

Sweet chili sauce is easy to buy, but nothing takes the place of homemade. You can buy green or red curry paste to prepare this sauce. The green curry paste is made from green chili peppers and the red curry paste is made from red cayenne peppers. One of my favourite sauces, it can be served with omelettes, wraps, soups and stews. —Nettie

MAKES 2 CUPS (500 mL)

⅔ cup (160 mL) granulated sugar	½ cup (125 mL) rice vinegar
4 tsp (20 mL) cornstarch	3 Tbsp (45 mL) green or red curry paste
1 tsp (5 mL) salt	2 cloves garlic, minced
⅔ cup (160 mL) water	¼ cup (60 mL) chopped fresh parsley

1. Combine the sugar, cornstarch and salt in a bowl. Set aside.

2. Combine the water, vinegar, curry paste and garlic in a saucepan. Bring to a boil over medium-high heat, stirring often. Stir in the sugar mixture. Reduce the heat and simmer, stirring constantly, for 5 minutes or until thickened. Cool and stir in the parsley.

3. Store in an airtight container in the refrigerator for up to 2 weeks. Bring to room temperature and mix well before using.

Chunky Red Pepper Sauce

This is the kind of sauce that is easy to make and so, so versatile. It keeps in the refrigerator for up to 4 days. I like to double the recipe and freeze it in 2-cup (500 mL) quantities. You can defrost it in the microwave while pasta is cooking, combine and toss for a super-quick homemade meal in under 30 minutes. It's bellissimo on crusty bread with some artisanal cheese for bruschetta, and if you purée it, you can drizzle it over vegetables and meat for a great finish. —Pat

MAKES 2 CUPS (500 mL)

Chunky
Red Pepper
Sauce

2 Tbsp (30 mL) coconut or avocado oil	3 cloves garlic, finely chopped
1 onion, chopped	1 can (19 oz/540 mL) diced tomatoes
2 red bell peppers, chopped	3 Tbsp (45 mL) chopped fresh rosemary

1. In a saucepan, heat the oil over medium-high heat. Add the onion and peppers and cook, stirring frequently, for 5 minutes or until soft. Add the garlic and cook for 2 minutes. Stir in the tomatoes and rosemary and simmer, stirring occasionally, for 12 minutes or until the sauce has thickened.

Romesco Sauce

I think of this recipe as a distant cousin to pesto sauce. I use this sauce as a dip and as a topping for burritos and pasta. You can adjust the heat with the amount of red pepper flakes. My son Cameron is always adding more pepper flakes. —Nettie

MAKES 1½ CUPS (750 mL)

⅓ cup (80 mL) slivered almonds

⅓ cup (80 mL) chopped hazelnuts or walnuts

⅓ cup (80 mL) panko or fresh breadcrumbs

1 clove garlic, minced

¼ tsp (1 mL) sea salt

1½ cups (375 mL) seeded and diced tomatoes, fresh or canned

1 jar (8 oz/250 g) roasted red peppers, drained and rinsed

2 Tbsp (30 mL) olive or avocado oil

1 Tbsp (15 mL) red wine vinegar

½ tsp (2 mL) paprika

¼ tsp (1 mL) crushed red pepper flakes

⅛ tsp (0.5 mL) black pepper

1. In a medium-sized skillet, toast almonds and hazelnuts over medium-low heat, stirring constantly, for 3 to 5 minutes or until browned. Remove from the heat.

2. In a food processor, pulse toasted nuts, panko, garlic and salt until finely ground. Add the tomatoes, red peppers, oil, vinegar, paprika, pepper flakes and black pepper. Process until smooth. Transfer to a serving bowl.

Béchamel Sauce

Béchamel sauce is a staple in Northern Italian cooking. I must admit to customizing the recipe to suit the occasion, using olive oil instead of butter or alternative milk instead of whole milk. This recipe is the real deal—the mother of all white sauces. It is used in lasagna, moussaka and quiches, with pasta and meatloaf. —Nettie

MAKES 2 CUPS (500 mL)

2 Tbsp (30 mL) unsalted butter	¼ tsp (1 mL) salt
2 Tbsp (30 mL) all-purpose flour	⅛ tsp (0.5 mL) white pepper
2 cups (500 mL) whole milk	⅛ tsp (0.5 mL) ground nutmeg

1. Melt butter in a heavy saucepan over medium-low heat. Add the flour and cook, whisking for 3 minutes, to make a roux. Add the milk in a steady stream, whisking constantly, and cook, continuing to whisk until it is thick and smooth. Whisk in the salt, pepper and nutmeg and simmer, whisking frequently, for 8 to 10 minutes or until the sauce is thickened.

RECIPE NOTE

Whisk in different cheeses to flavour the sauce. Grated Parmesan, cheddar, or Gruyère are excellent choices. Use ½ cup (125 mL) cheese and add when sauce has thickened.

Homemade Ricotta Cheese

I eat ricotta drizzled with maple syrup and mixed with cooked oats for breakfast. It is also a healthy dessert, served with ripe fresh fruit and honey. —Nettie

MAKES 2 CUPS (500 mL)

2 quarts (2 L) whole milk	½ tsp (2 mL) sea salt
1 cup (250 mL) 35% cream	3 Tbsp (45 mL) freshly squeezed lemon juice

1. Line a large sieve with a layer of fine-mesh cheesecloth or dampened paper towel. Place over a large bowl.

2. In a large pot over medium heat, slowly bring the milk, cream and salt to a rolling boil, stirring occasionally. Add the lemon juice, reduce the heat to low and simmer, stirring constantly, until the mixture curdles, about 2 to 3 minutes.

3. Pour the mixture into the lined sieve and let it drain for 60 minutes. Discard liquid, transfer the ricotta to a bowl, cover and refrigerate.

Vegan Cashew Sauce

A lot of people are seeking vegan alternatives to dairy-based sauces for food sensitivity and dietary reasons. My first choice in nutritional yeasts is Good Tasting Nutritional Yeast, from Red Star Yeast. It has a great taste and thickens naturally. I use Earth Balance shortening, which is vegan, made from non-GMO soy and canola oil, and contributes a wonderful texture. Discover the versatility of this delicious sauce: stir into cooked pastas or pour over your favourite vegetables and garnish with chopped parsley, or serve with bread chunks as a dip. —Nettie

MAKES 4 CUPS (1 L)

¾ cup (185 mL) raw cashews

½ cup (125 mL) nutritional yeast

2 tsp (10 mL) onion powder

1 tsp (5 mL) garlic powder

½ tsp (2 mL) black pepper

2½ cups (625 mL) rice, soy or almond milk

1½ Tbsp (22.5 mL) cornstarch

¼ lb (125 g) vegan shortening or ½ cup (125 mL) olive or avocado oil

2 tsp (10 mL) Dijon mustard

1 Tbsp (15 mL) apple cider vinegar

2 Tbsp (30 mL) tahini (see About Tahini, page 17)

1 Tbsp (15 mL) freshly squeezed lemon juice

1 tsp (5 mL) paprika

2 tsp (10 mL) salt

1. In a food processor, combine the cashews, yeast, onion powder, garlic powder and pepper. Pulse until the texture resembles a fine powder.

2. Heat the rice milk in a saucepan over medium-high heat. Add the cornstarch and shortening. Bring to a boil, reduce the heat and simmer, stirring frequently, for 8 to 10 minutes or until the mixture thickens.

3. With the food processor motor running, gradually add the rice milk mixture to the cashew powder. Blend for 2 minutes or until smooth and creamy. Add the mustard, vinegar, tahini, lemon juice, paprika and salt. Continue processing until smooth and creamy.

MAKE-AHEAD STRATEGY

Prepare the sauce in advance and refrigerate for up to 4 days.

desserts on the double

Chewy Granola Bars

Chewy
Granola
Bars

My 14-year-old son, the hockey player, told me these bars were good enough to sell. They are crunchy, sweet and very filling. —Nettie

MAKES 24 SQUARES

2½ cups (625 mL) large rolled oats

1 cup (250 mL) whole wheat pastry flour

½ tsp (2 mL) baking soda

½ tsp (2 mL) sea salt

½ cup (125 mL) dried cranberries or cherries

½ cup (125 mL) dried chopped apricots

½ cup (125 mL) semi-sweet chocolate chips

½ cup (125 mL) pecans, chopped

½ cup (125 mL) golden cane or brown sugar

½ cup (125 mL) cashew or almond nut butter

¼ cup (60 mL) coconut or olive oil

1 tsp (5 mL) pure vanilla extract

2 large eggs

1. Preheat the oven to 350°F (180°C).

2. In a large bowl, combine the oats, flour, baking soda and salt. Stir in the cranberries, apricots, chocolate chips and pecans. Mix well.

3. In a medium-sized bowl, whisk or beat together sugar, nut butter, oil, vanilla and eggs. Pour over the oat mixture and combine well, using a large spoon.

4. Spread mixture in a lightly oiled 9- × 13-inch (3.5 L) baking dish and pat down firmly. Bake for 25 to 30 minutes or until firm. Cool 10 minutes before slicing into bars.

Chocolate Chip Bark

When I was a vegan university student trying to eat organic, fair-trade chocolate desserts on a budget, almost every dessert I whipped up started with affordable chocolate chips. I like to nibble, hence the bark recipe. Little pieces of confection satisfy me for hours. —Nettie

MAKES 1 LB (500 G)

2½ cups (625 mL) chocolate chips	½ cup (125 mL) dried apricots, chopped
3 Tbsp (45 mL) cocoa powder	½ cup (125 mL) coarsely chopped walnuts
2 Tbsp (30 mL) coconut oil	½ cup (125 mL) chopped almonds
2 Tbsp (30 mL) crystallized ginger, finely chopped (see Recipe Note)	⅓ cup (80 mL) dried unsweetened coconut
½ cup (125 mL) dried cherries	

1. In the top of a double boiler or a heatproof bowl set over a pan of simmering water (don't let the bottom of the bowl touch the water), place chocolate chips, cocoa powder, oil and ginger. Stir until the chocolate is melted. Remove from the heat.

2. Add half of the cherries, apricots, walnuts and almonds and 2 Tbsp (30 mL) coconut. Mix well.

3. Spread mixture evenly onto a parchment paper–lined, rimmed baking sheet. Sprinkle top with remaining cherries, apricots, walnuts, almonds and coconut. Chill in the refrigerator for 25 minutes or until firm.

4. Peel off the parchment paper and break bark into bite-sized pieces before serving.

RECIPE NOTE

Store refrigerated for up to 1 week. It never lasts that long.

about dried fruits

Dried fruit should be treated as a perishable ingredient with a long shelf life. Store dried fruit in airtight containers at room temperature away from light, heat and above all, moisture. Stored properly, it should last at least 4 months.

Balsamic Roasted Strawberries

As easy as this dessert is, I always get compliments on it, I think because of the complex flavours and the tangy-sweet sauce. This is the kind of recipe that calls for good-quality balsamic vinegar. —Pat

MAKES 4 SERVINGS

4 cups (1 L) strawberries, hulled (16 oz/500 g)	1 vanilla bean, cut into 4 pieces
⅓ cup (80 mL) caster sugar	1 cup (250 mL) muesli (optional)
2 Tbsp (30 mL) balsamic vinegar	1 cup (250 mL) plain yogurt or ice cream (optional)
zest of 1 orange	

1. Preheat the oven to 400°F (200°C).

2. Cut 4 parchment paper rectangles, 12 × 15 inches (30.5 × 38 cm). Fold each rectangle in half, with the fold along the long edge. Starting at the top of the fold, cut out a half heart shape, cutting as close to the edges as possible so that the heart is as big as the rectangle allows. See image ❶.

3. In a bowl, combine the strawberries, sugar, vinegar and zest. Toss to mix well. Divide into 4 portions and spoon each onto one half of each parchment heart, close to the fold. Add a piece of vanilla bean to each. See image ❷.

4. Crimp and fold the cut edges together so that a sealed half-heart pocket is formed. Set on a rimmed baking sheet and bake for 7 minutes. See image ❸.

5. Serve sealed pockets to guests in a shallow bowl and let them slit open with a knife. Pass muesli and yogurt or ice cream, if desired.

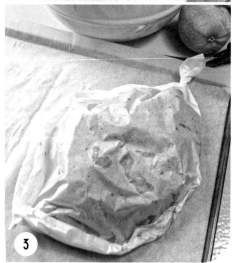

about caster sugar

Sometimes referred to as fruit sugar or superfine sugar, caster sugar is much finer than regular, granulated sugar. Caster sugar is used for sweetening fruit and in making cakes and pastries because it dissolves quickly. Don't confuse caster sugar with confectioner's or icing sugar, which is powdered and instantly dissolves, used for making velvety smooth icings and candies.

Balsamic
Roasted
Strawberries

using a zester

When a recipe calls for grated rind or zest, it means that only the bright, aromatic skin of the orange, lemon or other citrus fruit is to be scraped off and added to the ingredients. A paring knife is not recommended for this task because it cuts too deeply into the bitter white pith.

For this recipe, we wanted the small bits of orange to be visible in the roasted strawberries, so we used a tool called a zester, which gives you two options:

1. short, thin strands produced by using the sharpened holes at the top of the tool. See image ❶.

2. longer, wider strips achieved with the blade at the side of the tool. See image ❷.

Caramel
Pear Tarte
Tatin

Caramel Pear Tarte Tatin

Tarte tatin is a baked, French (of course!) fresh fruit tart with a caramel sauce that is prepared and cooked all in one pan—a skillet or specially made tarte tatin dish. After baking, the tart is flipped upside down to serve. Usually made with apples, ours features pears, but you can try almost any tree fruit in this classic recipe. —Pat

MAKES 4 TO 6 SERVINGS

¾ cup (175 mL) caster sugar

3 Tbsp (45 mL) unsalted butter

½ package (14 oz/397 g) puff pastry, thawed (see About Puff Pastry, next page)

3 pears, halved and cored

1. Preheat the oven to 375°F (190°C).

2. Heat a tarte tatin pan or an ovenproof skillet over medium-low heat for 2 minutes. Add the sugar and heat without stirring for 2 to 3 minutes or until the sugar begins to liquefy around the outside of the pan or in hot spots. Gently stir for 8 minutes. Turn off heat and keep stirring until all the sugar has melted. Immediately remove from the heat.

3. Beat butter into the caramelized sugar. Let cool, stirring occasionally. See image ❶.

4. Roll out 1 square of puff pastry to about 9 inches (23 cm) square. See image ❷.

5. Arrange the pear halves in one layer in the pan, on top of the caramelized sugar mixture. See image ❸.

6. Cover the dish with the puff pastry, tucking back the square edges all the way around. See image ❹.

7. Bake for 25 to 30 minutes or until the pastry has puffed up and is evenly browned. Let the tart rest for 10 minutes. See image ❺.

8. Position a serving plate over the tarte tatin pan and turn the plate and pan upside down so that the pears are on top of the pastry on the plate. See image ❻.

continued on next page ›

TIME-SAVING STRATEGY

There are some very good brands of ready-made caramel sauce. To save time, you can spoon your favourite jar of caramel sauce into the pan, arrange fruit over the sauce and top with the pastry, then bake as directed.

MAKE-AHEAD STRATEGY

Assemble the tart up to 4 hours ahead of time and keep it in the refrigerator. Be sure to bring to room temperature before baking.

about puff pastry

What is it?
Puff pastry is a simple dough that, when cooked, separates into several thin layers of light, flaky and crisp sheets. It is used in hors d'oeuvres, in savoury and sweet turnovers, as toppings for pot pies and for wrapping beef, as in beef Wellington.

Is it hard to make?
You can make puff pastry from scratch but it is time-consuming and a bit tricky. To make puff pastry, a simple dough of flour, salt and water is rolled into a rectangle. A flat disc of unsalted butter is placed on the centre third of the dough and the two ends of dough are folded over it. The dough is rotated a quarter turn, re-rolled into a rectangle and the two ends are folded over. This step is repeated once and the dough is refrigerated. After the dough is turned, rolled, folded and refrigerated 6 to 10 more times, the butter is evenly distributed between many thin layers of dough.

What makes it puff?
When baked, the air between the layers turns to steam, making the layers puff up into delicate and rich-tasting, flaky pastry.

How is it sold?
You can buy excellent quality, frozen, prepared puff pastry dough in grocery stores. It is sold in a 14 oz (397 g) box containing 2 squares of unrolled dough, or a 17.3 oz (490 g) box containing 2 sheets of rolled dough. When you open the package, you can remove one square or sheet and leave the remaining one in the box. Frozen puff pastry will keep in its original wrapping in the freezer for up to 3 months.

For this recipe, we used one square of the unrolled dough and saved the other square for later use.

How is store-bought puff pastry prepared?
Thaw the pastry by placing it in the refrigerator, leaving it in its sealed plastic, for about 4 hours or overnight. You can keep the sheet or square in the refrigerator for up to 2 days before using it as long as it is wrapped in plastic.

The rolled sheets may be used as they come out of the box, but the squares must be rolled out on a lightly floured surface.

about this recipe

What makes it great?
The presentation is spectacular, but it is the taste that people love. The caramel soaks into the puff pastry and makes it exceptionally delicious with the soft fruit.

Do I need a special pan to make tarte tatin?
You will need a pan that can be used on top of the stove and in the oven because this will save time. The base of the tarte tatin pan from Emile Henry is made of flame-proof, non-stick ceramic material that may be used over direct heat. A cast iron skillet works just as well.

Can I make tarte tatin ahead of time?
This dish is best when served hot from the oven (after resting). It does not freeze well and you likely won't have any left, but it does not store long in the refrigerator. Using ready-made caramel sauce and puff pastry makes this an easy-to-prepare dessert that cooks while you are enjoying the first course of your meal.

Red Chili Chocolate Cupcakes

Pair fresh red chilies and milk chocolate for this recipe. Heat and sweetness combine well together, especially in a dessert recipe. I recommend medium-hot chilies. —Nettie

MAKES 12 CUPCAKES

5 oz (150 g) bar milk chocolate

2 Tbsp (30 mL) finely diced fresh red chilies, stem, seeds and membranes removed (see Recipe Note)

¼ cup (60 mL) dried cherries

1½ cups (375 mL) all-purpose flour

½ cup (125 mL) unsweetened cocoa powder

1 tsp (5 mL) baking powder

½ tsp (2 mL) sea salt

¾ cup (185 mL) granulated sugar

2 large eggs

½ cup (125 mL) canola oil (see Recipe Note)

1 cup (250 mL) whole milk

1½ tsp (7.5 mL) pure vanilla extract

1. Preheat the oven to 400°F (200°C).

2. In a medium-sized bowl, coarsely grate the chocolate. Add the diced chilies and cherries. Stir together and set aside.

3. In a large bowl, sift the flour, cocoa, baking powder, salt and sugar. Add the chocolate-chili mixture to bowl. Stir together.

4. In a medium-sized bowl, beat the eggs and oil with a whisk until well blended. Gradually add the milk and vanilla. Whisk until foamy.

5. Pour the wet ingredients into the dry ingredients and stir until just combined.

6. Spoon the mixture into 12 muffin cups, lightly oiled or lined with paper cups, filling each cup two-thirds full.

7. Bake for 20 minutes. Allow to cool in pan for 5 minutes.

RECIPE NOTES

- We recommend using organic canola oil because it is made from non-genetically modified rapeseed and is not over-refined.

- Chilies are available in several varieties, whether fresh, dry, ground or canned. The most popular is jalapeño, available in green or red, with a medium to hot heat level. Poblano chilies are dark forest green, and range from mild to hot. If you touch the flesh of the chilies with your bare hands, be extra careful to wash your hands afterward. If you accidentally touch your eyes or mouth, the volatile oils will sting.

Salted Dulce de Leche Tarts with Chocolate Ganache

These tarts are easy to make, they're decadent and addictive and almost too rich for anything other than a very special occasion, so make them in cups just large enough to hold a chocolate wafer cookie. They take advantage of the very good specialty brands of international foods most urban dwellers and Internet users have at their disposal. —Pat

MAKES 8 TARTS

8 chocolate wafer cookies (store-bought)	¾ cup (175 mL) Chocolate Ganache (recipe follows)
1 cup (250 mL) Dulce de Leche (recipe follows)	2 tsp (10 mL) coarse sea salt

1. Assemble 8 small serving cups or bowls. In the bottom of each cup, place 1 chocolate wafer. Spread 2 tablespoons (30 mL) of Dulce de Leche over each wafer. If the Dulce de Leche is soft and runny, refrigerate for at least 30 minutes. See image ❶.

2. Spread 1½ tablespoons (20 mL) of Chocolate Ganache over the Dulce de Leche. Sprinkle salt over and chill the tarts for at least 1 hour before serving.

Dulce de Leche

Soft and tasting of caramel, this thick, pudding-like sauce is made by heating sweetened milk to the point where the sugars caramelize. It is popular in South American dishes. While very good, imported canned dulce de leche is available, not all brands are great. In fact, some are quite artificial in flavour, so we offer this recipe for making your own. —Pat

MAKES 2 CUPS (500 mL)

2 cans (12 oz/355 mL) sweetened condensed milk

1. Preheat the oven to 220°F (425°C). Using a spatula, scrape the milk into a 2-quart (2 L) ovenproof baking dish with a lid. Cover tightly with aluminum foil, then cover the dish with its lid.

2. Place into a 10- × 15-inch (4 L) deep-sided baking pan and pour boiling water into the large pan until it reaches two-thirds of the way up the sides. Bake for 1½ hours or until the milk is caramel coloured. Transfer to a bowl and whisk until smooth. Homemade dulce de leche keeps, tightly covered, in the refrigerator for up to 3 weeks.

TIME-SAVING STRATEGIES

· To make these tiny parcels of pure delight quick and easy, we substituted ready-made chocolate wafer cookies in place of a homemade chocolate or shortbread crust. Then we found ceramic tart cups that fit the wafers and saved all the time it takes to clean tiny tart tins.

· There is some very good ready-made dulce de leche that is imported from South America. I did try a well-known brand of condensed milk that is making dulce de leche and I found it to be artificial tasting and not to my liking, so you really have to taste the product before using. See image ❷.

Salted Dulce
de Leche Tarts
with Chocolate
Ganache

Chocolate Ganache

MAKES ¾ CUP (175 mL)

½ cup (125 mL) whipping cream	5 oz (150 g) dark chocolate, coarsely chopped

1. In a heavy-bottomed saucepan, bring the cream to a light boil. Stir in the chocolate and simmer, s tirring constantly, until the chocolate melts. Let cool before using.

Make-Ahead Chocolate Pots

Dessert is usually the last thing I think about when planning a menu for guests, partly because we don't usually eat dessert and partly because I'm not a baker, so I don't have cookies or muffins on hand. So when I developed this absolutely fabulous, freeze-ahead dessert, I loved everything about it. Add to that the fact that you don't have to thaw it before baking and you have the perfect quick and easy dessert, especially for people who, like me, don't think about dessert until the very last minute. The individual pots are rich and satisfying on their own, but you can serve them with a biscuit or garnished with fresh fruit such as raspberries or cherries. —Pat

MAKES 8 POTS

1 cup + 3 Tbsp (250 mL + 45 mL) unsalted butter	½ cup (125 mL) caster sugar (see page 192)
8 oz (250 g) 70% dark chocolate	½ cup (125 mL) all-purpose flour
4 large eggs plus 4 egg yolks	cocoa or icing sugar, for garnish
2 tsp (10 mL) pure vanilla extract	

1. In a small saucepan over medium-low heat, melt 3 Tbsp (45 mL) of the butter.

2. Brush the insides of eight 6 oz (¾ cup/175 mL) ramekins with melted butter, place them on a rimmed baking sheet and refrigerate until the chocolate filling is ready. See image ❶.

3. Combine the remaining 1 cup (250 mL) butter and the chocolate in a small saucepan and melt over simmering water, stirring frequently. Remove from the heat when the mixture is melted and smooth. See image ❷.

4. Using a stand mixer or electric beaters, beat eggs, egg yolks, vanilla and sugar for about 7 minutes or until doubled in volume. See image ❸.

5. Drizzle the chocolate mixture over the egg mixture and mix on low or whisk until combined. See image ❹. Sprinkle flour over and gently stir into the mixture. Spoon into chilled pots and cover tightly with plastic wrap. Freeze for up to 2 months.

6. To cook from frozen: Preheat the oven to 350°F (180°C). Remove the plastic covering and place the ramekins on a rimmed baking sheet. Bake for 20 to 25 minutes or until the mousse puffs up. Dust with cocoa or icing sugar and serve warm.

EQUIPMENT NOTE

RAMEKINS

The small, glazed, ovenproof ceramic or glass bowls known as ramekins are used for cooking and serving individual servings of hot or cold dishes. Probably most widely used for soufflés, they can also be used for soups (especially French onion), pâtés and hot dips, or for crème brûlée. Traditionally, ramekins are round white pots with a fluted exterior. Our colourful glazed ceramic ramekins are made in France by Emile Henry.

Basmati Chai Rice Pudding

If you like to add flavour and not fat to your grains, cook them in tea. Grains readily absorb the liquids they are cooked in, and mint, Earl Grey, chai and green tea all add a welcoming twist to the taste profile of such an easy-to-prepare dessert. —Nettie

MAKES 6 SERVINGS

2 cups (500 mL) water

3 cups (750 mL) unsweetened soy milk or low-fat milk, divided

3 black chai tea bags

1 cup (250 mL) basmati rice, rinsed

⅓ cup (80 mL) sugar

⅛ tsp (0.5 mL) sea salt

1 medium-sized Fuji or Spartan apple, cored and diced into small pieces

1 cup (250 mL) fresh or frozen blueberries, rinsed

¼ cup (60 mL) raisins or dried cranberries

½ tsp (2 mL) ground cinnamon

1. In a large saucepan over high heat, bring the water and 1 cup (250 mL) soy milk to a boil. Remove from the heat and add the tea bags. Cover and steep for 3 to 5 minutes. Remove the tea bags.

2. Stir rice, sugar and salt into the tea mixture. Bring to a boil over medium heat. Reduce the heat, cover and simmer for 8 minutes.

3. Add the remaining 2 cups (500 mL) soy milk and simmer, uncovered, 15 to 20 minutes or until the rice is cooked.

4. Stir in the apples, blueberries, raisins and cinnamon. Remove from the heat. Cover pot and let sit for 5 minutes. Serve warm or cold.

RECIPE NOTES

- You can use any unsweetened milk alternative to prepare this recipe, such as almond, rice or hemp milk.

- Mix and match the fruits as you wish, using one hard and one soft fruit for texture contrast: pears and kiwi, for example. My daughter Mackenzie has a sweet tooth and is always asking for more sweet flavour, but you can leave out the sugar if you prefer your desserts less sweet.

Glossary of Foods

Adzuki beans: Small, dark red beans used in traditional Japanese cuisine and easily digestible.

Agave nectar: Made from the sap of the plant from which tequila is distilled, agave nectar does not crystallize or solidify when cold, is sweeter than sugar and has a 3-year shelf life. A vegan alternative to honey, it's sold in light, amber, dark and raw varieties. We would recommend using one-third less agave than you would white sugar and one-quarter less than other liquid sweeteners. Baked goods made with agave brown more quickly, so reduce oven temperatures by 25°F (15°C).

Amaranth: The principal food of the Aztecs, this little yellow seed, high in protein and calcium, releases a starchy substance during cooking and has a gelatinous quality.

Apple cider vinegar: An inexpensive fruity-tasting vinegar that needs refrigeration if unpasteurized. Its low level of acidity (4 %) allows it to contribute flavour without overwhelming other ingredients, especially in salad dressings.

Arame: An edible sea vegetable that is sold dried, cut and packaged, it is reconstituted by adding water or stock and soaking for 5 minutes. Arame resembles black angel hair pasta and is used in soups, salads, casseroles, turnovers and strudels. Its sweet taste is due to mannitol, a noncaloric sugar present in many brown and black algae.

Avocado oil: With a rich, smooth, buttery flavour, avocado oil makes a great base for salad dressings and dips. It is also ideal for sautéing, basting and stir-frying at high heats. An excellent source of vitamin E, avocado oil contains no trans fats and is high in heart-healthy monounsaturated and polyunsaturated fats.

Balsamic vinegar: An Italian vinegar made from white Trebbiano grape juice that becomes deep amber when aged in wood barrels. The mellow sweet-sour flavour best suits vinaigrette salad dressings or splashed on steamed or grilled foods. Like most vinegars, it will keep indefinitely if stored in an airtight container and need not be refrigerated. It is expensive, especially if aged for 10 years or longer, but fortunately a little goes a long way.

Basmati rice: A type of long-grain rice with a delicate aroma and nut-like taste that suits many cuisines. White basmati cooks in 20 minutes, while brown basmati requires 45 minutes to cook.

Black beans: Small, plump kidney-shaped beans with a shiny black-blue coat and an earthy flavour.

Buckwheat (kasha): Buckwheat has a strong, earthy flavour and is very porous, so it cooks quickly. Rinse raw buckwheat groats quickly; otherwise, they absorb water and lose their shape. If you dry-roast buckwheat before adding it to liquids, its texture will be firmer and crunchier. When you combine an egg with uncooked groats, the egg albumen helps the groats retain their shape.

Bulgur wheat: Made from wheat berries that have been steamed, dried and crushed to create small grit-like pieces, bulgur is available in different textures. Medium ground is a good choice for most dishes. It will cook in 15 minutes or less. Never rinse bulgur; it will turn to mush and lose its shape.

Brown sugar: Brown sugar is refined white sugar with molasses added, and is available in light and dark varieties. The darker the colour, the more intense the flavour.

Canola oil: Extracted from rapeseed, canola oil is clear with little colour. It is lower in saturated fat than any other oil and contains cholesterol-lowering omega-3 fatty acids, but most brands are made from genetically modified plants and are highly refined. We recommend buying organic canola oil. It can be used for high-temperature cooking, such as stir-frying, as well as baking.

Capers: The flower buds of a Mediterranean shrub, pickled and used as a condiment.

Chickpeas: Small, round legumes with a tip and creamy beige colour. Garbanzo is the Spanish name for chickpeas. Available canned, frozen and dried.

Chili peppers: Chilies are available in many forms: fresh, dried, ground or canned. In general, the smaller the chili, the hotter it is. The most intense heat is in the seeds and surrounding membranes. Their volatile oils can cause a lot of discomfort if you touch your mouth or eyes. You can protect yourself by wearing thin rubber gloves, and always wash your hands after handling. We use ancho (mild), jalapeño (medium-hot) and cayenne (hot). We also use chipotle (smoked jalapeño), which produces a medium heat.

Cocoa powder: When combined with dark or bittersweet chocolate, cocoa powder adds intensity to the flavour of a recipe. Cocoa beans are bitter and cannot be eaten raw. They are fermented, roasted and aged, and then shelled and ground. In the process, the beans' natural fat, cocoa butter, is released. When this is removed, a dark paste known as cocoa liquor remains, which contains the flavour and aroma of chocolate. Cocoa powder is produced from the cocoa liquor, leaving a dry cake that is ground into a fine powder.

Coconut milk: Made by soaking shredded fresh coconut in hot water. When using canned coconut milk, make sure you mix the thin liquid at the top with the bottom, thick, creamy layer. Refrigerate leftover coconut milk for a maximum of 3 days.

Coconut oil: A healthy replacement for butter and margarine in recipes, coconut oil is a saturated fat that contains no cholesterol and is not hydrogenated or deodorized. Coconut oil is made when the pulp is grated, cold-pressed and filtered. Good for cooking on high heats, the other ingredients do not absorb the coconut oil when stir-frying and deep-frying. It is an excellent ingredient to introduce to a natural foods kitchen.

Coconut water: Coconut water has a slight almond flavour and is extracted from the centre of young coconuts, then pasteurized. It is very nutritious, and especially high in potassium and other minerals.

Flaxseed: Ground flaxseed binds ingredients together, and is a great egg replacer for vegan dishes, especially for baking, and an excellent source of vitamin E and omega-3 fatty acids. Store ground flaxseed in the freezer for up to 6 months.

Grapeseed oil: Grapeseed oil is made by pressing the seeds of grapes. We occasionally suggest it as an alternative to olive oil in recipes.

Kidney beans: These versatile kidney-shaped beans can be red or white. They tend to hold their shape during prolonged periods of cooking and so are often used in soups and stews.

Kombu: A sea vegetable often used as a base for soup and stock in Asian cooking. Do not rinse it off before cooking. A strip of kombu cooked with water releases glutamic acid, a white powdery coating that contains a lot of flavour. Glutamic acid is the natural version of the synthetic flavouring agent mono-sodium glutamate (MSG).

Lemongrass: An herb with a delicate lemon scent and flavour. Remove the dry, fibrous outer layers and use only the lower 6 inches (15 cm) of the stalk.

Lentils: A type of legume that is small and disc-shaped, with a firm texture. Because they are flat with thin seed coats, they do not need to be pre-soaked. There are many kinds and colours of lentils: black, brown, green, orange and red. We store my lentils in a glass jar, away from direct light.

Maple syrup: A sweet syrup made from boiling the spring sap tapped from sugar maple trees. This national treasure can be used in place of sugar and honey when baking and is often served over pancakes and French toast. Graded according to its colour, flavour and sugar content, the stronger-flavoured medium and darker grades are good for baking and cooking.

Miso: Miso is to vegetarian cooking what beef bouillon or gravy is to a meat-centred diet. This salty, fermented paste is made from aged soybeans and usually grains. Thick and spreadable, it's used for flavouring a wide variety of dishes and as the basic ingredient in soups. It can also replace salt in recipes. Miso is available in the refrigerated section of most large supermarkets, Asian and health food stores. It is available in several varieties. Dark miso tends to be saltier and have a stronger flavour than lighter varieties. Shiro, or white miso, has a pale yellow colour and a mild taste. Miso will keep for 6 months when refrigerated in an airtight container.

Molasses: The syrup left over in sugar cane processing once the sucrose has been removed from the boiled juice. Thick, with a strong flavour, molasses is used as a background ingredient in gingerbread, baked beans, barbecue sauces and licorice. Store in a cool, dark place for up to 6 months.

Non-dairy milks: Of the various non-dairy milks, soy milk most closely mimics the properties of cow's milk. Plain or original flavour works best in savoury recipes; vanilla and other flavours work well in dessert recipes. Available fortified with calcium and B vitamins, soy milk is sold fresh or in Tetra Paks. Once opened, it will keep for 1 week refrigerated. For baking, other non-dairy beverages such as almond, rice, hemp and coconut milk can be substitute for soy milk.

Non-hydrogenated shortening: The only non-hydrogenated shortening we recommend is Earth Balance, which contains no trans fat and is made from non–genetically modified palm fruit, soybean, canola and olive oils. Vegan baked goods have arrived! Store in the refrigerator.

Nori: A sea vegetable with a briny flavour that has been dried and pressed into sheets, or sold as flakes. Use for wrapping sushi rolls and as a garnish, cut into thin strips or shredded. Sprinkle on corn on the cob and popcorn.

Nut butters: Pastes made from finely ground nuts or seeds are called "butters." Almond, cashew, hazelnut and sesame are all available in stores. The fat of nuts and seeds is monounsaturated and polyunsaturated. Nut butters contain no cholesterol but can be high in calories and are best eaten in small amounts. Only buy nut and seed butters that do not contain added sugar or refined oils.

Nutritional yeast: Not to be confused with baking yeast, this yeast is not a leavening agent but a condiment that is added to sauces, casseroles and

salads for its nutritional value and cheeselike flavour. Available in flakes or powder form, nutritional yeast can be used in place of cheese or substituted for half the amount of grated cheese in a recipe. It is terrific on popcorn. Store in an airtight container for up to a year.

Olive oil: Olive oil is pressed from olives. The first, "virgin" extraction is a simple pressing that does not heat the oil above room temperature and is filtered to remove pulp. Virgin and extra virgin olive oil are recommended for cooking up to medium temperatures only, as well as for dressings and other uncooked uses. Buy good-quality olive oil, packaged in dark-coloured glass to protect it from sunlight.

Phyllo: Paper-thin sheets of flaky pastry dough, available frozen in supermarkets.

Pine nuts: The seeds from the cones of several species of pine trees, pine nuts are also called pignolias or piñons. These perishable nuts need to be refrigerated or kept in the freezer for up to 6 months. They can be eaten raw or toasted.

Pinto beans: Half the length of kidney beans and oval in shape, pinto beans' speckled coats range from brown to cranberry. A staple in Mexican cuisine, they are used in burritos, chili and refried bean dishes.

Quinoa: A grain the size of a sesame seed, quinoa is a nutritional powerhouse. It was one of three staple foods, along with corn and potatoes, of the Inca civilization. Quinoa contains more protein than any other grain: an average of 16.2%. The grains are covered in saponin, an extremely bitter, resin-like substance, and the grain must be rinsed before cooking, in a fine-mesh sieve under cold running water for 3 to 5 minutes or until the water runs clear. Quinoa is also available as flour and pasta, and in flakes. Toast flour before using to remove saponin traces.

Rice vinegar: A light, honey-coloured, sweetish vinegar made from fermented rice, with a mild acidity level of 4%. Do not buy "seasoned" rice vinegar: the seasoning interferes with the natural flavours.

Soba noodles: Long, thin Japanese noodles made from 100% buckwheat flour or a combination of buckwheat and unbleached or whole wheat flours. Soba noodles are eggless and less sticky than Italian pastas.

Soy sauce and tamari: Good-quality soy sauce is made from organic soybeans mixed with a bacterial culture and a grain—usually cracked roasted wheat.

The mixture is fermented, salted and left to age for up to 2½ years. Some brands carry a wheat-free soy sauce. Salt-reduced soy sauce needs to be refrigerated after opening because the lower salt content decreases its shelf life.

Spelt flour: One of the ancient grains, spelt is a strain of wheat. Its texture is similar to standard wheat but it has a different genetic profile. It can be substituted for soft or pastry whole wheat flour.

Tahini: A thick, smooth paste made of hulled, ground sesame seeds, this Middle Eastern staple is used as a spread and as an ingredient in dressings, sauces and dips.

Tempeh: A high-protein cultured food made from soybeans and grains. Invented in Indonesia, tempeh is traditionally made by culturing cooked, cracked soybeans with the mold *Rhizopus oligosporus*. Fermentation enhances the flavour and the mold enzymes break down the complex proteins, fats and carbohydrates of the soybean, making them easier to digest. Tempeh has a firm, chewy texture and a mild, mushroom taste. It can be steamed, fried, deep-fried, braised, crumbled and poached. Sold fresh and frozen, frozen tempeh can be kept up to

6 months and will thaw overnight in the refrigerator or in 3 hours on the countertop.

Toasted sesame oil: Made from toasted sesame seeds, this oil is darker in colour than plain sesame oil. It has a wonderful aroma and flavour.

Tofu: Sometimes called bean curd, tofu is a white, neutral-tasting, easily digestible soy food. To make tofu, soybeans are soaked, drained and ground, then simmered in water, strained and pressed to produce soy milk. A coagulant added to the soy milk causes curds to form. The curds are placed in perforated boxes, with varied weights placed on top according to the desired firmness. Pre-packaged tofu should always be rinsed before use. Once opened, any unused portion can be submerged in water and refrigerated for up to 5 days, changing the water every second day. Tofu can be frozen for up to 6 months but will have a crumbly, spongy texture when thawed.

Whole wheat flour (soft or pastry): Finely ground, it is made from softer wheat than regular whole wheat flour, and is lower in protein but contains some of the wheat bran and germ. It is used for cakes and pastries.

Resources

Organizations and Companies

Browne & Company distributors of fine kitchen products, including Emile Henri bakeware and Cuisipro equipment: www.browneco.com

Canadian Organic Growers, a directory of organic farmers and information about organic farms and food: www.cog.ca

Canadian Manomin wild rice, from lakes in northwestern Ontario: www.canadianwildrice.com

Cookin' Greens, quality flash-frozen spinach, kale and Swiss chard: www.cookinggreens.com

Cuisine Camino, Fair Trade chocolate: www.cuisinecamino.com

Eden Foods, organic canned foods: www.edenfoods.com

Far North wild rice is cultivated, organic wild rice grown in Manitoba: www.wildrice.mb.ca

Green Being Farm, organic CSA farm: www.greenbeingfarm.ca

Green Pan, non-stick cookware: www.green-pan.com

Honibe Pure Canadian Honey, pure honey and innovative honey products: www.honibe.com

KitchenAid, maker of fine kitchen appliances: www.kitchenaid.ca

Maison Orphée, organic condiments and oils: www.maisonorphee.com

Nuts To You Nut Butters Inc., organic nut butters: P.O. Box 21059, Paris, Ontario, Canada N3L 4A5

Olivado Oil, fine quality avocado oil: www.olivado.ca

Ontario CSA Farm Directory: www.csafarms.ca

Ontario Natural Food Co-op, source of organic food products: www.onfc.ca

President's Choice Organics, a line of organic food products: www.pc.ca

Soya Nova organic and smoked, hand-crafted tofu: soyanova.com

Upper Canada Cheese Company, purveyers of fine cheese including their Gurnsey Girl haloumi cheese: www.uppercanadacheesecompany.com

Waiola, 100% Coconut Water: www.waiolalife.com

Zwilling J.A. Henckels, knives and kitchen tools: www.zwilling.com

Books and Websites

2013 Canned Tuna Sustainability Ranking (Greenpeace): www.greenpeace.org

The Adaptable Feast, Ivy Manning (Sasquatch Books)

The Café Brenda Cookbook, Brenda Langton and Margaret Stuart (Voyageur Press)

Eat Well, Eat Happy, Charity Ferreira (WeldonOwen Books)

Fairtrade Canada: www.fairtrade.ca

International Seafood Sustainability Foundation iss-foundation.org

The New Mediterranean Diet Cookbook, Nancy Harmon Jenkins (Bantam Books)

PETA (People for the Ethical Treatment of Animals): www.peta.org

Pure Vegan, Joseph Shuldiner (Chronicle Books)

Rebar: Modern Food Cookbook, Audrey Alsterberg and Wanda Urbanowicz (Big Ideas Publishing Inc.)

River Cottage Veg, Hugh Fearnley-Whittingstall (Random House)

Slow Food International: www.slowfood.com (includes "Too Much at Steak," a guide to choosing meat)

The Vegetarian Resource Group: www.vrg.org

VegNews magazine: www.vegnews.com

A Year in a Vegetarian Kitchen, Jack Bishop (Houghton Mifflin Company).

Acknowledgements

Acknowledgements from Nettie

This book is a result of inspiration, guidance and support.

Thank you Pat, for being so generous with your knowledge and experience. I continue to learn so much from you.

Many thanks to: Mary Ambrose, Mary Catherine Anderson, Barbara Barron, The Big Carrot Natural Food Store, David Bird, Jocie Bussin, Marilyn Crowley, Alison Fryer, Naji Harb, Mary Luz Mejia, Gina St. Germain, Judi Schwartz, Mary Sharpe, Dorice Tepley, Vanessa Yeung.

And to my family: Helen Cronish, Suzie Siegal, Cameron, Mackenzie and Emery Urquhart, and my wonderful husband, Jim, who puts away the sharp knives.

Acknowledgements from Pat

Thanks to Nettie, who walks the vegetarian talk, but is graciously inclusive of all food choices at her dining room table.

I'm grateful to my local organic farmers, Simon de Boer, Cory Eichman, Tarrah Young and Nathan Carey (Green Being Farm), Devan Penney (Fairfields Farm), and Leslie Moskovits and Jeff Boesch (Cedar Down Farm) for helping me to eat mindfully.

We would like to thank Nick Rundall and Jesse Marchand of Whitecap Books.

We tested the recipes for this book using exceptional products and we thank all the fine companies that supported the recipe development and photography. For contact information, see the Resources section.

Cookin' Greens are dark leafy greens that are farm picked within six hours. They are double-washed, blanched, chopped and quick-frozen for convenience. Sold as straight packages of kale, rapini and spinach or as blends of greens that include white beans, red pepper, onion and yellow beans. Thanks to Toby Davidson.

Cuisine Camino supplies high-quality fair trade and organic baking ingredients. We used their cocoa, chocolate chips, shredded coconut, semi-sweet baking chocolate and sugar (muscovado and turbinado). They are owned by La Siembra Co-operative, established in 1999 in the Ottawa Gatineau region. Thanks to Jennifer Williams.

Eden Foods is the oldest natural and organic food company in North America and the largest independent manufacturer of dry grocery organic foods. All of the soybeans in their miso and soy sauces are non-GMO, United States–midwestern organic. Thanks to Janet Tovey and Jonathan Wilson.

continued on next page >

Emile Henry, founded in 1850, produces some of the finest glazed ceramic bakeware and cookware at its factory in Marcigny, Burgundy, France. Its ceramics are certified ISO 9001 and bakeware pieces created with the company's Flame process are freezer-, oven-, stovetop-, microwave- and dishwasher-safe. Thanks to Browne & Company.

Green Being Farm is a Grey County sustainable farm and its stewards, Tarrah Young and Nathan Carey, raise Pat's winter CSA share of fresh, root-cellared vegetables. Their lamb, Berkshire pork and chicken are exceptional.

Green Pan is a Belgian cookware manufacturer that created a non-stick cookware using a non-stick mineral coating that offers a healthier, safer and more environmentally friendly cookware. The ceramic coating is high-heat resistant. Nettie tested recipes using Green Pan skillets and woks. Thanks to Kathy Themelis.

Honibe from Charlottetown, PEI have innovative honey products such as dried, pure honey baking sprinkles as well as unique honey flavours. Thanks to Lindsay Mulligan.

KitchenAid supplied our stand mixers and we have come to discover that there are certain tasks only a stand mixer can perform. It will whip faster, beat longer, cream and knead to perfection. A good stand mixer will last you a lifetime.

Maison Orphée supplied us with the best-quality canola, coconut, grapeseed and olive oils. Their vinegars, sea salt and mustards (our favourite mustard was made with turmeric) are of the highest quality. They blend flavour and nutritional value well. Thanks to Nathalie Plamondon.

Nuts To You is a Canadian-owned, full-range nut butter manufacturer selling excellent quality, delicious, organic and conventional nut and seed butters. Their line of almond, cashew and tahini nut butters is available in two different sizes. Thanks to Sam Abrams and Anne Lawrence.

Ontario Natural Food Co-Op is a long-established food distributor that provided us with southwestern Ontario field-ripened, canned diced tomatoes. They also carry frozen berries, dough, fish, jarred sauces, salsas, soups, canned tomatoes, tofu and beef. Thanks to Kim De Lallo and John Landsborough.

President's Choice Organics is a well-known label to Canadians. Nettie teaches cooking classes at PC Cooking Schools in the Toronto vicinity and uses the PC Organic line in many of her hands-on and demonstration cooking classes. We used their line of organic canned black beans and diced tomatoes.

Upper Canada Cheese Company supplied us with Guernsey Girl, a halloumi-based cheese that can be grilled or fried and will retain its shape. Using specially sourced milk, this cheese is a delicate shade of ivory with a pale lemon undertone. Thanks to Vivian Szebeny and Mary Luz Mejia for supplying and introducing us to this delicious cheese.

Waiola coconut water is pure, with nothing added. Because it is a nutritious water with a delicious taste, we include it in recipes whenever possible. (Waila is Hawaiian for "water of life.") Thanks to Brendan Fallis.

Zwilling J.A. Henckels have been in business for over 280 years, supplying households with knives, cookware, kitchen tools, scissors and flatware. Their bamboo cutting boards, stainless steel whisks, pasta spoons and grater were useful for properly testing recipes. Having the right tools is just as important as having the correct ingredients. Thanks to Marlene Verissimo.

Index